Retreat and Rearguard 1914

To Joan

who travelled with me in the footsteps of Gerald Smyth

Retreat and Rearguard 1914

The BEF's Actions from Mons to Marne

Jerry Murland

Pen & Sword
MILITARY

First published in Great Britain in 2011 by
Pen & Sword Military
an imprint of
Pen & Sword Books Ltd
47 Church Street
Barnsley
South Yorkshire
S70 2AS

ISBN 978-1-84884-391-2

A CIP catalogue record for this book is available from the British Library.

Typeset in 11pt Ehrhardt by
Mac Style, Beverley, E. Yorkshire

Printed and bound in the UK by CPI

Pen & Sword Books Ltd incorporates the Imprints of Pen & Sword Aviation,
Pen & Sword Family History, Pen & Sword Maritime, Pen & Sword Military,
Pen & Sword Discovery, Wharncliffe Local History, Wharncliffe True Crime,
Wharncliffe Transport, Pen & Sword Select, Pen & Sword Military Classics,
Leo Cooper, The Praetorian Press, Remember When, Seaforth Publishing
and Frontline Publishing.

For a complete list of Pen & Sword titles please contact
PEN & SWORD BOOKS LIMITED
47 Church Street, Barnsley, South Yorkshire, S70 2AS, England
E-mail: enquiries@pen-and-sword.co.uk
Website: www.pen-and-sword.co.uk

Contents

Acknowledgements

I owe a great debt of gratitude to the men of the retreat who chronicled their experiences and left them for future generations to read. Without their observations and accounts of the two weeks of the retreat this book would have been impossible to write. In tracking down those accounts I must thank the late Professor Richard Holmes and Major Stewart Sampson, Toby Helm for permission to quote from Cyril Helm's diary, the Institution of the Royal Engineers for permission to quote from the RE Journal, the Imperial War Museum, the National Archives and the Leeds University Archive. I must also record my gratitude to Mark Whyman for his help and assistance with locating the Pennyman diary and the National Trust for their kind permission to publish the photograph of James Pennyman. James Pennyman's photographs which he took during the retreat are published with the permission of the Teesside Archive. The photographs of Cyril Helm were supplied by his daughter Caroline Price and those of Mons and St Symphorien by David Rowland. Patricia Godsell very kindly gave permission for the photograph of Kenneth Godsell to be published.

It would have been difficult to write an account of the retreat without following in the footsteps of the men who took part. To those who accompanied me in 2010 – David Rowland, Tom Waterer and Paul Webster – I give thanks for their patience in what proved to be an enlightening five days that began at Mons and ended at Rozoy en Brie, albeit in considerably more comfort than those who undertook the journey in 1914. In particular I must thank Yvon Debuire who welcomed us into his home at Néry and spent a day with us exploring the battlefields of the three rearguard actions of 1 September. He has also given permission to publish the photographs of his house at Néry and the estaminet at Vaucelles from his collection. Thanks must go also to Rebecca Jones at Glory Designs in Coventry who has once again produced some first class maps and made a number of design suggestions that have improved my initial sketches considerably.

Finally I must register my thanks to the members of the Great War Forum on the Long Long Trail website who have assisted me considerably with their expertise and personal knowledge and to Jon Cooksey, my editor, for his encouragement and assistance.

In all instances every effort has been made to trace the copyright holders where any substantial extract is quoted. The author craves the indulgence of literary executors or copyright holders where these efforts have so far failed.

1914

War broke: and now the Winter of the world
With perishing great darkness closes in.
The foul tornado, centred at Berlin,
Is over all the width of Europe whirled,
Rending the sails of progress. Rent or furled
Are all Art's ensigns. Verse wails. Now begin
Famines of thought and feeling. Love's wine's thin.
The grain of human Autumn rots, down-hurled.

For after Spring had bloomed in early Greece,
And Summer blazed her glory out with Rome,
An Autumn softly fell, a harvest home,
A slow grand age, and rich with all increase.
But now, for us, wild Winter, and the need
Of sowings for new Spring, and blood for seed.

Wilfred Owen

Introduction

The action of the British Expeditionary Force (BEF) at Mons on 23 August 1914 ended with a tactical withdrawal that, hours later, rapidly developed into retreat. Over the next thirteen days, sixteen Victoria Crosses were won as the BEF was pursued relentlessly by the Germans to a point south of the River Marne. There the tables were finally turned in a battle which was forever to bear the name of that same river astride which it was fought and retreat was transformed into advance.

When Britain went to war on 4 August 1914, overall command of the BEF was placed in the hands of Field Marshal Sir John French; his Chief of Staff was Lieutenant General Sir Archibald Murray, with Major General Henry Wilson as his deputy. The principle staff officer with responsibility for operations (GSO1) was Brigadier General George Harper, and GSO 1 (Intelligence) was Lieutenant Colonel George Macdonogh. This core group of senior staff officers formed the nucleus of the British General Headquarters (GHQ) whose task it was to exercise overall command and control of what was, when compared to some of the large conscript armies of continental Europe, a very modest BEF.

Compounded by fears in England of a German invasion of the home country and the recent trouble in Ireland over Home Rule, the British Government was initially cautious and had committed only four of its six available infantry divisions and one cavalry division to the BEF. Thus the fighting strength of the British force which went to war was made up of I Corps (1st and 2nd Divisions) commanded by Lieutenant General Sir Douglas Haig, II Corps (3rd and 5th Divisions) commanded by Lieutenant General Sir James Grierson and the Cavalry Division under the command of Major General Edmund Allenby. In addition there were five infantry battalions designated for the protection and maintenance of the lines of communication. Sadly Grierson died from a heart attack on the way to Le Cateau on 17 August and was replaced by General Sir Horace Smith-Dorrien two days later.

Today, the retreat of the BEF during the summer and autumn of 1914 is marked only by the trail of military cemeteries scattered along a route which is punctuated by the occasional memorial. The ground over which much of the retreat was conducted has changed very little since the thousands of boots of the BEF made their mark on the landscape, and it is the men that filled those boots and the rearguard actions they fought with which this book is primarily concerned. More specifically it focuses on nine of those actions fought during the course of the retreat, some of which – like those at Le Cateau and Néry – are relatively well-known while others such as the struggles at Le Grand Fayt and Maroilles are less well remembered and lie almost forgotten in battalion war diaries and regimental histories. When taken together, however, they present a quite remarkable chapter in the history of the British Army.

As the BEF withdrew from Mons on 23 August 1914 the role of cavalry regiments and their supporting Royal Horse Artillery (RHA) batteries proved to be of vital importance in providing an essential screen between the pursuing enemy and the infantry rearguard. Major John Darling, who served in the 20th Hussars as a captain during the retreat, was aware that many felt the cavalry had a much easier time than the infantry in the 200 mile long retirement. 'Constantly we find a German attack was developing just as the time had come for us to retire', he wrote, 'or that we retired just as an attack was developing'. But this was 'the very essence of a rearguard action – to make the enemy deploy, thus wasting his time, then, when he had made his maximum deployment, to slip away, thus causing him further delay in reforming column of route'. A fact perhaps not fully appreciated by the footsore infantryman, was that their cavalry counterparts performed this duty time and time again; their regimental war diaries being replete with tales of minor rearguard skirmishes carried out on an almost daily basis.

That is not to say that the infantry battalions and other units involved did not suffer from similar running skirmishes with German forces which had slipped through or around the cavalry screen. Drummer George Whittington wrote in his diary on several occasions of his battalion of the Royal Sussex Regiment coming under harassing artillery fire and cavalry attack. Corporal Bernard Denore of the Royal Berkshires also noted the presence of marauding Uhlans and remarked on the fact that every night there appeared to be fewer men to answer their names when read out at roll call. It was a story not unfamiliar to the units of the Royal Field Artillery (RFA), the gunners constantly having to deploy in reply to harassing enemy shellfire. Eric Anderson, a lieutenant with 108 Battery – who fought at Mons and Le Cateau – recalled several occasions on which his battery engaged the pursuing enemy; and on one occasion, at Villeret on 27 August, the gunners were needed to reinforce the infantry firing line with their rifles against enemy cavalry and their supporting Jäger infantry who had been getting perilously close. There was a degree of unease as the brigade fell back from this engagement, so much so that Anderson noted the presence of Brigadier General Freddie Wing – Commander of Royal Artillery in the 3rd Division – directing operations personally.

Nevertheless, every rearguard action fought – whether a major action or a passing skirmish – was instrumental in creating and maintaining the vital gap between the pursuing German forces and a very tired, and often extremely hungry, BEF. Several of these encounters must be regarded as critical actions which contributed to the successful escape of the BEF from the clutches of the German First and Second Armies. General Smith-Dorrien's historic stand at Le Cateau was one such as was the fight at Néry which immortalized the men of L Battery, Royal Horse Artillery. Néry was one of three rearguards fought on 1 September 1914 and although its outcome would impact to some extent on the Battle of the Marne six days later, the actions fought further east at Villers-Cotterêts and at Crépy-en-Valois were still vital in maintaining the integrity of the BEF. At no time during the retreat was the BEF completely safe from pursuit, a factor that Sir John French and his staff at GHQ were only too well aware of.

Much of the literature appertaining to August and September 1914 has elevated the men of Mons and the retreat to almost legendary status. Historians have drawn attention to the professional British Army that stood its ground at Mons and Le Cateau in the face of overwhelming odds, and which, despite the rigours of the retreat, turned defeat into victory at the Battle of the Marne alongside their French allies. British accounts of the retreat tend to gloss over the fact that in the great scheme of things the BEF was very much a minor player over an ever extending battleground that saw six French and seven German armies in the field. To an extent this account of the retreat is guilty of the same omission but the British soldier on the ground would have been only too well aware of his French allies being alongside him and in some cases even competing for the same stretch of road along which he would be compelled to retire.

So what was it about this 'contemptible little army' that enabled it to survive one of the longest retreats in its history? The British *Official History* claimed that the BEF was incomparably well trained, well organized and equipped. Well trained it might have been, but when it came to fighting in a major European conflict there were still some harsh lessons which had to be learned. One of these was the value of good staff work and its impact upon effective command and control. It became clear as the retreat unfolded that the lack of experience of senior officers in handling large bodies of troops on the battlefield certainly contributed to errors of judgement on occasion. At battalion and brigade level the decisions made by Lieutenant Colonel Abercrombie in the deployment of his Connaught Rangers at Le Grand Fayt has to be questioned as does Brigadier General Ivor Maxse's handling of the Etreux episode in which the men of the 2nd Battalion of the Royal Munster Fusiliers (2/RMF) were forced to fight a desperate rearguard action.

At the very senior level, the lack of control by GHQ over operations as a whole is painfully apparent as is its increasing level of isolation from events after

Le Cateau. This is perhaps understandable when the concept of a GHQ as such had not existed in peacetime and on the only occasion when it had been rehearsed it had been felt to have been 'an unwieldy instrument'. Captain Charles Deedes, a serving staff officer with GHQ, felt they were handicapped by 'difficulties in mobilization, ignorance of each other's duties and functions [and] a tendency to work in watertight compartments', all of which made 'the machine creak and groan considerably'. But was it was the creaking and groaning described by Charles Deedes or just plain incompetence that led to the issuing of operational orders that were notorious for their ambiguity? High on that list is the contentious Operational Order Number 8 that split the BEF and left II Corps alone at Le Cateau, a close second must surely be the amateurish wording of the orders issued on 31 August that led, indirectly, to the Néry encounter of 1 September.

Just how far events were influenced by the rivalries that existed between the senior commanders is uncertain but again, questions inevitably arise. Did Douglas Haig drag his heels intentionally on 25 August and allow Smith-Dorrien to face the enemy alone at Le Cateau as Brigadier General Bulfin suggested in his diary? And what was really behind Haig's decision to retire along a separate course for the following five days? Historians will no doubt continue to debate these issues but ultimately the reader must form their own opinion. In mitigation it must be said that Sir John French and his commanders were faced with a huge task in August 1914, a task which placed a massive burden of responsibility on men who had very little or no experience of manoeuvring such large masses of troops over extended periods of time. The performance of GHQ during the initial clashes and the ensuing retreat may be viewed, to use a fashionable phrase of recent years, as a 'learning curve' of astonishing steepness and whilst it might be argued that the retreat was indeed a considerable feat of arms, it could equally be argued that it was accomplished in spite of the actions taken by GHQ.

What was obvious to many at the time, including Brigadier General Aylmer Haldane, commanding 10 Infantry Brigade, was that by agreeing to fight on the French left flank, the BEF was also committed to the French tactical doctrine of *offensive à outrance* – the belief that battles could be won by mass attack and the spirit of offensive. To a degree this was true. With the correct balance of strategic leadership and tactical command much could be achieved in this manner, but both of these attributes were lacking in the French army of August 1914 and, as the junior partner, the BEF was obliged to fall in with French movements.

Compared to the huge conscripted European armies, the British Army was considered insignificant by its rivals, indeed Bismarck once famously quipped that, if necessary, he would send a German policeman to arrest it! By 1914, however, after almost a century of reform and reorganization, it was a highly professional and experienced force of volunteers which had been battle-hardened and honed by its colonial engagements all over the globe. It may not have been fully prepared for operations in a European war but its great strength lay in a regimental system that fostered a regimental pride and *esprit de corps* that was at the very heart of British military tradition. It was this culture of devotion to duty and sacrifice – probably more than anything else – that 'won' the retreat and enabled the BEF to hold together.

I wrote in *Aristocrats Go To War* that the officer corps of 1914 was composed of men of a different character and disposition than those who followed and that they were part of the last legions of Edwardian gentlemen: chivalrous, privileged, stubbornly proud of their traditions and patriots to the core. Above all, I felt, they epitomized the professional British soldier of 1914, earning the devotion of their men and the respect of their opponents. One only has to read the diary of Lieutenant James 'Jim' Pennyman, the young machine-gun officer who fought with his battalion of King's Own Scottish Borderers at Mons and Le Cateau and trudged the whole 200 miles alongside his men on the retreat, to appreciate the inner-strength and quality, not only of Pennyman himself but of the men he commanded.

It was, however, an army that relied upon a large proportion of reservists to bring it up to war strength. The bulk of reservists were former soldiers who had served their period of active engagement and had an obligation to return to the colours in time of national emergency. These were supplemented by men of the Special Reserve. The Special Reservists were similar in many ways to the part-time territorial soldiers in that they were essentially civilians who undertook regular periods of military training, but unlike the Territorials, they were liable for overseas service. The actual number of reservists who went to war in August 1914 is quite staggering, it is estimated that 60 per cent of the BEF's manpower came from its reservists and it was these men who suffered the most due to problems arising from their lack of military fitness on the long march from Mons.

Many units had, in fact, already been on the road for two or three days before arriving at Mons on 22 August; in some cases marching up to forty miles or more from railheads such as that at Landrecies. For a many reservists it was forty miles too far in new boots. Jim Pennyman observed that:

'It is a curious fact that all the reservists' boots were too small for them. When a man leaves the colours he states the size of his boots, and boots of that size are given him when he is called up. The men cannot all be vain enough to ask for sizes too small for them, so the conclusion is either that their feet expand during fat civilian life, or that hard marching makes their feet swell abnormally. Anyhow the state of their feet was appalling'.[1]

It was a problem that would intensify over the course of the retreat as punishing daily marches in the heat of an August sun took their toll of men who were unable to keep pace with their units. Although the march discipline in many units kept the men together, Drummer George Whittington, who had been a regular soldier since 1911, remembered that on some days, it was 'so hot that the men were falling out and even dropping down in the road in dozens'. The more fortunate were collected up in carts and wagons but many of the stragglers were invariably left behind.

Apart from the problem of fitness and new boots, the BEF of 1914 was an army that had been shaped by the need to adapt and develop in the face of new circumstances and challenges. There had been plenty of setbacks in the past, the most recent being in South Africa where the fast-riding and accurate shooting of the Boers shook the army to the core as a seemingly ragged army of farmers succeeded in denting British pride and forced its army to examine its lamentable performance in the field. But some lessons had taken longer to absorb. While the army had learned much in the light of its South African experience, not least in the value of good shooting with the new Mark III Lee Enfield rifle, it still clung to outmoded theories of the superiority of shock tactics by mounted cavalry – the *arme blanche* – over the fire power of machine guns and artillery. The folly of such tactics was driven home in a costly lesson at Audregnies on 24 August when 2 Cavalry Brigade lost heavily against German artillery and machine-gun fire.

This action stands in contrast to the cavalry encounter at Cerizy on 28 August – involving Brigadier General Chetwode's 5 Cavalry Brigade – which was conducted so successfully that it must be regarded as a classic cavalry rearguard action. At Cerizy a single brigade of cavalry and a battery of horse artillery successfully prevented units of the German I Cavalry Corps from exploiting the increasingly large gap that had been created between Douglas Haig's I Corps and Smith-Dorrien's II Corps and did so largely by the effectiveness of their dismounted rifle and machine-gun fire.

Whereas much of the spotlight inevitably falls on the lot of the infantry and cavalry soldier it is all too easy to forget that very often the last of a rearguard force to retire were the men of the Royal Engineers. The sappers worked tirelessly to prepare positions and blow bridges during the retreat under the most trying and dangerous circumstances. This vital work began with blowing the bridges of the Mons-Condé Canal and concluded with the destruction of the Marne bridges. Their story provides continuity over the 200 miles of the retreat as we follow the fortunes of the Royal Engineer Field Companies during their march south. The diary of Second Lieutenant Kenneth Godsell, a sapper officer with the 17th Field Company (17/Field Company), is a wonderful chronology of the retreat from the perspective of a young man barely out of his teens. As you would expect, his view of events contrasts starkly with those provided by the campaign diaries of Generals Aylmer Haldane and Count Gleichen, but it is through the diary accounts of Kenneth Godsell that we get the opportunity to march alongside him and share the discomforts and frustrations of a junior subaltern. The lot of the sapper during the retreat was described somewhat succinctly by Major (later Major General) Ian Playfair in the *RE Journal* of March 1932:

> '*A field company in the retreat seems to have been rather like a dog being taken for a country walk. Master sets himself a fairly definite course, to which dog has generally to conform or else he gets lost. But dog covers twice the distance! He scampers ahead; then darts off to one side; then to the other; and every now and again he gets left and has to be whistled up*'.

One of the more distressing aspects of the retreat was the plight of the wounded. Such was the speed of the retirement that large numbers of the more seriously wounded had to be left behind to fall into German hands. Private Ben Clouting, a cavalryman serving with the 4th Dragoon Guards (4/Dragoon Guards), was heartbroken at having to leave his pal Thomas Cumber behind at a dressing station at Audregnies after he had rescued him under fire. Cumber was taken prisoner along with the field ambulance staff who remained with the wounded. The story of the retreat would also be incomplete without reference to the countless medical officers and RAMC personnel who unflinchingly saw the care of their patients as their primary duty. In the finest traditions of the medical profession Captain Eburne Hamilton, a medical officer with 7 Field Ambulance, remained at St Symphorien on 23 August caring for the wounded and dying men who had fought in the Nimy salient that day. He and five other medical officers were taken prisoner on 23 August and eventually sent to Germany. After the action at Villers-Cotterêts, Captain Marmaduke Wetherell remained with his wounded commanding officer, Lieutenant Colonel Ian Hogg, until he died in the tiny village of Haramont the next day. Like his colleagues, Wetherell was taken prisoner.

Fortunately Lieutenant Cyril Helm – the medical officer attached to the 2nd Battalion King's Own Yorkshire Light Infantry (2/KOYLI) – avoided capture but his observations of the retreat and the costly rearguard action the battalion fought at Le Cateau provide a fascinating account from the perspective of a non-combatant. At Le Cateau his battalion aid post was close to the guns of XXVIII Brigade, he saw for himself the effects of German counter-battery fire. 'It was a ghastly sight eventually seeing all the guns silenced one after the other. From one battery only one man escaped, all the officers being killed'. It was the opinion of Helm and many of his colleagues that the breakdown of horse transport during the retreat had a paralysing effect upon the efficient evacuation of the wounded by the field ambulances. Had there been enough of the relatively new motor ambulances in service in August 1914, the imprisonment of many of the wounded who fell into captivity may well have been avoided and many more lives may well have been saved.

Casualty figures are probably some of the most massaged and inaccurate statistics available, particularly when it comes to an estimation of enemy casualties, but I would argue that casualty figures themselves are not the key factor in an engagement; it is the impact which that engagement has on future events that is of greater consequence. The *Official History* records British casualties between 23 August and 5 September as a little over 15,000 – the majority of those being from units of II Corps – a quite shocking number until it is realized that casualties is a generic term that covers those killed, wounded, missing or taken prisoner. Quite literally a soldier is considered to be a casualty if he is missing from roll call and thus unable to be counted as an effective fighting man.

In fact the numbers of British actually killed during the retreat was relatively light – although some battalions were hit harder than others in this respect. Where the BEF suffered most heavily was in the numbers of men taken prisoner, either after engagements such as Mons, Le Cateau and Etreux, or as a result of men being left behind on the march, exhausted, wounded or in some cases simply unwilling or unable to continue. Men became easily detached from their parent unit in the confusion and were consequently posted at missing at roll call that evening, only to turn up days later having tagged along behind another unit. On 5 September some 20,000 men were absent from the original numbers of the BEF, of which a large proportion rejoined later.

There is little doubt that the BEF gave a good account of itself at Mons but there is now a body of opinion that suggests German casualty figures at Mons and, three days later at Le Cateau, were not nearly as high as British sources would have them. A similar question mark hovers over the popular belief that German forces attacking at Mons were convinced that they were facing a large number of machine guns, an impression given apparently by the sustained and devastating rifle fire from British infantry. British sources also hold fast to the belief that the infantry of II Corps, holding the line of the canal at Mons, cut the advancing 'grey hordes' down in their hundreds, a view that is at odds with the casualty figures recorded in German war diaries and histories. Any view that brings this into question is likely to be unpopular as the events at Mons and Le Cateau have become ingrained in the British military psyche and are held as almost sacred in the minds of many individuals.

There is also a misconception in some minds as to exactly why the BEF had to retreat from their Mons positions. What has to be appreciated is that on 23 August 1914 Sir John French anticipated advancing north on the left flank of General Lanrezac's Fifth Army and the Mons positions were purely a jumping off point for that advance. Instead he was forced into a defensive encounter from which the BEF only escaped by the skin of its teeth and, despite Sir John's protestations, the battle of Le Cateau was an inevitable and necessary adjunct.

Essentially the British retreat from Mons was precipitated by two factors: Lanrezac's retirement on the British right and the weight of German forces that had penetrated deeply into the British centre, had taken Mons itself and threatened both flanks of the BEF. Sir John French may have placed the blame on Charles Lanrezac for exposing his right flank, but in reality he had no other choice. Had he remained and committed I Corps to the fight, the BEF would almost certainly have been destroyed – he was in no position to operate independently of the French.

Chapter 1

Prelude

German military forces crossed the border into Belgium at 2 minutes past 8 on the morning of 4 August 1914 and as Belgian gendarmes opened fire near the frontier town of Gemmerich, war was ignited. It was a war which the Chief of the German Army staff, Helmuth von Moltke, felt would 'decide the course of history for the next hundred years.'

German forces in the west numbered some 1,500,000 men who were deployed in seven army groups along the Belgian and French borders with the First Army on the extreme right opposite Liège and the Seventh Army holding the left flank in Alsace. Their invasion strategy for France and Belgium – first formulated by Count Alfred von Schlieffen in 1905 – had been planned to the last detail, taking into account what they hoped would be every unforeseen event that might impact on the timetable of attack and advance. Schlieffen's plan was for a war on two fronts: a swift and decisive incursion into France which would be concluded before Russian forces in the east would be able to mobilize effectively. Staff officers at German General Headquarters (OHL) were confident that their calculations of Russian railway mileage and the limitations this would impose on Russian Army mobilization would allow their armies in the west to overwhelm France and then move enough divisions to the east to defeat the Russian Bear.

Thus in August 1914, as the countdown to war began, the Sixth and Seventh German Armies were in position along the Alsace and Lorraine front, the Fourth and Fifth Armies were poised to invade France through the Ardennes and Luxembourg and on the right wing, the First, Second and Third Armies were ready to advance through neutral Belgium. The three armies of the German right wing were commanded by relatively old men, two of whom, General Alexander von Kluck, commanding the First Army and General Klaus von Bülow of the Second Army, were veterans of the Franco–Prussian War of 1870. Although both commanders were 68-years-old, the more energetic and aggressive command style of von Kluck often clashed with that of the more cautious von Bülow.

Von Kluck's First Army was deployed on the extreme right wing of the German force in the west. His orders were to attack the left flank of the French

Army and drive them back, ultimately enveloping Paris before turning east to trap the French between the Franco–German border and the German armies advancing from Alsace and Lorraine, thereby bringing a rapid conclusion to the war. Although the First Army had the greatest offensive striking power, a density of about 18,000 men per mile of front, they had the longest distance to march. It was von Kluck's men who would first clash with the BEF at Mons.

At 4.30 pm on 4 August 1914, British land forces were ordered to mobilize for war against Germany in response to the violation of Belgian neutrality. Almost immediately nearly 70,000 reservists began to pour into regimental depots as the smooth machinery of mobilization organized Britain's Army for its first war on the continental mainland of Europe in almost 100 years. Screened by the ships of the Royal Navy, the embarkation of the BEF began on 11 August with up to thirty-seven ships per day carrying men, equipment and supplies to Rouen, Le Havre and Boulogne. After landing in France troops were dispatched to nearby rest camps before embarking on lengthy train journeys to the BEF forward assembly area near Maubeuge. By 20 August assembly was complete and apart from the odd hiccup, it had all gone like clockwork.

The Royal Flying Corps (RFC), under the command of Brigadier General Sir David Henderson, had only officially come into being in April 1912 but over the course of the next few weeks this fledgling force of aviators would establish the reconnaissance role of aircraft as a vital necessity and in doing so would write the opening chapter of the history of the first air war. The vanguard of the RFC consisted of Aeroplane Squadrons 2, 3, 4, and 5 and an Aircraft Park, the main body of the ground personnel and stores going by sea and the aircraft of 2, 3 and 4 squadrons flying across the channel on 13 August. The first to arrive at Amiens at 8.20 am was the 2 Squadron pilot Lieutenant Hubert Harvey-Kelly in his BE2a.[2] Number 5 Squadron arrived two days later. By the evening of 15 August over fifty aircraft of all shapes and sizes were parked at the Amiens airstrip waiting to fly to the forward airbase at Maubeuge the next morning.

If the architect of the BEF was Lord Haldane then Major General Henry Wilson – a fluent French speaker and enthusiastic Francophile – was a willing acolyte.[3] Convinced of the inevitability of war with Germany, Wilson had planned for the BEF's role in support of the French since 1909 when he began touring the border areas France shared with Germany and Belgium. In 1911, when he was Director of Military Operations, he committed the British Army through an unofficial memorandum with the French Chief of Staff, General Auguste Dubail, to a deployment of six infantry divisions and a cavalry division that would concentrate at Maubeuge and be ready to fight thirteen days after mobilization. Apart from his considerable intellect and obvious charisma, Wilson was also a devious intriguer upon whom Sir John French relied heavily for advice, advice that was not always supported by accurate intelligence. It was Wilson's advice on the strength and deployment of German forces that significantly contributed to the climate of confusion which existed prior to the engagement at Mons on 23 August 1914.

Sir John French was 61-years-old in August 1914 and had made his reputation commanding the British Cavalry Division in the South African War. His command of the celebrated cavalry charge at Klip Drift and the subsequent relief of Kimberley propelled his face and name onto the front pages of the British press and at the end of the war he was one of only a handful of senior officers to emerge with their reputations intact. Nevertheless, this brave and resourceful soldier, who was more at home leading troops in the field, lacked the basic mastery of the management of strategic command. He was one of the few senior officers in the BEF who had not attended the Staff College at Camberley and in the opinion of historian Nikolas Gardner, 'lacked the intellectual focus necessary to direct a force as large and complex as the BEF'.

To be fair none of the then current crop of senior officers in the British Army had experience of commanding a force larger than a division during active operations. At corps level Sir Douglas Haig was the only commander to have a permanent staff prior to mobilization and even then it required several inexperienced newcomers to bring it up to full establishment. Apart from the capable Brigadier General Forestier-Walker as his chief of staff, Smith-Dorrien's II Corps was initially very poorly staffed and suffered greatly from inexperienced and indifferent staff officers. Unbelievably, the Cavalry Corps had no permanent staff officers at all prior to August 1914. Colonel John Vaughan was appointed Chief Staff Officer – an individual described as more at home instructing horsemanship than grappling with senior staff work – and if it were not for the ability of Lieutenant Colonel George de Symons Barrow as Chief Intelligence Officer and Major 'Sally' Home, Allenby would have encountered even greater difficulties than he actually did during the retreat.[4] Predictably these problems with the staff structures would come back to haunt the BEF time and time again in 1914.

Furthermore, and potentially more harmful, was the unhealthy triangle of tension that existed between Sir John French and his two corps commanders. In spite of a general agreement that the 1914 British Army was a highly professional force, in the higher strata of command there was still an importance placed on social traditions, individual personalities and friendships which often led to professional rivalries. The careers of many promising officers were all too often at the mercy of circles of patronage that would favour certain individuals in their quest for promotion to the higher ranks of command, a system that could block promotion as well as enable it. This was by no means unusual of course. Circles of patronage exist in many organizations, particularly those where opportunities for senior positions are limited.

The tensions between Sir John French and Sir Horace Smith-Dorrien, for example, stemmed from the second South African War where Smith-Dorrien's early career flourished under the patronage of Sir Evelyn Wood and Lord Roberts. Like Sir John, his reputation as a field commander during the South African campaign had provided him with a professional pedigree that opened the gateway to further promotion. Even though they were on good terms during the early parts of their respective careers, their professional relationship came to a head after Smith-Dorrien's appointment in 1907 as General Officer Commanding (GOC) Aldershot Command. His predecessor was Sir John, whom, as a former cavalry officer, laid great emphasis on the value of cavalry training and the importance of the sword and lance in the massed cavalry charge. Smith-Dorrien – in a far sighted move that underlined his deepening understanding of the developing role of cavalry – laid a greater emphasis on dismounted work and musketry training, demanding that the cavalry be every bit as effective as the infantry with the Short Magazine Lee Enfield rifle.

The third personality in the triangle was Douglas Haig, who at 53-years-old was the youngest of the three men. He served as Chief of Staff to Sir John French during the South African campaign and afterwards had benefitted considerably from Sir John's patronage. But Haig's self interest in advancing his own career did not fall short of criticism of his former chief. Whatever doubts he may have harboured, it was only when French had been appointed to command the BEF that Haig's criticism surfaced. He missed no opportunity to exploit his access to the Royal Family to voice his concerns over Sir John's leadership capability.[5] Shortly before leaving for France on 11 August Haig used his privileged access to the King to express his doubts about Sir John's suitability as Commander-in-Chief.

Unquestionably Haig saw himself as the more suitable choice for the top job and after the demise of Grierson must have viewed the arrival of a more senior colleague in the form of Smith-Dorrien as a setback to his ambitions. Haig apparently felt no personal hostility towards Smith-Dorrien but there were several occasions when it appeared he deliberately avoided supporting his II Corps colleague. Nevertheless, allowing professional jealousies and personal ambition to surface and fester did nothing to ease the unprecedented burden of responsibility that the senior BEF commanders had to face and master in 1914.

The BEF's assembly area was a narrow strip running from Maubeuge in the north east to Le Cateau in the south west where Sir John French had established his GHQ in a school house in the centre of the town. On its right was the XVIII Corps of the French Fifth Army and on its immediate left the French 84th Territorial Division. The French Plan XVII, as it became known, was outlined to Sir John at French Supreme Headquarters (GQG) by the French Commander-in-Chief, General Joseph Joffre. In concept it was quite simple: the Third and Fourth French Armies were to strike northeast through the Ardennes against the rear of the German Army advancing through Belgium, while the French Fifth Army of General Charles Lanrezac together with the

BEF would advance into Belgium north of the River Meuse and outflank the right wing of the German Army in a pincer movement. It was a plan in keeping with the French military strategy of *offensive à outrance* and like many such plans that had been dreamt up on the map tables of GQG, it looked good on paper. Unfortunately the optimism expressed by the French Commander-in-Chief was not shared by Lanrezac who was becoming increasingly concerned, and quite rightly as it turned out, by reports of the true strength of the advancing German forces, a factor apparently being ignored by Joffre at GQG in spite of intelligence to the contrary.

* * *

The British advance into Belgium was a short one; the German First and Second Armies were rapidly closing from the north and to make matters worse, the German Third Army under General Max von Hausen was moving swiftly towards them from the east. Lanrezac's reluctance to advance in accordance with the wishes of GQG almost certainly saved the Fifth Army and the BEF from destruction. However, none of this was apparent early on 22 August as the BEF moved into their positions at Mons to align with Lanrezac's Fifth Army then assembled along the line of the River Sambre between Namur and Charleroi.

Regular and effective liaison between army commanders is vital if they are to co-operate with one another and share intelligence. Unfortunately the relationship between Sir John French and Charles Lanrezac got off to a disastrous start and never really recovered thereafter. From the moment of their first meeting on 17 August at Rethel both men took an instant dislike to each other. Lanrezac's obvious sarcasm and distrust of his British allies was not lost on those who were present at the meeting and as Lieutenant Edward Spears – acting as a liaison officer between the BEF and the French Fifth Army – later observed, Lanrezac's indifference to the BEF and complete disregard for any form of co-operation had a profound impact on the opening phase of the campaign, the consequences of which resulted in a running sore of distrust that remained a permanent obstacle between Sir John and his Fifth Army counterpart. Thus with GQG still minimising intelligence reports regarding the strength of the German right wing and communication with the Fifth Army almost non-existent, the BEF was very much thrown back on its own ability to gather intelligence.

Unfortunately that intelligence was largely disregarded by GHQ. On 21 August George Barrow rode into Mons and took over the railway telephone office. For the next twelve hours he contacted all 'the possible and impossible places in Belgium not known yet to be in German hands'. From the replies received he was able to get a fairly accurate picture of the German advance, a picture that indicated the German right wing was much further west than had at first been realized. GHQ chose to ignore this new intelligence suggesting it was exaggerated, adding the instruction that the Cavalry Division was not to become seriously engaged. Not surprisingly, this reply was signed by Henry Wilson.

It wasn't long before British cavalry patrols reported their first clashes with the forward units of the German 9th Cavalry Division and this, together with reconnaissance provided by the RFC, began to reveal the advance of the German IX and III Army Corps and the presence of the German II Army Corps marching southwest along a route that would bring it outside the British left flank at Mons. But what the British had failed to detect in time was the presence of the German IV Army Corps which was far more of an immediate threat than the II Army Corps which was still two days march away.

The RFC reconnaissance flights had been filing reports on German troop movements since 19 August. On Saturday 22 August, twelve reconnaissance flights revealed the presence of large bodies of troops moving in the direction of Mons and several aircraft reported coming under fire. But it was the flight undertaken by Captain Lionel Charlton and Second Lieutenant Vivian Wadham which finally confirmed the scale of the approaching storm. Having landed near Grammont it did not take the British airmen long to discover that:

> 'We had landed absolutely in the middle of a large concentration of German troops, the nearest of which was about a quarter of an hour's walk away. After collecting some quite good information … we hurriedly switched on the engine and started off hoping for the best. When about 500 feet up, we flew plumb over a German brigade halted for the dinner hour … I imagine someone must have said: "By Jove! There goes an English aeroplane: let's have it" At any rate every man jack jumped to his feet and loosed off at us.'[6]

On landing, the aircraft was found to have over forty bullet holes in addition to a badly damaged spar. They had been very fortunate. Charlton himself had a very near miss; as he clambered out of the machine he found his safety belt had been shot through by a German bullet.

Incredibly, Sir John's reaction to this intelligence was lukewarm and it was not until he had confirmation – in the form of a very concerned Lieutenant Spears – that he began to place any faith in it. Just why he did not appear to take his own intelligence reports seriously perhaps provides the first clue as to the poor quality of advice he was receiving from his staff – Henry Wilson in particular.

The predicament that faced the Commander-in-Chief on 22 August hinged on GHQ's understanding that both the BEF and the French Fifth Army were to advance at the earliest possible moment. With the BEF moving up to positions along the Mons-Condé Canal, Sir John was actually on his way to discuss the joint offensive with Lanrezac when he met Spears on the roadside. The young lieutenant had actually been on his way to see Sir John and took the opportunity to relay his fears that Lanrezac was seriously considering remaining on the south bank of the Sambre and not advancing as had been intended. He also shared with his commander-in-chief the view from the Fifth Army Intelligence Bureau that the far-flung German movements to the west could only mean an enveloping movement on a huge scale. More importantly he confirmed the presence of the II German Army Corps which had been identified by the RFC reconnaissance flights.

The pincer movement envisaged by Joffre and Plan XVII was now taking place in reverse and the BEF was in danger of being attacked on two sides. The fact that this information was relayed to the BEF via Spears and not through official channels gives some indication of the extent of the ill-feeling extant between Sir John and Charles Lanrezac. Consequently, Sir John French's planned meeting with Lanrezac on 22 August 1914 never took place. On hearing from Spears that the Fifth Army commander was at Mettet, Sir John judged it too far to travel and despite Spears almost pleading with his commander-in-chief to change his mind, Sir John returned to Le Cateau.

When Spears arrived back at Fifth Army HQ he found the opening blows of the Battle of Charleroi well underway with units of the German Second Army attacking along the length of the Sambre but it was a battle that was lost before it was fought. Lanrezac was half-hearted and dispirited with a fatalism that was not improved by bad news filtering through from the French offensive in the east: there the twenty divisions of the French Third and Fourth Armies pushing into the Ardennes had blundered into the German Fourth and Fifth Armies suffering enormous losses and near rout in the process. Joffre's plan and doctrine of headlong offensive had been dealt a fatal blow and the BEF, now in position along the Mons-Condé Canal, was about to feel the weight of the German First Army onslaught.

On the evening of 22 August any shred of optimism that might have prevailed was dashed when the French Fifth Army was alerted to the presence of the German XII Saxon Corps at Dinant threatening the Fifth Army's right flank. Lanrezac concluded that his only course of action was to fall back to a new position and he thus informed Joffre. To his shame he did not see fit to share his decision with Sir John French who was still under the impression that all was well on his right flank. Once again it was the resolute Spears who brought the bad news to GHQ, finally prompting Sir John to cancel the planned advance of the BEF. There was a further rather bizarre episode that night when an officer from Lanrezac's staff arrived at Le Cateau with a request for the BEF to attack the right flank of the German Second Army. It was an impossible demand and the British reply was cordial and to the effect that they would hold their current positions at Mons for twenty-four hours.

While GHQ was apparently unaware until a few hours before of the actual strength of the German forces confronting them, von Kluck was just as surprised to find both corps of the BEF at Mons. On the morning of 22 August the German First Army was still under the impression that the BEF would appear in the Lille area and had landed six divisions at Boulogne and Calais. Even though German First Army intelligence had reported British troops in the Mons area and British aircraft had been observed over Louvain as early as 20 August, First Army orders for 23 August anticipated an easy day's march south expecting to meet the BEF either at Lille or Maubeuge.

One possible explanation for this failure was von Bülow's rather single-minded focus on the Second Army's battle with Lanrezac on the Sambre. Even though he had overall responsibility for the right wing, he deprived von Kluck of much of his cavalry screen. Up until late on the 21 August the only cavalry assigned to the First Army was one cavalry division, the remainder being deployed north of the Sambre with von Bülow. It was only on the morning of the 22 August that the German 9th Cavalry Division encountered elements of 4/Dragoon Guards on their way to Ath and reported it. So intent was he on continuing his wide sweeping movement to the west that von Kluck chose to ignore the possibility that the skirmish with British cavalry and the presence of RFC reconnaissance aircraft was an indication that the BEF lay in his path.

On the morning of 23 August 1914 the BEF was in position thus: Smith-Dorrien's II Corps lined the canal between Mons and Condé facing north while Haig's I Corps was posted along the Beaumont–Mons road facing northeast. To the west the cavalry guarded the canal crossings as far as Condé. It was not the ideal battleground. The canal position had a serious weakness at its eastern point where it formed a salient around Nimy, a weakness that worried Smith-Dorrien to such an extent that he had prepared a more defensible line a few miles further back along a line that ran through Dour –Frameries – Paturages.

But the drama was building quickly and events to the east now dictated the next moves of the BEF. At 8.00 pm on 23 August, GHQ at Le Cateau finally received word from Joffre that French intelligence had underestimated the strength of German forces opposing the BEF, information that was already only too apparent to Smith-Dorrien's II Corps, which, by now, was retiring to its second position south of Mons. Yet even in possession of this conclusive evidence, Sir John stubbornly clung to his belief that advance was still a possibility, his message to II Corps timed at 8.40 pm that evening ordered them to stand firm and strengthen their new positions during the night. By the time the British II Corps received this signal General Lanrezac had already ordered the general retirement of his Fifth Army and once again had not seen fit to inform the British.

It was left to Spears to make the journey to Le Cateau to inform Sir John, whom, with no alternative left open to him, finally decided, at midnight, to retire. The young lieutenant had, through his dogged persistence and sure grasp of the overall strategic picture, in effect saved the British Army. The retreat had begun.

Chapter 2

23 August – A Very Short Fortnight

Lieutenant Thomas Wollocombe had been a regular soldier for nearly six years. After leaving Wellington College in the summer of 1906 he began his army career as a gentleman cadet at the Royal Military College Sandhurst and was commissioned into the Middlesex Regiment as a subaltern a year later. Promotion to lieutenant came after three years and shortly afterwards, he was appointed adjutant of the regiment's 4th Battalion. Late in the afternoon of 22 August 1914 he and his commanding officer were approaching Mons at the head of the battalion under orders to move north and defend the eastern sweep of the wide loop of the Canal du Centre. Just south of Hyon the battalion was halted:

> 'In front of us was a large wooded hill called Bois le Haut [sic] and the road led along the south of it and round the western end where Hyon was situated ... the CO and I rode onto [Hyon] in advance of the battalion to talk to the advance guard cavalry commander, Lieut. Whittle of the 15th Hussars. He had not much news except our protective cavalry screen were in touch with the Uhlans who had bolted at the first sight of our cavalry.'[7]

31-year-old Cyril Whittle was a troop commander with A Squadron, 15th The King's Hussars (15/Hussars), which was attached to the 1st Division as divisional cavalry. Deployed as a forward cavalry screen, he and Second Lieutenant Charles Hoare with their respective troops had been in contact with German cavalry intermittently all that day and by the time they met Wollocombe at Hyon, had been in the saddle for over ten hours. It was a similar story elsewhere. Since early that morning cavalry patrols had been in contact with German forces north of the canal; further east, and rather more worrying, a patrol of the Royal Scots Greys from 5 Cavalry Brigade had encountered a strong enemy column moving south east from La Louvière. This force, comprising of the German 13th Infantry Division (13 ID) and part of von Richthofen's I Cavalry Corps, was the right wing of von Bülow's Second Army which had already crossed the canal and was on course to attack the right flank of the BEF through the gap left by the retirement of Lanrezac's Fifth Army.

The 4/Middlesex was one of four infantry battalions in the British 8 Infantry Brigade commanded by Brigadier General Beauchamp Doran. 4/Middlesex was brigaded with the 2nd Battalion Royal Irish Regiment (2/Royal Irish), 1st Battalion Gordon Highlanders (1/Gordons) and the 2nd Battalion Royal Scots (2/Royal Scots), all of whom would be in action to a greater or lesser extent over the next 24 hours. As the Middlesex were marching up towards their canal positions, the Gordons and Royal Scots were digging in along the eastern edge of the Bois la Haut to secure the right flank of the salient, while the Royal Irish, who would play such a vital part in the next day's fighting, were ordered to stay in reserve at St Symphorien and Villers St Ghislain.

Having had Whittle's assurance that the ground ahead of them was unoccupied, Wollocombe rode back to fetch the rest of the battalion. He took with him his commanding officer's orders to form a defensive line running along the south side of the canal loop which also included three bridges which would become the focus of early German attacks the following day. Lieutenant Colonel Charles Hull, 4/Middlesex's commanding officer, was a particularly proactive leader and although he was limited in the deployment of the battalion by the line of the canal, he and Wollocombe spent much of the late afternoon and early evening visiting each of their four companies, making adjustments and improvements to their defensive positions. D Company had moved quickly to occupy the canal line to the right of the two bridges near Obourg railway station whilst B Company had dug in to their left to link up with the right of the 4th Battalion Royal Fusiliers (4/Royal Fusiliers) busy preparing the western face of the canal bend for defence. The men of C Company were behind the line of the canal just east of the Convent on the Obourg-Mons road and A Company was in position to their left, south of the railway line between Obourg and Nimy.

Brigadier General Doran's 8 Brigade was accountable to Lieutenant General Hubert Hamilton commanding the 3rd Division. Of the division's three brigades, it was Doran's Brigade together with Brigadier General Frederick Shaw's 9 Brigade which would bear the brunt of the fighting in the canal bend that formed the Nimy salient. The remainder of Smith-Dorrien's II Corps was deployed along 18 miles of the canal stretching west of the 4/Middlesex positions at Nimy. Standing to the left of the 3rd Division, where the canal formed a straight reach to Condé, was Major General Sir Charles Fergusson's 5th Division, west of them, standing sentinel over the canal crossings as far as Condé, was Allenby's Cavalry whose task was later taken on by 19 Infantry Brigade.

Concerned at the vulnerability of II Corps' positions, particularly those in the Nimy salient, Smith-Dorrien had not only established a fall-back position south of Mons but had immediately set in motion plans for the demolition of the bridges along the canal should he be compelled to give ground. The second line of defence also had the advantage of flattening out the sharp angle which formed the junction with Haig's I Corps. The sector of canal defended by II Corps was crossed by no less than eighteen road and rail bridges in addition to the numerous locks which could easily be negotiated by infantry on foot. Even if there had been a demolition plan in existence it would have been a tall order for the sappers of the Royal Engineers (RE) to prepare and blow all the crossing points. Nevertheless, on the evening of 22 August the four RE Field Companies with II Corps and the 1/Field Squadron attached to the cavalry began their reconnaissance of the not inconsiderable task which lay ahead.

20-year-old Second Lieutenant Kenneth Godsell had arrived in France on 18 August with 17/Field Company and after what felt like a seemingly endless journey by sea, rail and latterly on foot all the way from the sprawling army barracks at the Curragh, some fifteen miles from Dublin, he had finally pitched up in Belgium His unit had spent most of 21 August on the road, marching up towards Mons, Godsell noting in his diary that, 'the weather was terribly hot, boots were new, socks were new and sore feet were prevalent.' The next day as they approached Mons he recorded another hot and dusty march with the infantry 'falling out like flies'. Also marching with 17/Field Company that day was Lieutenant Gerald Smyth, a charismatic Irishman from County Down who had been posted to the unit from Gibraltar in 1913.

On the night of 22 August, Gerald Smyth and Kenneth Godsell were at St Ghislain engaged in digging trenches on the north bank of the canal and loop-holing houses and walls for defence. At 5.00 pm they were visited by Sir Charles Fergusson who stopped to chat to Gerald Smyth; both men knew of each other from hunting in Ireland and spent several minutes passing the time of day. The general's parting words, as he turned to leave with his escort of lancers, contained advice to the effect that Smyth ought not to 'work too hard as we should probably have a fortnight to prepare the position'. Fergusson continued on his tour of the canal and a little further on came upon the sappers of 59/Field Company who were preparing the Les Herbières bridgeheads for defence. Calling 24 year-old Lieutenant James Pennycuick over to explain what his men were doing, the young officer took the opportunity to ask the general what was happening as they 'knew nothing, had not seen a German or heard a shot fired.' Pennycuick remembered the general's laughing reply: 'I can't tell you much,' said Fergusson, 'we may be here for a week or two or perhaps go on tomorrow.' As Kenneth Godsell later remarked in his diary, it was to be a 'very short fortnight'!

* * *

Sunday 23 August dawned misty with a light drizzle. The 4/Middlesex stood to arms at 4.30 am and afterwards Lieutenant Colonel Hull left battalion HQ in the Chemin du Carron on a tour of the Middlesex positions leaving his adjutant in charge. Wollocombe had just finished his breakfast when he was handed a signal from 3rd Division HQ to the effect that the 56/Field Company RE had been detailed to prepare the bridges on the canal from Nimy to Ville-sur-Haine for demolition. Although the first contact of the day came shortly afterwards at 6.00 am when D Company reported a skirmish with German infantry of Infantry Regiment 86 (IR 86), the extent to which German forces were already in strength on the north bank of the canal loop had not become immediately apparent to the Middlesex; an impression that rapidly changed when sappers of 56/Field Company approached the bridges early that morning.[8]

Major Norman Hopkins, the Officer Commanding 56/Field Company, had personally reconnoitred the bridges on the previous evening and asked permission to prepare them for demolition immediately. He was told to do nothing before 6.30 am the next morning. Now it was too late. Handicapped by German snipers and having difficulty identifying their targets, the accompanying two platoons of C Company of 2/Royal Irish under Captain James Fitzgerald, were unable to provide enough covering fire to allow the sappers to move onto the bridges. The exact details of what happened next is unclear, but one section led by Lieutenant Herbert Holt was overcome on the Rue des Bragons Bridge which left Holt dead and the remainder of the section captured.[9] The other two parties were equally unsuccessful, forcing Fitzgerald to withdraw and issue orders for his men to strengthen D Company at Obourg railway station. Thus the bridges were left intact and this, together with the now unguarded crossing points along the canal to the east of the Middlesex positions, exposed the weakness of the Nimy salient and set in train the inevitable withdrawal which occurred later in the afternoon.

The initial contacts and skirmishes soon gave way to an artillery barrage that not only heralded the opening of the battle but also announced the arrival of the sunshine. Compared to the shelling the BEF was to experience on the Aisne a month later in September and at Ypres during October and November the bombardment was not unduly ferocious, but for men coming under shellfire for the first time it must have been a frightening introduction. At the Middlesex HQ the opening round of the battle was announced just as Lieutenant Wollocombe was preparing to take an early lunch:

'... *consisting of tea and a plate of beef steak which was almost too tough to eat, but which I managed to get through. It was immediately followed by a signal from the Germans that the battle had started in the shape of a shell which burst at the head of the quarry somewhere. It was quickly followed by another, like my first mouthful of beef.*'[10]

Lieutenant Baron Allistone, a special reserve officer who had fallen out on the march up to Mons with sore feet, chose precisely this moment to report to Wollocombe having just been discharged by the battalion's medical officer:

'He wanted to know what to do so I sent him off to his company at Obourg station. I am to say that this was the most unfortunate company in the action and he never returned. He was one of the missing after the action.'[11]

Allistone had chosen a singularly bad moment to rejoin his company. D Company with its commander, Captain Harold Glass, was at that very moment under very intense machine-gun and shellfire and although initially keeping German forces at bay was being very sorely pressed and taking heavy casualties.

By 10.30 am German infantry of IR 86, using the captured bridges to cross the canal, were beginning to establish a firing line on the south bank and moving round the right flank of the detachment at the railway station. It had been a courageous defence but the men of D Company were now ordered to retire by Captain Glass. Leaving many wounded and dying comrades behind, the remnants of D Company fell back through the dense woodland to the rear. The last man to leave the railway station at Obourg was Lieutenant Allistone.[12] Interestingly Allistone does not make any mention of the lone Middlesex soldier who was reported to have remained on the roof of the station to cover the withdrawal. He and the six men with him were soon captured on the Havre-Mons road but not before they had realised that the Germans had worked their way round the rear of their positions.

Now wounded and with his second-in-command, Captain Kenneth Roy, killed, Glass sent an urgent message back to battalion HQ for reinforcements, a request that went unheeded by the remaining Middlesex companies as they were also fully engaged with the Germans advancing from the north and east of their positions. With the pressure building, Brigadier General Doran now ordered up his reserve battalion, the 2/Royal Irish, which responded immediately by sending two companies to extend the left flank of the Middlesex who had been pushed back east of the cemetery across the Obourg road. Reinforced by the men of the Royal Irish, the remaining Middlesex men of its C Company – now in an arc facing roughly north east – put up a stiff resistance around the communal cemetery.

But the Irish were soon in difficulties themselves. Soon after 3.00 pm Lieutenant Colonel St John Cox, the Royal Irish CO, was badly concussed by a high explosive shell whilst on the high ground east of the hospital, command falling temporarily to Major Stratford St Leger. Known throughout the battalion as 'Zulu', a nickname he had acquired in South Africa during the second Boer War, St Leger's reputation as a brave and resourceful officer was second to none amongst his contemporaries. Like many senior officers of his generation he had been under fire before and this was certainly not the first time he had been outnumbered by enemy forces in a precarious situation. Fourteen years earlier in South Africa he had been in command of a company of mounted infantry at the disastrous action at Sannah's Post. During that action as his company had been obliged to retire under heavy Boer rifle fire a wounded man was seen running towards them. Under heavy fire St Leger had returned to pick him up and bring him to safety. Now, in command of a very heavily-pressed battalion, he gave orders which initiated what was probably the finest fighting withdrawal of the day and which enabled the beleaguered survivors of 8 Brigade to slip away.

The fighting which took place that afternoon and early evening, commencing on the rising ground of the communal cemetery and concluding on the southern edge of the Bois la Haut, was often at close-quarters and ferocious in its intensity. German infantry had infiltrated the Irish and Middlesex positions by using the confusion of streets and wooded areas that surrounded the cemetery and, whilst maintaining a desperate defence, the two battalions were taking heavy losses from the advancing Germans. The Middlesex had lost a considerable number of their officers and NCOs and the Irish too were becoming severely handicapped by the number of their own officers who had been killed, wounded or had simply gone missing. By 5.15 pm the Germans were within 250 yards of the Irish and Middlesex positions and the situation had become desperate. St Leger, in consultation with Colonel Hull of the Middlesex, selected the open ground in front of the hospital on the Faubourg-Barthelmy road as a fallback position. It was to be the first of three more deliberate and disciplined retirements that the Irish would make that day.

With the second position temporarily secured by St Leger's men, small parties of Middlesex were being directed by Wollocombe to the relative security of the road running alongside the wooded slopes of the Bois la Haut.

'*We retired* [through the Royal Irish lines] *along this road where the ambulance wagons were gradually filled up and the doctors were very hard at work with shells bursting all around them. We continued to retire to Hyon, the place we had left the night before.*'[13]

On the outskirts of Hyon the Middlesex were ambushed and there Colonel Hull and his men fought a final action before managing to extricate themselves in order to retire to the relative safety of Nouvelle.

Once Colonel Hull and the Middlesex had retired, Major St Leger moved back to his third position just north of Hyon and finally, at 7.00 pm, to the wooded slopes of the south eastern corner of the Bois la Haut where they joined up with the 1/Gordons. It was not long before the first German infantry of IR 76 were seen closing in on the Gordons and Royal Scots from the north east but from their partly-concealed positions a heavy dose of rifle and machine- gun fire put paid to any further German advance that evening. In the final act of the day the Royal Irish were ordered to entrench with the Gordons around the remaining guns of XL Brigade, RFA. Many of the exhausted men must have thought this corner of Belgium would be their last stand; but fortune chose to smile, German forces halted at dusk and at 10.00 pm orders were received to:

> '... *manhandle the guns as quietly as possible on to the road. Bayonets were fixed, the necessity of marching in absolute silence and without light having been impressed upon all, with small advanced and rear guard, the remainder of the battalion strung out on each side of the guns in the pitch blackness of the night retired to Nouvelles at about 12 midnight without opposition'.*[14]

One more story of gallantry took place during the late afternoon and evening of 23 August. Back up on the crossroads, where the roads from Beaumont and Charleroi met, Regimental Quartermaster Sergeant Thomas Fitzpatrick had collected about forty cooks, grooms and store men and was engaging the forward units of IR 35 and IR 85 advancing from the east. He had the advantage of being on the high ground and having a good field of fire, a task much improved by the arrival of one of the damaged Royal Irish machine guns which was repaired by Sergeant Michael Redmond and brought into action. Incredibly he and the survivors held on until midnight to escape and rejoin the battalion the next day.

As the wounded men of both battalions were pouring back down the Beaumont road, 28 year-old Captain Eburne Hamilton, a doctor serving with 7/Field Ambulance was attending to as many of the walking wounded as he could. Hamilton had just received orders to fall back with his section when:

> '...*a bugler galloped up from the direction of the road we had just left knocking sparks from the cobbled pavement and said a major of the Gordons was lying along the road with his leg smashed up. My bearers were falling in at the end of the foot path which we intended to go back along but I asked for 2 stretcher bearers and a stretcher and sent the rest in charge of the sergeant straight back. It was awfully hot and as we were expecting rifle bullets all the time, we took whatever cover we could – rested for a few seconds – and then ran on as fast as the load of stuff we carried would allow us'.*[15]

Hamilton and his party eventually found Major Charles Simpson, who had suffered a compound fracture of the leg, and evacuated him to the château at St Symphorien where the owner, Monsieur Boiulliart de Saint, had opened up its doors as a temporary hospital:

'It had a large Red Cross flag flying in front, the three of us went in. I asked if there was a doctor there, there wasn't. A scene of disorder met me in the hall and was visible in the room opposite. Men – some bleeding from visible wounds – some collapsed and apparently dead were lying about on the floor or on beds and chairs

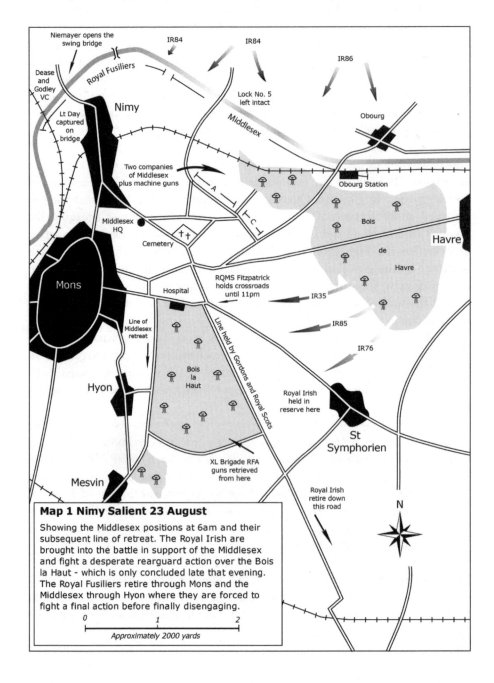

Niemayer opens the
swing bridge

IR84

IR84

IR86

Dease
and
Godley
VC

Royal Fusiliers

Lock No. 5
left intact

Obourg

Lt Day
captured
on
bridge

Nimy

Middlesex

Two companies
of Middlesex
plus machine guns

Obourg Station

A

Bois

Middlesex
HQ

C

Havre

Cemetery

de

Havre

Mons

Hospital

RQMS Fitzpatrick
holds crossroads
until 11pm

IR35

IR85

Line of
Middlesex
retreat

IR76

Line held by Gordons and Royal Scots

Hyon

Bois
la
Haut

Royal Irish
held in
reserve here

St
Symphorien

Mesvin

XL Brigade RFA
guns retrieved
from here

Royal Irish
retire down
this road

N

Map 1 Nimy Salient 23 August

Showing the Middlesex positions at 6am and their
subsequent line of retreat. The Royal Irish are
brought into the battle in support of the Middlesex
and fight a desperate rearguard action over the Bois
la Haut - which is only concluded late that evening.
The Royal Fusiliers retire through Mons and the
Middlesex through Hyon where they are forced to
fight a final action before finally disengaging.

0   1   2

Approximately 2000 yards

and some women were doing their best to fix them up. I saw there was a lot of work here for me but as I realized that it probably meant being taken prisoner I sent the two stretcher bearers straight back.'[16]

In company with many medical officers who were in action over the coming days, he remained behind with the wounded and dying and was taken prisoner. However, before he was transported to Germany as a prisoner, Hamilton was allowed by his captors to remain at the château for the next two weeks where he treated British and German wounded and organized search parties to find and bury the British dead.

There were a lot of dead and wounded and most of those in the Nimy salient were men of the Middlesex and Royal Irish. The casualty return for 23 August sent in by Major St Leger detailed 2 officers killed and another, 19-years old Lieutenant John Shine, the battalion machine-gun officer, as wounded. Shine would later die of his wounds.[17] 7 other officers were posted as wounded and missing including Major Long the battalion medical officer who also remained behind with the wounded. From a battalion of over 900 men some 300 NCOs and private soldiers were wounded or missing. A similar picture was reflected in the Middlesex returns. Lieutenant Wollocombe listed 15 officers killed wounded or missing along with 467 NCOs and men of which 73 were killed in action. Captain Perry, the battalion medical officer, like his colleague in the Royal Irish, elected to remain behind with the wounded. By far the largest number of Middlesex casualties came from D Company who lost well over half their number. None these casualty figures reflect the number of men who later died of their wounds. IR 86 which had been engaged all day with both battalions recorded a total of 30 enlisted men killed and 6 officers and 90 enlisted men wounded, although given the intensity of the day's fighting, the IR 86 casualty figure does appear to be a little on the light side.

As the men of 8 Brigade began their retirement so too did the two companies of 4/Royal Fusiliers which were holding the canal bend to the left of the Middlesex. Their positions along the canal were far from perfect; there was no real field of fire and the enemy had every opportunity for cover provided by the wooded areas on the opposite bank. Early that morning the sappers of 57/Field Company had arrived to prepare the three bridges that spanned the canal for demolition. One of these, a swing bridge, had been opened by the Fusiliers to prevent enemy infantry from crossing, leaving the large railway bridge and the road bridge to be destroyed. Detailed to blow the road bridge Corporal Alfred Payne and six sappers set their charges and having no hand generated electrical exploder, were forced to light the fuses of six separate charges before running back across the bridge and onto the road. The resulting explosion was masked by the noise of bursting shells but their success in the form of large pieces of bridge flying through the air was evident.

By 1.00 pm the overall situation of the Fusiliers had become desperate. The Nimy railway bridge, defended by men of C Company and the machine-gun section under Lieutenant Maurice Dease, was under heavy assault by IR 84 and despite one machine gun being knocked-out, one was still firing. Each time the gun stopped firing Lieutenant Dease went forward to see what was wrong. The battalion history recorded the action:

> 'The machine-gun crews were constantly being knocked out. So cramped was their position that when a man was hit he had to be removed before another could take his place. The approach from the trench was across the open ... to do this once called for no ordinary courage. To repeat it several times could only be done with real heroism.'

Under these very difficult conditions Corporal Payne's section commander, Lieutenant Alfred Day, now waited to set his explosives on the railway bridge which he considered to be of greater tactical value to the Germans than the swing bridge. He only had enough explosives for one bridge and this one was by far the larger structure. Events now escalated as Lieutenant Dease was mortally wounded and Private Sidney Godley ran forward to continue firing as the bridge party withdrew. Lieutenant Day's efforts were to be in vain, Godley was soon wounded and the gun was hit and put out of action. It was probably at this point in the fight that Day tried to reach the leads and blow the bridge. He was too late. Caught in the final rush across the bridge by IR 84 the young RE officer was overcome and taken prisoner. The bridge was intact and in enemy hands. As for the swing bridge it was opened by a very gallant German soldier, *Musketier* Oscar Niemayer of 8 Company, who swam the canal under fire and returned with a boat enabling his section to get across while he swam the canal again and opened the bridge. Sadly this brave young man was shot dead, but not before the second bridge fell into German hands. Had he been a British soldier he would have surely been recommended for the Victoria Cross.

The regimental history of IR 84 tells a slightly different story to that of the official British history and indeed, that of the Royal Fusiliers. There is no mention in the German account of being held up by the two machine guns of the Fusiliers and it appears from their records that they captured the two machine guns on the bridge and made prisoner about sixty men who surrendered. This is presumably when Lieutenant Day was captured. What isn't made clear in the German account is that the captured Fusilier machine guns were useless, the water jackets of both had been 'riddled with bullets'. Godley's selfless act probably allowed some of the surviving C Company to escape capture but there is no strong evidence to support the story that he threw his shattered machine gun into the canal. What probably went into the canal were the working parts of the weapon.

The Fusiliers began falling back through Mons towards Ciply some time after 1.40 pm. The IR 84 account indicates there was brutal house-to-house fighting as the Fusiliers fought a desperate fighting retreat but they appear to have disengaged from the pursuing enemy once they were clear of Mons. South of Mons the 1st Battalion Lincolnshire Regiment (1/Lincolns) had not been in contact with the enemy at all and was dug in across the main road at Cuesmes. By the middle of the afternoon the first trickle of retiring men from the salient reached the Lincolns where the battalion medical officer, Captain Gerard Kempthorne, and his medical team began patching up the growing tide of wounded men. One of the first men he attended to was one of the surviving Middlesex officers:

'The transport officer came by leading a subaltern of the Middlesex on his horse. He turned out not to be wounded but in a state of complete exhaustion. He said his regiment had been under constant fire since early morning, that it was absolute hell, and they were all so tired that they didn't mind if they were shot or not. All his platoon was shot down and a quarter of the officers were casualties.'[18]

Soon afterwards the bulk of the Fusiliers appeared, but without Lieutenant Dease or Private Godley. Although the battalion history records the Fusiliers retired in good order, it did not record the state of the shocked and tired men that marched away from the canal. The majority would have been under fire for the first time and none would have experienced the horrors of sustained shellfire on such a scale. Kempthorne would afterwards record the 'glazed look' in the eyes of many of the Fusiliers as they filed past him. Combatants in more recent wars would dub that phenomenon 'the thousand-yard stare'.

After being wounded, Godley was taken prisoner and Dease died, of his multiple wounds, in the arms, it is said, of Lieutenant Frederick Steele. Both Dease and Godley were later awarded the Victoria Cross. As for casualties, the figure for the Fusiliers varies, the official history has it that they did not 'greatly exceed 100', other sources list 24 other ranks killed and some 125 missing and wounded. IR 84 records declare 94 casualties of which only 24 were killed.[19]

With the German infantry getting closer, the Lincolns prepared to withdraw under fire from German machine guns; Kempthorne watched horrified as the last man of the battalion ran the gauntlet of German fire:

'As the last man withdrew the bullets in the road became more frequent and the Germans opened with a machine gun from somewhere among the trees. He came sloping along the road, either careless or ignorant of the danger. The suspense of watching him was too much for me, he was about twenty yards from safety when I found myself yelling for him to run. At that moment he was bowled over.'

The Lincolns had spent the night of 22 August bivouacking in and around the square at Cuesmes. It had been a pleasant evening and most of the inhabitants were out in the streets fraternizing with the troops. On the morning of 23 August, with the noise of battle to the north, the reality of war descended upon the small town as the Lincolns erected barricades to block the approaches to Mons. Serving with the Lincolns was Lance Corporal George Beeton, a regular soldier with seven years service behind him and now a regimental policeman. He remembered barricading the main road using paving stones and trees hewn down in haste:

> '*Next day, which was a Sunday, we were having a walk around the square of the town ... just three miles from Mons, when suddenly we had the order to send all the men in and get dressed, I myself was on the Regt. Police and had to hurry up after seeing them in. We went towards Mons about 30 minutes from our billet this side of the town and took up position at the end of the main road.*'[20]

The Lincolns' war diary records two casualties on 23 August, Second Lieutenant Rupert Cave-Orme who was slightly wounded in the hand and one private soldier wounded in the back – the man whom Kempthorne witnessed being hit as the battalion withdrew. It would be a very different story for the men of Lincolnshire the next day.

Chapter 3

23 August – A Slow Burning Fuse

West of the Nimy salient the battle spread slowly along the straight reach of the canal as more of von Kluck's First Army completed its wheeling movement to the south and encountered the BEF. The German pivot flank was opposite Nimy, thus accounting for the early contact with the two brigades in the salient. David Ascoli's description of the battle as spreading 'like a slow fuse along the straight length of the canal,' was a very apt one. The slow fuse of battle that had been lit at Nimy took another four hours to reach Kenneth Godsell at St Ghislain. He was preparing the girder road bridge for demolition with his section sergeant 'when the enemy's first salvo was fired at 10 am – it made a funny noise which we could not make out until the shells burst, then we knew.' Yet despite this opening ranging shellfire, the battle did not really get going on 13 Brigade's front until around 11.00 am on 23 August.

Brigadier General Gerald Cuthbert's 13 Infantry Brigade was posted along a three mile section of the canal with the 1st Battalion Royal West Kent (1/RWK) covering the bridges west of St Ghislain and the 2nd Battalion King's Own Scottish Borderers (2/KOSB) defending the sector up to the railway bridge at Les Herbières. Both the KOSB and the West Kents had been mobilized in Ireland and had left Dublin docks aboard the *SS Gloucestershire* on 13 August. The march up to Mons had been uneventful but nevertheless Lieutenant James Pennyman, the KOSB machine-gun officer, remembered it as 'long and weary'. As the battalion crossed the Belgian border on 22 August, it had been a difficult day:

'*A dreadful march through Dour and Boussu. The inhabitants had heard that we were starving, and all classes loaded us with fruit, mostly unripe, cigarettes, tobacco, matches and wine. A great many of our men were 3 year men, who had lost most of any discipline they may have had. It was an awful job getting the battalion along through these towns, and I shall never forget it.*'[21]

By 5.00 pm 'Jim' Pennyman and his battalion were established on the canal where they took up their posts for the night, Pennyman and his machine-gun section positioned their guns on the Lock 4 abutment where a barricade had been erected and the lock keeper's house fortified:

'*Before going to sleep, Leigh* [Major Chandos Leigh], *Kennedy* [Captain Charles Frazer Kennedy] *and I sat on the seat outside the house on the lock and had a long talk with the owners. These good people whose house we had put into a state of defence and consequently made a dreadful mess of, were awfully good to us, and shared all their little stock of food with us.*'[22]

The West Kents arrived a little later that evening but by dusk the battalion's C and D Companies were at the bridges north and northeast of St Ghislain with the remaining two companies in reserve. At dawn on 23 August, A Company under the command of Captain George Lister, was sent across the canal to support patrols of the 19th (Queen Alexandra's Own) Royal Hussars (19/Hussars) and the Divisional Cyclists with orders to take up a defensive position at the crossroads south of the village of Tertre. Lister's own account was written after the war:

'*These preparations were scarcely complete when I saw four cyclists with an officer coming at full speed down the road from Tertre. On arriving at our position they flung themselves down by me, and the officer in charge stated the remainder of his detachment had been blown to pieces by the enemy's artillery fire.*'[23]

Barely five minutes later, A Company had themselves come under fire from a large body of the 1st Battalion of the 12th Brandenburg Grenadier Regiment advancing out of Tertre. Still with no word of the fate of the 19/Hussars patrol, Lister was advised to retire if 'things were getting too hot.' By 11.30 am it was certainly getting 'too hot' and Lister wisely began to withdraw his men to the safety of the barricade across the road bridge, but with only 90 men of the 200 who had passed over the bridge at daybreak. The casualties included Lister himself who was wounded in the shoulder and taken prisoner. The members of the cavalry patrol were also prisoners; having bumped up against the advance guard of the Brandenburg Grenadiers. Captain Walter Bloem described his encounter with one of the British cavalrymen and the difficulties of accurate fire with a service revolver:

'*We were approaching one of the scattered farm buildings in the meadow, and being the first I went in, and noticed at once a group of fine looking horses, all saddled up ...I had scarcely spoken when a man appeared not five paces away from behind the horses ...meantime the fellow had raised his arm, a sharp report, a wisp of smoke, and the whisk of a bullet passed my head. In the same second I had pulled out my loaded pistol and fired – peng! Missed too.'*[24]

Meanwhile Jim Pennyman and the KOSB, who had been up before sunrise in anticipation of a dawn attack, had had time to prepare a more suitable location for the battalion's two machine guns when the German onslaught had failed to materialise. Although he admitted it was 'a rather doubtful place', the only position where he could get a suitable field of fire was from the top floor of one of the houses lining the south bank and as he and his men sandbagged the windows, the men of A and C Companies lined the canal bank in front of them, Major Alfred Haig, the senior major in the battalion, joined Pennyman to await developments. Haig had deployed D Company under Major Chandos Leigh across the canal to defend the bridge and was anxious to get a clear view of what was happening:

'*We could see the Germans debouching in extended order across a road 900 yards straight to our front ... unfortunately a large number of them were able to approach into a wood behind the houses in front of me, without coming under fire. A and C Companies took these on. My sergeant (Gilmartin) pointed out to me two groups of two Germans, each lying in the open. We thought these might be machine gunners and decided to open fire on them. I took the range accurately and we laid out all four in the first traverse. ... This was our first experience of killing people: it was rather horrible, but satisfactory.'*[25]

Amongst the men of the machine-gun section was Private Charles Harding, a reservist from Bethnal Green who had been called up on 5 August. He and a number of the other men in the section were old hands but even so had never experienced fighting of this nature against a professional European army. Described by Pennyman as a 'dependable and useful man to have around', Harding would prove his mettle at Le Cateau and in the days that followed.

As Pennyman had predicted it wasn't long before the German infantrymen began to target the building they were firing from. Sergeant Gilmartin had just asked his officer if the sandbags were bullet-proof when red hot rounds began to punch their way through the walls and drop on the floor beside them. With the answer to his question now lying glowing on the floor in front of him, it was clearly time to move! As the section dragged the machine guns out of the building Pennyman noted the CO, Lieutenant Colonel Charles Stephenson, 'walking up and down, sucking his old pipe and not caring a damn.' The white house and its machine guns had been a thorn in the side of B Company of the Brandenburg Grenadiers ever since they had advanced beyond the natural cover of the woods. Their company commander, Walter Bloem, had lost several men to Pennyman's machine guns already:

> *'Another effort was made to silence the machine gun in the upper room of the white house. "Two rounds each at the white house, aim just below the eaves in the roof!" Through my glasses I could see … that at least no window pane was left. The gun was silent for a while, maybe altogether, I never knew.'*[26]

Both the West Kents and the KOSB were continually shelled from midday to dusk, but German forces, although working up quite close in some cases, never really developed a sustained attack in the face of the rifle and machine-gun fire of the British infantry and clearly suffered considerable losses, particularly on the West Kent frontage. 41-year-old Major Percy Hastings, who commanded C Company of the West Kents, was on the barricade across the road bridge for most of the day:

> *'A few infantry attacks were made on us, but when fired on from our position, the enemy got under the cover of a ridge and passed along from east to west towards Pommeroeul. All the houses near us were shelled heavily … After dark the German infantry came in quite close, but did not open fire upon us. The enemy positions varied from 150 to 500 yards from us.'*[27]

Further along the canal to the left of the West Kents, Jim Pennyman was searching for a new position to site his machine guns:

> *'I went all along the YLI* [King's Own Yorkshire Light Infantry] *and West Kent positions on our right, and the East Surrey's positions on our left, but could find no possible position for the section. By this time shells were coming all over the shop and a new house went sauté every minute, but we did not seem to be losing very heavily and were still in position all along the line.'*[28]

They may well have all been in position but as far as General Smith-Dorrien was concerned the time had come to begin withdrawing. The order to blow the bridges along the 5th Division front had gone out to 17/Field Company at 2.00 pm but it was not until the early hours of 24 August that all the bridges – apart from the lattice girder bridge over Lock 4 which was still intact – were successfully blown. Lieutenant Charles 'Valdo' Pottinger, having laid his charges at Lock 4, found to his dismay the exploder he was using failed to work. Unable to get back onto the bridge owing to the heavy German fire he drew his revolver and tried to set off the detonator by firing at it. Perhaps it was fortunate that he was unsuccessful. If he had scored a direct hit he would have blown himself to atoms as well as the bridge.

Kenneth Godsell, who was at the railway bridge with Gerald Smyth and Corporal John Geraghty, was reflecting on his day – although still mourning the loss of Corporal Edwin Marsden, who had been shot in the head and killed earlier- his section had been very successful in blowing all their allotted bridges. His diary described the moment the bridges went up:

'When most of the infantry had crossed there was a sudden burst of fire which rather upset everyone but it proved to be a false alarm. The bridge was blown up at 1.30 am. This was the signal for the demolition of the other bridges and all went well. The demolition parties joined the section which proceeded along the Wasmes road behind the infantry.'[29]

Further east the sappers of 57/Field Company had been busy preparing the bridges from Jemappes station to Mariette for demolition and Lieutenant Percy Boulnois and No. 3 Section had been at work from 7.15 am. Mounted on bicycles and with their equipment in a forage cart, they allocated twenty-five slabs of guncotton to each of the drop bridges that spanned the canal, leaving long lengths of electric cable ready to be attached to the exploder. At 11.00 am the German attack was already in progress at Lock 2 and the 1st Battalion Royal Scots Fusiliers (1/Royal Scots) had been driven back from their barricade at the north end of the bridge but were still clinging on to the south side. Whilst all this was taking place, Lance Corporal Alfred Jarvis and Sapper Charles Neary were underneath the bridge, working from a small boat and fixing their charges. Each time they returned to their cart to fetch more explosives they ran the gauntlet of fire from the enemy who were only a matter of yards away. Jarvis received the Victoria Cross for his work that day.

Percy Boulnois, better known to his contemporaries as 'PK', must have felt quite exposed as he bicycled up and down the towpath visiting the men working on the other bridges. Accompanied by Sergeant Alfred Smith they carried with them the drum of electrical cable and the single exploder that was intended to blow all the bridges. At around 2.00 pm they met Captain Theodore Wright who was in a car and was still suffering from a head wound received at Lock 2 whilst visiting Jarvis and Neary. They hardly had time to compare notes when their meeting was interrupted by news of a general retirement and orders to blow the bridges.

The sappers now had a problem. With only one exploder they had the job of blowing all five bridges along a front of three miles, and it had to be done quickly. Wright immediately left to order Lieutenant Day to blow the Nimy bridge – a task we know now was unsuccessful – whilst Lieutenant Boulnois and Sergeant Smith cycled to Lance Corporal Jarvis' bridge at Jemappes station and blew the bridge there at 3.00 pm. With time running out Boulnois decided to bypass the other bridges and headed straight for the Mariette bridge which was on the main road. Pedalling furiously he was on his way down the towpath when he again bumped into Captain Wright who was making his way back from Nimy. After a brief exchange Wright decided to take the Mariette bridge himself and sent Boulnois off to see to the remaining bridges.

B Company of the 1st Battalion Northumberland Fusiliers (1/Northumberland Fusiliers) was about to retire when Captain Wright arrived at the bridge and after a short conversation with the company commander, Captain Beaumont St John, he got down to work. St John and the men of B Company could only watch on in admiration:

> He [Wright] *reported that the Germans were over the bridges on both our flanks so that things did not look too rosy. However he got to work on his job but found that the man who had laid the charges had only provided leads for the main canal and had not taken the second waterway into consideration, nothing daunted he went out in front of the barrier and got under the bridge of the canal, dragged himself through the water to the centre tow path and wriggled about trying to find which leads connected to the charge. Unfortunately he could not find them and so he returned. It was a plucky action, particularly as he was wounded at the time. I reported this instance and was glad to see the officer got the VC for it.*'[30]

In actual fact Wright was pulled from the water by Sergeant Smith after he had lost his grip through exhaustion and they had to leave the bridge intact. Wright's forlorn hope under fire left a profound impression on the men of B Company of 1/Northumberland Fusiliers. Two days later at Bavai the march weary Fusiliers recognized Wright riding past them and gave him a spontaneous cheer. Lieutenant Boulnois had also been unsuccessful in detonating his bridges and consequently, of the eight bridges allocated to 57/Field Company, only the one closest to Jemappes station had been rendered useless to the enemy.

Fortunately James Pennycuick and his sappers of No. 1 Section, 59/Field Company, had a little more success. They successfully blew both the railway and road bridges at Les Herbières, the destruction of the railway bridge being the signal for Corporal Dorey to light the fuse at the drop bridge further west near La Hamaide which was defended by the 1st Battalion East Surrey Regiment (1/East Surrey) which held the line on the left of the KOSB down to the road bridge at Pommeroeul. At the Les Herbières railway bridge the houses on the north bank ran down to the bridge itself and in order to get a good field of fire C Company of 1/East Surrey was moved to an advanced position on the north bank, supported by A Company which held the bridge on the south side. Aware of the forward position of the KOSB on their right, Major Tew sent Lieutenant Harold Schomberg along the towpath to Major Chandos Leigh to ensure that neither battalion would withdraw without informing the other. Leigh was an experienced officer who had been commissioned in 1895 and had won a DSO as a lieutenant with the battalion in South Africa. He would not withdraw unless the situation became indefensible.

At 1.00 pm, as the attack by the German IR 52 developed, 1/East Surrey began to take casualties. One of the first was C Company's officer commanding,

36-year-old Captain John Benson, who had crossed the canal as soon as the attack began using a barge which had been moored under the railway bridge. Benson was mortally wounded and despite being brought back over the canal died at the dressing station. Across the canal German infantry were now advancing in extended order and were trying to cross the railway embankment which led up to the bridge. They were fortunately kept at bay by the fire from Lieutenant Thomas Darwell's machine-gun section on the south side of the canal, which was shooting directly up the railway line. The 2nd Battalion Suffolk Regiment (2/Suffolk) has also been involved in 1/East Surrey's fight at the bridge. Two platoons of C Company had been on the north side of the canal supporting the bridgehead and the battalion had suffered its first casualties of the war with 3 men killed and Lieutenant Vere Phillips wounded and taken prisoner. At 7.00 pm both the 1/East Surrey and 2/Suffolk withdrew across the River Haine. For the Suffolks this was their baptism of fire but unfolding events would shortly bestow upon them a permanent place in British Army legend.

For the men holding these rather precarious positions at the bridgeheads, however, the situation was becoming increasingly tense. Looking up the canal, Major Tew could see that Chandos Leigh and his Borderers of D Company were also under severe pressure, accordingly at 6.00 pm he ordered his men back across the canal. Unfortunately Tew's orders did not reach the platoons on the right of the railway embankment and they fought on to the inevitable end as the rest of the battalion looked on helplessly from across the canal. On the KOSB frontage things had also 'hotted up': Major Tew being proved correct in his appraisal of Chandos Leigh's situation. German artillery, firing almost at point blank range, destroyed the KOSB barricade at Lock 4 forcing Chandos Leigh to order a similar retirement. He never made it back. Jim Pennyman wrote in his diary that one of the D Company men told him that Chandos Leigh 'was wounded in the hand and had given them an order to leave him and retire.' Clearly his wounds were more serious as six months later, returning prisoners of war reported that he had died of his wounds. The KOSB began withdrawing quietly at about 6.00 pm. A company of 2/KOYLI covered the retirement and apart from a few horses being hit by chance bullets and the battalion doctor being wounded, they got away largely unscathed.

Compared to the opposite end of the canal at Nimy, however, the western extremity of the British positions was relatively quiet with no hint of the drama that befell 8 Brigade. The 1st Battalion the Duke of Cornwall's Light Infantry (1/DCLI), at the road bridge at Pommeroeul, easily beat off an attack by German cavalry and infantry from IR 26 which developed from the direction of Villers-Pommeroeul in the late afternoon and by the time the independent 19 Brigade relieved the Cavalry Division later still in the afternoon, only the occasional burst of fire disturbed the British positions. The bridge at Pommeroeul was blown by Lieutenant Robert Egerton of 1/Field Troop, RE, a mounted unit attached to the Cavalry Division. According to Egerton, who witnessed 1/DCLI's fire fight, once the men of B and C Companies had returned to the south bank of the canal and begun their retirement, the sappers moved in quickly to demolish the bridge:

> *'Was told to go and prepare the bridge over the canal at Pommereul (sic) for demolition, but not to let it off without orders. It was a drawbridge of 18ft span ... At 5.25 the DCLI retired, and the Germans being about sixty feet away, I touched it off; it went fairly well indeed. Retiring was a ticklish job, as we were under fire at the time from 100 yards or so.'*[31]

The DCLI withdrew taking up new positions on each side of the road behind the bridge over the Haine. Lieutenant Robert Flint and his No. 3 Section from 59/Field Company were waiting at the bridge. There they had a short yet sharp engagement with enemy artillery before the bridge was finally demolished.

Soon after midnight on 23 August the bulk of II Corps had retired from the canal positions and was back on the high ground of the Dour-Frameries-Paturages line. The decision by Sir John French to stand and hold the canal line for 24 hours had thrown a temporary spanner in the working of the timetable that von Kluck held so central to victory. But 'temporary' was the key word. By dusk German engineers had thrown pontoon bridges over the canal where the physical crossings had been destroyed and fighting was already taking place south of the canal. For some retiring battalions this fighting was at close-quarters and took place in the maze of narrow streets that characterized the sprawling urban area south of the canal. Captain St John and two companies of 1/Northumberland Fusiliers had to defend every street corner as they withdrew through Quaregnon on their way to Frameries:

> *'This retirement was one of the most exhausting things I remember so far as I was concerned. We had no time to waste and my job was to post covering parties. We had to defend every street corner until the column had turned the succeeding corner and the result was that by the time I had placed one post I had to run on and catch the column up and tell off and place the next.'*[32]

* * *

While there is little doubt that, given the circumstances, the British Army accounted for itself extremely well at Mons on 23 August, we cannot ignore or undervalue the German achievement. By early afternoon elements of the German IX Corps had crossed the canal at Jemappes which effectively rendered the already precarious 3rd Division positions in the Nimy salient completely untenable. Moreover, the initial German surprise at finding the BEF along the canal at Mons was quickly turned from what began as a route march into a successful encounter engagement. I find it very hard to take seriously some of the popular accounts of the British battalions mowing down hundreds of German infantrymen as they advanced shoulder to shoulder into the withering rifle fire of the British. There is no hard evidence that has been produced to date that supports the popular contention that, in the face of the British rapid rifle fire, the Germans thought they were facing numerous machine guns. This anecdote is deeply embedded in the British story of Mons and can probably trace its origins to the British *Official History* in which Sir James E Edmonds wrote, 'The Germans imagined that they were everywhere opposed by machine guns only, not realizing the intensity of British rapid fire.'

There are, however, numerous accounts of German infantry advancing in close-order formation and there are several eye witness accounts of this taking place. Major Stratford St Leger, for example, in describing the German attack on the Gordons and Royal Scots had this to say:

'The advance of the German infantry during the attack on the Gordon Highlanders and Royal Scots in the evening [of 23 August] *was carried out with every confidence and in faultless formation in dense lines. Fire appeared to be completely reserved and to all appearances, the idea seemed to be to overwhelm our line with weight of numbers by charging at dusk. There was no artillery to assist them, and personally, I did not notice any Machine Guns, which probably accounts for the advance being made without covering fire. The outburst of rapid fire that met them was no doubt a revelation.'*[33]

Using the Mark III Short Magazine Lee Enfield Rifle (SMLE), British infantry in 1914 were able to fire fifteen or more aimed rounds per minute – the so called 'mad minute.' This level of sustained infantry fire was devastating against an advancing enemy; a platoon of 40 men could in theory fire over 600 targeted rounds in a minute. However, it is not possible – or tactically prudent – to maintain this rate of fire for long periods or, as is often assumed, indefinitely! Aside from the purely physical and material demands that an unbroken period of fifteen rounds per minute would place on every man involved, the tactical situation on the ground as seen by platoon and company commanders would inevitably lead to an adjustment in the rate of fire. Fifteen rounds a minute also requires regular live firing practice, something many of the reservists had not taken part in for some time; indeed older reservists who had left the service before 1907 would not have used the Mark III SMLE at all before rejoining their units in August 1914. Some of the descriptions of the British action at Mons in current battlefield literature defy belief and serve only to contribute to feeding myth and legend. Not by any stroke of the imagination can I support the notion that German infantry at Mons were 'cut down in their thousands.'

That said, some German units did indeed suffer heavy casualties, the 12th Brandenburg Grenadiers who faced the West Kents and 2/KOSB being the most quoted example, but as far as overall casualties are concerned, a recent assessment of German battle casualties at Mons based on careful analysis of regimental histories provides a revised estimate of 2,000 who were either killed or wounded in action.[34] Whether this is nearer the truth or not, it cannot be dismissed as an unreasonable evaluation.

British casualties at Mons were 1,600 killed, wounded and missing. Even if we accept that about 50 per cent of the British casualties at Mons were men who were taken prisoner – and many of those would also have been wounded – we are left with a casualty figure of between 800 to 1,000 men who may have been killed in action. Looking at these figures purely dispassionately, the loss ratio of 2:1 in favour of the British does give some credence to the effectiveness of British rifle fire; a characteristic of the 1914 fighting soldier that has always been acknowledged by German sources.

There was, however, a prevailing feeling amongst many of the British soldiers who fought at Mons that the casualties they had inflicted on their enemy were quite substantial. Lieutenant Arthur Chitty who was fighting with the West Kents was under the false impression that some 3,000 German dead were buried along with 50 British in front of the battalion's trenches at St Ghislain. Quite where he got this notion from is anyone's guess but it certainly annoyed the German doctor who was treating him in the military hospital at Mons! Chitty had been hit through the lung and wrist whilst with A Company and having successfully regained the battalion's positions across the canal was carried to St Ghislain hospital. Left for dead by his battalion he was later taken to the Les Saeurs Convent Hospital where he was betrayed to the Germans three weeks later by the local Burgomaster. Had he remained at the convent undetected he was convinced he would have recovered and escaped. As it was he was transferred to Mons where he remained until he was fit enough to travel to Germany.[35]

Large numbers of British wounded were taken to the railway station at Mons which had been turned into a makeshift transit hospital. Private Edwards was wounded in the left thigh as the KOSB were retiring, unable to move he lay in the field for two days during which time he was 'more or less unconscious'. In the late afternoon of 27 August he was found by German soldiers who stripped him of most of his clothing and eventually took him to the railway station where he was 'treated very fairly'. A week later he was removed to the hospital at Mons where he says there were about 60 other wounded British casualties. Private Arthur Watkiss, serving with 4/Middlesex, was one of the first of his battalion to be wounded. A gunshot wound to the knee ended his war and after being picked up by a Belgian farmer he was taken to the Belgian Red Cross hospital close to the Hotel de Ville in Mons. There he remained for eleven days before being taken to the railway station and on to Germany.

Another Middlesex soldier, Private Arthur Price, who had been badly wounded in the face and right arm by shrapnel also ended up in the Military Hospital at Mons where he was in the charge of a Belgian doctor until transferred to Germany in mid-November 1914. A Londoner from Upper Holloway, Price had lost the sight of his left eye and most of his nose which contributed to the decision to repatriate him a year later. Arthur Price was typical of the badly wounded and maimed individuals who were discharged from the army as no longer fit for service and left to survive on a pension. The Great War rendered over 300,000 British servicemen physically disabled from wounds received in the fighting with a further 67,000 scarred with the effects of mental illness. Mons was just the beginning in more ways than one.

Chapter 4

24 August – A Very Trying Day

By dawn on 24 August the majority of the retiring II Corps had realigned along a 17 mile frontage facing roughly north east with its centre some 3 miles south of Mons. Unaware of the behind-the-scenes drama which had already set in motion the retreat that would eventually end south of the River Marne, the men of the BEF were still under the impression that they were to stand and fight that morning. In contrast to Douglas Haig's I Corps which had taken little part in the Mons action and was now retiring south west, the units of Smith-Dorrien's II Corps were more scattered. The men of the 3rd Division were roughly aligned through Nouvelles, Ciply and Frameries, Fergusson's 5th Division had fallen back to a line running through Paturages, Wasmes and Hornu, while 19 Brigade was further west at Thulin, Elouges and Audregnies. Allenby's Cavalry was at Quiévrain on the Mons-Valenciennes road.

Sir John French's decision to order the retreat on the 23rd took little account of the logistics of military movement. That aside, the manner in which he chose to inform his corps commanders of his decision was in many ways responsible for the very costly rearguard actions that Smith-Dorrien's two divisions and the Cavalry Corps had to fight over the course of 24 August. Many of Sir John's difficulties stemmed from the poor quality of the advice he was receiving from Sir Henry Wilson and the French GQG but others arose due to his remoteness from the battlefield. At Le Cateau, GHQ was in direct contact with I Corps, but there was no such link with Smith-Dorrien and II Corps or with Allenby's Cavalry HQ at Elouges. Consequently when the three Chiefs of Staff were summoned to Le Cateau to be informed of the decision to retire, Gough was able to wire the orders informing Haig of the change of plan through to I Corps almost immediately. With new instructions issued from I Corps HQ near Bonnet at 2.00 am, the 1st Division began its retirement at 4.00 am followed three quarters of-an-hour later by the 2nd Division with 4 (Guards) Brigade detailed as rearguard. Despite some shelling and the attentions of small – scale German cavalry patrols, their movements were largely untroubled.

But 24 August was to be a very different day for II Corps. Forced to drive the 35 miles back to Sars-la-Bruyère, Forestier-Walker was only able to place the new orders in front of Smith-Dorrien at 3.00 am on the 24th along with the rather surprising revelation that he and Haig were to sort out the detail themselves. By the time the orders had passed through divisional and brigade staffs it had been light for several hours and the opening shots in the series of rearguard actions which were to be fought by II Corps had already been fired. Smith-Dorrien must have realized that the next few hours would prove crucial and that it would be 'touch and go' for his divisions. The foremost task was to clear the roads of the heavy unit and divisional supply transport which had been brought forward in expectation of an advance from Mons. This in itself was a major undertaking made all the more difficult by the swelling numbers of civilian taking to the roads and fleeing ahead of the advancing German army.

Once the divisional transport was underway, Smith-Dorrien turned his attention to the logistics of moving his two divisions. In 1914 an infantry brigade on the march probably took up the equivalent of 3 miles of road and took in the region of 2 hours to pass a given point. In each brigade of field artillery – notwithstanding the ammunition and supply wagons – a team of six horses was required to pull each gun and with six guns to a battery and three batteries per brigade the numbers soon begin to stack up! Along with the other transport, it was not uncommon for a field artillery brigade to have somewhere in the region of 750 horses. Whilst their comrades in the Royal Horse Artillery rode, the gunners in the Royal Field Artillery usually marched. Add to this the companies of engineers, field ambulances and other support units and the size of the task confronting Smith-Dorrien's staff begins to become apparent.

Mindful of the destruction of the Belgian forts of Liege and Namur by German siege batteries, Sir John French had wisely decided to avoid the tempting prospect of falling back to the fortified confines of Maubeuge, choosing instead to plot a south westerly course to Bavai. For II Corps this involved a potentially complex crossover manoeuvre, whereby the 3rd Division would move southwest to the right flank of II Corps, allowing the retreat of 5th Division from Wasmes to be shortened as it fell back due south and assumed its new position on the left. Orders were dispatched to Sir Charles Fergusson not to withdraw until the 3rd Division had successfully disengaged.

The German artillery attack began just before dawn on 24 August and whilst it initially focused on Frameries and Ciply, it soon extended along the whole of the II Corps front as far as Wasmes and Hornu. At 5.15 am German infantry were beginning to attack in strength at Frameries where Captain St John and his 1/Northumberland Fusiliers had arrived late the previous evening and had spent much of the night barricading the Mons road. At dawn, still weary from the previous day's fighting and marching, St John had just lit his pipe when 'a regular inferno of shell fire burst on us and round us. I made rapid tracks to my trench and got safely in it'. It was the beginning of a 'very trying day' and it was not long before the surrounding buildings were ablaze.

Gerard Kempthorne and 1/Lincolns had also arrived in the dark from Cuesmes and halted on the northern edge of Frameries at around 10.00 pm. The arrival of dawn was announced by the opening artillery rounds which began bursting over the orchard where they had spent the previous night. Kempthorne was standing on the road with his commanding officer, Lieutenant Colonel Wilfred Smith, when the first high explosive shell burst nearby, sending them scurrying for cover. At first the shells were short but the German gunners soon got the range of the farm across the road and both men watched as the buildings were systematically demolished: 'they hit the cottage full in the middle, the whole thing seemed to bend and then a great bit came away with part of the roof in a cloud of dust.' It wasn't long before Kempthorne had plenty of work to do as the cottages on the Rue des Dames and the neighbouring rope factory shop began filling with wounded, many of whom were dispatched back towards Frameries as soon as they had been patched up.

The Lincolns had been detailed as brigade rearguard. Still unsure of exactly where they were when they dug-in for the night, they only got a clearer picture of their positions at first light when the battalion stood to arms. They were not ideal:

> 'We were on a road, [Rue des Dames] *the ditch on the far side of which was occupied by our men kneeling or sitting in a mess of evil smelling black slimy mud. Just across the road was a small two storied cottage ...the rest of the men lined two sides of an orchard enclosed by a blackthorn hedge ... on the road were a few small houses and to our front and left was open ground with a view of chimneys and mine shafts in the distance and a great mound of waste rising about a mile and a half to our right front.'*[36]

Major Herbert Stewart found himself in Frameries on the morning of 24 August desperately trying to move the motor and horse drawn vehicles of the 3rd Division Supply Train through the shell-torn town towards Le Quesnoy. A task which was easier said than done. Stewart and his Army Service Corps (ASC) column had been one of the first ASC units to be ordered south and had been on the road since 4.00 am. Despite the hour, they had already encountered what was to become an increasing problem during the early part of the retreat: civilian refugees sharing the available road surface with the retreating army. His account of the retreat set down in his book *From Mons to Loos* provides an interesting alternative view of the retreat from the perspective of a supply officer. As his column moved into Frameries on the Ciply road he found 9 Brigade:

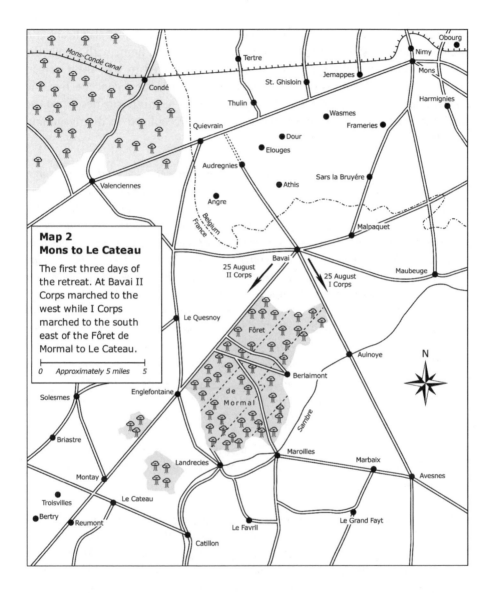

**Map 2
Mons to Le Cateau**

The first three days of the retreat. At Bavai II Corps marched to the west while I Corps marched to the south east of the Fôret de Mormal to Le Cateau.

0   Approximately 5 miles   5

'...*hotly engaged with greatly superior numbers. Up the streets pointing towards the German position the bullets were flying continuously, knocking up splashes of dust in the road or chipping brick and mortar off the sides of the houses. Overhead was the incessant crack of the shrapnel, and as fast as one group of the little white clouds, caused by the burst of the shells, dissolved into the still morning air, another group appeared.*'[37]

Frameries was under attack from IR 20 and IR 24 of the German 6th Infantry Division. The Lincolns had already been drawn into early contact with the

German infantry who were taking full advantage of the myriad of slag heaps and mine workings. Although the German attack was pressed home with vigour the equally resolute fire discipline of the Lincolns managed to stall the German attack. The unit history of the German IR 24 would later concede that the 'British defence was extraordinarily tough.' Gerard Kempthorne described the final stages of the action before the Lincolns were obliged to disengage and withdraw:

> '*We were by this time in the thick of it, the appalling noise, the smoking buildings, the crash of falling walls and the dead and wounded lying about suggested the end of the world more than anything else. Of the enemy we could see very little. Occasionally a figure showed on the slag heap, one of our two machine guns would open from the orchard and the figure would disappear. The position of the machine guns was soon located by the enemy and their neighbourhood was the hottest part of the line. I found one at the corner of the orchard. The machine gun officer [Captain Cecil Crampton Holmes] was himself firing it. He had sat on his gun since the commencement of the action with the greatest coolness and gallantry. It was obviously only a matter of time before he would be knocked out. He was mortally wounded in the groin first just as I came up, even then it was with some difficulty I could persuade him to let me help him to the rear. As I dressed him in the comparative shelter of one of the cottage walls nearly the whole of the neighbouring house collapsed with a roar and a rattle. He was carried back into the town on a ground sheet but was never heard of again.*'[38]

Having seen the divisional supply vehicles safely through the town on their way to Sars-la-Bruyère, Major Stewart remained behind with his driver assisting groups of wounded men:

> '*Presently a doctor, hearing I had a car close by, ran up and inquired whether I would take a badly wounded officer to the hospital. What a splendid fellow that doctor was! With clothes and hands covered in blood, he looked more like a butcher than a surgeon. He seemed wearied to death … but, his one anxiety was to get his patients where they could receive proper attention. The officer whom he wished me to take to hospital was, I think, a subaltern in the Fusiliers, and his shattered arm was a horrid sight.*'[39]

Most likely the doctor Stewart mentions in his account was Captain Malcolm Leckie, the battalion medical officer with 1/Northumberland Fusiliers. Leckie, an England international hockey player, had been serving with the RAMC since 1908 and for much of the time had been attached to the Egyptian Army in the Sudan and Upper Egypt. In 1906 his sister Jeanne had married the novelist Arthur Conan Doyle who himself had served as a doctor in the Boer War.

Leckie was not to survive Frameries, an eye witness account by a local district nurse told of his bravery in attending the wounded under heavy shellfire until he was severely wounded himself.[40] He died of his wounds on 28 August in the convent hospital at Frameries but such was his devotion to duty that his efforts did not go unrewarded; the award of the Distinguished Service Order (DSO) was announced in the *London Gazette* in December 1914.

Shortly after 1.00 pm on 24 August units of the German IR 24 and IR 20 entered the shattered streets of Frameries. Most of the prisoners they took were wounded men, the remainder of 9 Brigade having made an orderly, albeit hurried, withdrawal. There is plenty of evidence from both British as well as German sources to suggest it had been a costly affair, one battalion of IR 24 alone had been reduced from 1,065 officers and men to 560 men and 9 officers. The 1/Lincolns in their rearguard position at the orchard lost 4 officers and 134 other ranks killed, wounded or missing and 1/Northumberland Fusiliers left behind 12 men killed in action and another 40 wounded.

Further to the east, Brigadier General Frederick McKracken's 7 Brigade was under artillery fire from early in the morning and later there developed some scrappy skirmishing between A Company of the 3rd Battalion Worcestershire Regiment (3/Worcesters) and elements of IR 64. After the Worcesters withdrew the 2nd Battalion South Lancashire Regiment (2/South Lancs) was left rather exposed on its left and in the ensuing retirement the South Lancs lost nearly 300 men before the brigade finally broke off contact with the enemy.

The 3rd Division retreated in two columns, one moving through Genly and in touch with the 2nd Division of Douglas Haig's I Corps, the other through Eugies and Sars-la-Bruyère. Between the latter column and the retiring 5th Division, however, a gap had opened up which 15/Hussars had been ordered to fill. From reports filed by Second Lieutenant Edward Rouse-Boughton's troop it appeared that enemy cavalry had already penetrated the gap and had been sighted in the vicinity of the village of Blaugies. Accordingly, Lieutenants Whittle and Hoare with three troops of hussars from A Squadron were sent to investigate. Finding the southern outskirts of the village empty they continued at a gallop down the main street with swords drawn until their progress was finally blocked by a barricade. In his impetuous enthusiasm Whittle had blundered into an ambush and all hell was duly let loose. Caught in a devastating crossfire, the leading men were shot down in the street; those that managed to jump the barricade were caught at a second.

Both Whittle and Hoare were killed along with five of their men, two more later dying of their wounds at the Ursuline Convent in Blaugies.[41] Those at the rear of the column were more fortunate and in the course of managing to escape the fate of their comrades were forced to leave the wounded and the dismounted men behind. The surviving troopers successfully returned to the regiment at Bavai that evening with the news that 35 NCOs and men of the squadron had been lost. It would be another six months before confirmation of the death of 21-year-old Charles Hoare, who had only been with the for regiment eight months, would be relayed to his parents at Bicester by one of the wounded and captured men who was repatriated in February 1915.

* * *

With Frameries in flames, the men of 13 and 14 Brigades positioned a little under 2 miles to the west at Wasmes, were also under a severe bombardment. The village was overflowing with troops and the heavy supply columns of the ASC which were attempting to get away ahead of the infantry. On the ridge above the town the 2nd Battalion Duke of Wellington's Regiment (2/Duke of Wellington's) was dug-in on an arch around the northern perimeter of the village with three companies of 1/Dorsets from 15 Brigade on the western outskirts. In the village itself were troops from both battalions in addition to Jim Pennyman and the 2/KOSB. The first salvoes from the German artillery on the 24th woke Jim Pennyman and the men of his machine-gun section who had found a pile of straw on which to snatch a couple of hours sleep. A couple of hours was precious little but it was considerably more than Lieutenant Rowland Owen, a Special Reserve officer in D Company of 2/Duke of Wellington's, had been able to catch for he had been marching all night and had only arrived at Wasmes at dawn:

> *'Arrived Wasmes – knew nothing of what was happening, had happened or likely to happen; except that we seemed alone in the world – excluding Allemanders, of course. I was not in the hottest part of the battle. Position horseshoe shaped; D Coy spread all along (having come last) I was at one end – So I only got what missed the rest and hardly saw anything.'*[42]

Hot on the heels of Lieutenant Owen and his men were the West Kents who had marched from St Ghislain and had passed through 2/Duke of Wellington's outpost line just as the firing started. Having halted in the village square the shelling began in earnest and Major Charles Pack-Beresford and B Company were sent up to the outpost line to strengthen 1/Dorset's left flank. Private Harry Beaumont was happily ensconced in the local brewery, imbibing free beer being doled out by two Belgians, when his sojourn was abruptly curtailed by Captain William Phillips who ordered him up to the outpost line. On the ridge above the village the West Kents found themselves on the edge of a cornfield. Extending into open order, the company moved through the corn stooks towards the trenches they were to occupy:

> *'We had not covered more than thirty yards when the Germans rose from those very trenches we were intending to occupy, and met us with a withering fire at*

close range which wiped out most of that gallant platoon before anyone realized what had happened ... My position was on the extreme right of our line, and immediately following the enemy's burst of fire I felt a sharp stab in my groin. I knew that I was hit.[43]

Beresford and Phillips were killed along with 21-year-old Second Lieutenant Maximilian Broadwood.[44] For Harry Beaumont, lying wounded in the stubble of a cornfield far from home, his war as a fighting soldier was over was over – for the moment at least. Eventually taken prisoner, his remarkable story of escape and evasion was only just beginning.

For many others holding the line on the ridge above the village it was to be a different story. At 11.00 am, just as the German attack by units of IR 8 and IR 52 began to gather momentum and the British battalions were put under increasing strain, General Sir Charles Fergusson received permission to begin the retirement of his 5th Division. The plan was for 14 Brigade to retire towards Bavai, followed by 13 Brigade with 15 Brigade acting as rearguard. The order came not a moment too soon for the hard pressed West Kents and Dorsets who managed to get clear of the village by 1.00pm.

In the case of the besieged 2/Duke of Wellington's, the order to retire did not reach Lieutenant Colonel Gibbs who remained in position along with two guns of 121 Battery RFA. At about 1.00 pm, after a final sharp encounter and in the realization that they were now alone, Major Ballard ordered the guns to be limbered up and withdrawn. Drivers Burnett and Street along with Second Lieutenant Chapman were later mentioned in despatches for their gallantry under fire. The remaining Dukes then retired south to their assembly point at Warquignies after a rearguard action that had cost the battalion 11 officers – including the CO, Lieutenant Colonel Gibbs, who was taken prisoner – and 316 other ranks killed, wounded and missing. Lieutenant Owen and the remnants of D Company were some of the last men of the 2/Duke of Wellington's to leave their positions in what was evidently a great deal of confusion:

'About 120 men under Carey [Lieutenant Robert O'Donoghue Carey] *and myself with another subaltern wandered away– we knew nothing about where we were to retire to or what was happening or had happened etc. The place must have been swarming with Germans, as they were miles south. We simply went south, thro' a wood – we found a single file path. Nobody ever expected for a minute to get through – everyone was completely exhausted, very hungry and imagining that we were all that was left. The inhabitants came to the rescue with fruit and drinks – I drank all sorts of mixtures and beer and milk, all on a very hot empty stomach, and it made me as strong and cheerful as possible. Eventually got over the frontier and fell in with other troops and marched to somewhere near Bavai, where we met the rest of the regiment'.*[45]

Fortunately Jim Pennyman's experience was a little less traumatic. The battalion had only one man killed from shellfire at Wasmes and at 10.30 am Brigadier General Gerald Cuthbert ordered them to begin their retirement at which point the machine-gun limber lurched heavily to one side as one of the wheels gave way. With no choice but to carry as much of the equipment as possible, they continued on their way:

> '*It was by this time fiendishly hot and we had to carry by hand guns and all our ammunition* ... [then] *a wretched refugee woman came along leading a pony and cart. There was nothing for it but to commandeer this. It was most heart breaking, but it had to be done. The pony was the miserablest creature I ever saw, so we christened him "Eep Eep Ouray" which is what all the country folk always said when they saw us ... in spite of his looks he turned out to be a champion worker'.*[46]

At Warquignies Pennyman recalled 'a bit of a muddle' as the regiments sorted themselves out, 'I remember the Dukes reported 135 present, but I knew things weren't as bad as all that as I had seen many of them singly on the road'.

For a while it looked very much as though Fergusson's 5th Division had managed to successfully extricate themselves from the pursuing enemy forces. But it was the lull before the storm, the whole weight of the German IV Corps, which had been largely undetected in its wide sweeping march on the First Army's right flank, was now about to fall on Brigadier General Edward Gleichen's 15 Brigade.

Chapter 5

24 August – Audregnies

Brigadier General Count Edward Wilfred Gleichen had royal connections in that he was a half-nephew of Queen Victoria. Commissioned into the Grenadier Guards in 1881, he served in the short-lived Guards Camel Regiment in the Sudan campaign in 1884, saw action with the Egyptian Army in the Dongola Expedition in 1896 and again in the second Boer War in South Africa. In 1911, despite having not served with troops for 10 years, he was appointed to command 15 Infantry Brigade, a brigade that drew its battalions from county regiments the length and breadth of England. Mobilization swelled its ranks considerably with reservists and by the time the brigade arrived south of the canal at Mons on 22 August it numbered 127 officers, 3,958 NCOs and men and 258 horses.

On 23 August the brigade was in reserve and during the early part of the day could only speculate as to what was taking place to the north on the canal line. Later, as the brigades on the canal fell back, the 1/Dorsets and 1/Bedfords lost a number of men as German infantry pushed on through the maze of slag heaps and mine workings that abounded to the south. Eventually Gleichen's men fell back on the Wasmes-Paturages line and withdrew with the 5th Division on 24 August with orders to act as the divisional rearguard. Detailed for this task were the 1st Battalion Cheshire Regiment (1/Cheshires) and the 1st Battalion Royal Norfolk Regiment (1/Norfolks). By late morning on the 24th, as the guns of the advancing German IV Corps opened up from north of the main Valenciennes road, the full implications of the rather premature retirement of 19 Infantry Brigade and the Cavalry Division earlier in the morning became apparent: the left flank of the 5th Division was wide open and was about to be enveloped by the two divisions of von Armin's IV Corps.

Units of the German 7th Infantry Division (ID 7) had crossed the canal in the early hours of 24 August and at first light IR 66 advanced on Thulin. Here they came up against the British cavalry screen which defended the town 'energetically' before falling back on the railway line south of the town. Lieutenant John Ainsworth and his troop of 11th (Prince Albert's Own) Hussars

(11/Hussars) along with troopers from 1 Cavalry Brigade dismounted and held the line allowing the last of 19 Brigade to march south almost unmolested.[47] Lieutenant Algernon Lamb, fighting with the 2/Dragoon Guards (Queen's Bays), remembered being in position 'on the northern slope of a deep railway cutting with a magnificent field of fire' for about two hours before falling back southwest of Audregnies under the cover of L Battery, RHA.

With all this activity unfolding on the flank it remains a mystery why Fergusson was not informed of the extent of the threat to his division earlier and why he only realized his situation was deteriorating considerably at 11.00 am. However, that said, he responded quickly in dispatching an urgent request for help to Allenby and counterattacking with his only reserves: the divisional rearguard from Gleichen's 15 Brigade supported by 119 Battery RFA.

Two brigades of the cavalry were retiring on Angre when word reached them of Fergusson's plight. Allenby's orders sent Brigadier General Hubert Gough's 3 Cavalry Brigade post-haste to the heights above Angre to seize the spur between the Honnelle and St Pierre rivers, and de Lisle's 2 Cavalry Brigade to Audregnies, where it halted near the railway station. Meanwhile, Brigadier General Charles Briggs and 1 Cavalry Brigade had already reached Roisin when the call for help sent them galloping the three miles back to Angre to take up a position on the right of Gough's 3 Brigade. The village of Angre was on the extreme right of the German IV Corps advance and it was units in the vanguard of the German 8th Infantry Division (ID 8) which first encountered the dismounted cavalry as the forward companies of IR 93 left the cover of the small village of Baisieux. From their advantage on the high ground and in the woods north of Angre, the combined fire of the cavalry managed to check the German advance effectively.

Against the two battalions of IR 93 – now clearing the wooded area to the south of Baisieux- the cavalry held their ground for a little over 3 hours before retiring at around 4.00 pm. With the added firepower from D and E Batteries, RHA, Lieutenant Kenneth North and his 4/Hussars machine-gun section prevented any advance up the Honnelle valley.[48] A little further east, Captain Charles Blackburne and C Squadron of 5/Dragoon Guards managed to charge a platoon of German infantry in a nearby wood and after turning them out, brought an enfilading fire on the grey-coated infantry struggling up the valley. The Dragoons lost 4 men wounded and 3 horses killed, considerably less than the Hussars, who in what was their first action of the war, lost 35 men and 45 horses. German sources reported 14 killed and 77 wounded.

In contrast to the successful cavalry action at Angre, two of 2 Cavalry Brigade's regiments, 4/Dragoon Guards and 9/Lancers, were about to suffer a different fate. They had in the meantime moved north of Audregnies, their new location now being astride the old Roman road that ran north-south through Audregnies and which was in the direct line of the advance of the

German ID 8. To the right of Lieutenant Colonel 'Soarer' Campbell's lancers were L Battery and Gleichen's Cheshires and Norfolks with the six guns of 119 Battery deployed along the low ridge which ran east to Elouges. Half a mile northwest of Elouges two squadrons of 18/Hussars were in the shelter of the railway cutting.

L Battery's bone-rattling dash from the high ground south of Elouges had not been without mishap; galloping under fire they lost one wagon to shellfire and another which was smashed to pieces when crossing a sunken road. To his relief Lieutenant Jack Giffard arrived intact with his gun crews after some tricky route finding:

> *'We had to cross a narrow railway bridge and wheel sharp right down one field, across a dyke with only one crossing into the next field behind a hedge. Three batteries got onto us before we were over the railway and we galloped into action right under very heavy shellfire.'*[49]

As L Battery's six 13-pounder guns unlimbered and came into action they concentrated their shrapnel fire on the infantry of IR 72 advancing south of Quiévrain. A mile and-a-half further east on the Audregnies – Elouges road, 119 Battery with their heavier 18-pounders had already been in action for 30 minutes, targeting the German gun line on the main Valenciennes road.

With this rather unequal artillery duel getting underway, Allenby arrived on the scene and after a hurried consultation with General de Lisle, the decision was taken to instigate one of the most costly and controversial cavalry charges of 1914. If accounts of what actually took place during this infamous charge have since become hazy due to 'the fog of war', General de Lisle's orders to the brigade at the time were quite clear:

> *'I saw a strong enemy force advancing southeast from Quiévrain ... I rode back to the village, met Lieutenant Colonel Campbell, commanding 9th Lancers, and ordered him at all costs to check the advancing infantry. I ordered Lieutenant Colonel Mullens, 4th Dragoon Guards, to support the 9th Lancers.'*[50]

Watching the charge from the railway cutting was Major Charles Leveson of 18/Hussars. He and his squadron had a grandstand view:

> *'Suddenly there was a tremendous increase in the hostile gun and machine-gun fire on our left. I looked in that direction straight down the railway line and I saw our cavalry moving forward at the gallop ... the first three squadrons carried lances and were in open column of squadrons, the remainder had no lances and appeared to be in column of troops as near possible, but in both cases, the formation, if even made, was being rapidly lost as they were being exposed to a terrific shell and*

machine-gun fire ... I could distinctly see men falling off their horses – others evidently wounded just clinging on'.[51]

It must have been a remarkable spectacle as some 800 horses and men galloped into battle, but what had begun in some semblance of order quickly became disorder. The line of galloping cavalry charging up both sides of the Roman road soon ran into trouble. Captain Arthur Osburn, the medical officer attached to 4/Dragoon Guards, thought the ground over which they were charging totally unsuitable for cavalry, 'hundreds crashed amongst the railway lines, horses tripped over the low signal wires or pitched headlong- riders breaking their necks – into ballast pits near the railway'.

One of those who fell was 17-year-old Private Ben Clouting who had lied about his age when he had enlisted in 4/Dragoon Guards in 1913. Machine-gun fire had wreaked havoc on the horses and men of his troop and he recalled being 'brought up by agricultural barbed wire' which was strung out in front of them. Responding to a bugle call ordering a right wheel he had just pulled his horse round when:

'I hit the ground at full tilt and with my sword still firmly attached by a lanyard to my wrist, was lucky not to impale myself. Dazed I struggled to my feet ... A riderless horse came careering in my direction and, collecting myself, I raised my hand in the air and shouted "halt" at the top of my voice. It was a 9th Lancer's horse, a Shoeing Smith's mount and wonderfully trained, for despite the pandemonium, it stopped on a sixpence'.[52]

Lieutenant Alexander Gallaher was at the Head of A Squadron, 4/Dragoons, when he was brought down:

'I saw a flash which seemed right in front of my eyes, and my horse went down. When I came round I was lying on my right side, with one leg under my dead horse. My head was bad ... All was quiet for a moment. Dead and wounded lay all around and everything seemed strangely still.'[53]

Private William Bull serving the guns with L Battery saw the 9/Lancers make their 'gallant charge which was spoken of as a second Balaclava'. Gallant it may have been but in a matter of minutes de Lisle's 2 Cavalry Brigade had lost 234 officers and men killed and wounded and men and horses lay scattered across the line of advance. Tragically they had still been half a mile from the German guns when both regiments became utterly mixed up in the whirlwind of gunfire which had become concentrated upon them. Desperate to get out of the killing zone, some sought refuge at the nearby sugar factory or used slag heaps as cover whilst others made for the railway cutting where 18/Hussars were situated.

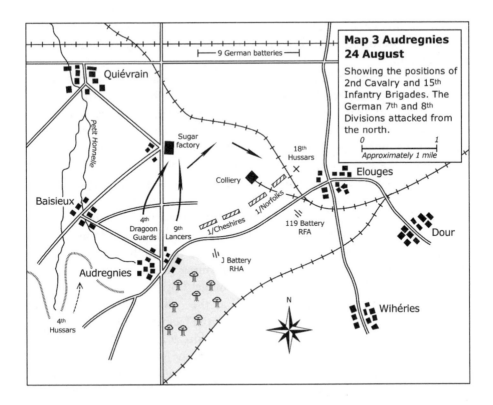

Map 3 Audregnies 24 August

Showing the positions of 2nd Cavalry and 15th Infantry Brigades. The German 7th and 8th Divisions attacked from the north.

Unquestionably the charge had little impact on the events of the day. For de Lisle to have ordered a charge over 1,200 yards of broken ground devoid of cover against an unknown number of infantry and guns had bordered on the reckless. Whether the mounted effort had been thwarted by wire fences, ballast pits, enemy fire or a combination of all three, it would have been far more effective if the cavalrymen had fought dismounted from established firing lines as their counterparts on the heights above Angre were doing.[54] As it was, over half the brigade had been lost for what one subaltern described as, 'no reason whatever'. Sadly, as the survivors found to their cost, against artillery and machine-gun fire the sword and lance was of very little use.

As the remnants of the shattered cavalry squadrons galloped across the frontage of 1/Cheshires and 1/Norfolks they masked the targets of their own infantry, preventing the frustrated riflemen from providing supporting fire. But this was the least of their worries. The two battalions were under the temporary command of 1/Norfolks commanding officer, Lieutenant Colonel Colin Ballard. Sir Charles Fergusson's orders to Ballard were to hold on at all costs initially, an order that was later amended allowing Ballard the discretion of retirement should he feel it necessary. Rightly or wrongly, Ballard assumed that Lieutenant Colonel Dudley Boger who commanded the Cheshires was in receipt of the same orders. Crucially he was not and had already issued instructions to his company officers to fight to the end. Another disaster was about to unfold.

Three of 1/Norfolks companies were between the Elouges–Baisieux road and the railway and the fourth was north of the railway bridge on the Elouges–Audregnies road with one platoon a little forward of the colliery buildings. The Cheshires were a little more spread out from the railway line – where D Company linked up with the Norfolks – down to the junction of the Audregnies-Wihéries road, and furthermore, owing to the undulating nature of the ground, visual contact between the companies was not always possible. To the north of the railway line the 1/Norfolks right flank was being seriously threatened by IR 66 which was also advancing on Elouges, a movement that would put them behind Ballard and block his retreat. The Norfolks history tells us that three messages were sent to the Cheshires and another to Major Ernest Alexander, commanding 119 Battery, informing them of the retirement, messages that regrettably failed to reach Colonel Boger. Similar messages also failed to reach the platoon of Norfolks at the colliery and they, with the Cheshires, continued to fight on, oblivious to the fact that Ballard had retired.

By the time Colonel Ballard had decided to retire at 2.30 pm the Norfolks had already suffered heavy losses; Major John Orr, the second-in-command and adjutant Captain Francis Cresswell had been killed along with Captain Ernest Briard, whilst Lieutenant Harold Openshaw and at least 250 NCOs and men lay dead or wounded on the slope.[55]

Once the Norfolks had left the field German infantry managed to work round to the right of 119 Battery and attack the two guns of Lieutenant Classon Preston's section which was about 500 yards to the right of the other four guns. Ordered to retire by his battery commander, Preston and Sergeant McCartney managed to limber up their guns and get them away along the Elouges road under heavy shell fire. Moments later, one of the lead horses on McCartney's gun was killed and had to be cut free and the young Irish lieutenant was wounded in the process. Despite the mounting casualties amongst the men, however, Preston brought his guns into action once more on the left of the battery and opened fire on German cavalry to his front, being wounded for a second time. The cavalry threat soon gave way to be replaced by advancing infantry who closed to within 800 yards before Preston ordered McCartney's gun to retire whilst he remained firing shrapnel to dispel any thoughts the Germans might have entertained of rushing the guns. Preston's devotion to duty saw him wounded twice more as he and the last gun team sought cover. Sergeant McCartney's last act of assistance for his courageous officer was to see him safely bundled into an ambulance as he brought the section away.

The remaining guns of 119 Battery continued firing for a little longer before Major Alexander felt the threat from the right made it necessary to move his guns before they were lost. He was almost too late. German infantrymen were by now just 600 yards away, firing from the cover of slag heaps and several German batteries had begun to concentrate their fire on the British guns. For a moment or two Alexander must have wondered just how he would be able get the guns away amid such a maelstrom when, quite incredibly and just at the very moment his help was needed, Captain Francis Grenfell of 9/Lancers with a party of officers and men materialized and the guns were manhandled over the carnage of dead and dying men to the gun limbers and safely wheeled away. The battery had lost 30 officers and men during their engagement and Grenfell and Alexander subsequently received the Victoria Cross for their part in saving the guns.[56]

It wasn't long after 119 Battery had retired that Major the Hon Walter Sclater-Booth was also considering retirement. L Battery, which prided itself on the fact that it was one, if not the, finest horse artillery battery in the British Army, had fired over 400 rounds of shrapnel and in the words of Jack Giffard, 'did considerable execution amongst the infantry and enabled what was left of the cavalry brigade to withdraw.' Sclater-Booth's decision to retire was taken for him by the Brigade Major of 2 Cavalry Brigade who appeared, galloping towards them, shouting 'Good old L.' The guns were limbered up to their horse-drawn teams in a matter of minutes and the battery escaped relatively intact down the line of the hedge. Their retirement towards Villers Pol left 1/Cheshires alone on the battlefield.

The stand of the Cheshires was defiant to the very last. Only one officer, Captain John Shore actually received any orders to retire and he was on the left flank with half of B Company firing on the German infantry advancing out of the Bois de Déduit and up the Petite River valley. Eventually at 3.00pm, after being ordered to retire by a staff officer, he left with the 70 or so men who had survived alongside him. On the other flank, Captain Ernest Jones with men of D Company must have seen the Norfolks retiring and assumed the Cheshires were doing the same. Accordingly he began moving his men down the mineral railway towards Wihéries. At 4.00 pm, unaware that the troops on both his flanks were retiring, Colonel Boger was becoming increasingly anxious about the attack now developing on the A and C Company fronts. Unable to contact Jones, he and his adjutant, Captain Victor Tahourdin, left Major Bryan Chetwynd-Stapylton behind in charge of battalion headquarters and set out to see for themselves what the situation was. Finding no trace of Captain Jones and D Company and alarmed by heavy rifle fire from the direction of the Elouges-Quiévrain railway they retraced their steps with the realization that the battalion was outflanked on the right. Retirement was the only option and even that option was quickly becoming unviable.

Meanwhile, the fight which was centred on A and C Companies was giving Captain Wilfred Dugmore some anxiety. They were holding the German infantry off but, despite calls for fresh supplies which were not forthcoming, ammunition stocks were dangerously depleted. Unbeknown to him his reserve supply of small arms ammunition had disappeared in the opposite direction; loaded onto the back of a company mule and even now retiring into the distance along with the support platoons of D Company. At 4.30 pm Dugmore took it upon himself to order those men that could to retire. Organizing them into two groups they split up and headed south to Audregnies where it was thought Colonel Boger was attempting to reassemble the battalion. The rest of the story of the Cheshires is one of courage and devotion to duty. The battalion was by now practically surrounded and in the ensuing attempts to escape towards Audregnies Wood and Wihéries the battalion's fight became fragmented into isolated actions and single acts of extreme bravery.

Colonel Boger was wounded in the foot sometime after the withdrawal of Dugmore and his men, command falling to 41-year-old Chetwynd-Stapylton but by now there was precious little of the battalion left to command. Dugmore and his party of Cheshires – along with a smattering of Norfolks he had collected along the way – were cut off by German troops crossing the railway line to his north and in ordering his men to scatter only one, Private William Sharples, evaded capture. Sharples managed to wriggle out of one end of Wihéries as the Germans entered the other.

One of the bravest acts of the day was led by the 'singularly quiet and unassuming' Captain Arthur Dyer. In a desperate attempt to silence a German machine gun firing on the left flank and allow the remaining men a chance to get away, he drew his sword and with a small group of men from A and B Companies charged the enemy firing line. Joining him were Captains Joliffe and Bertie Massy and Lieutenant Cuthbert Matterson, the battalion scout officer:

> '*I remained to the last with a few men covering the withdrawal. Masses of German infantry could be seen advancing and appeared to be enveloping our left flank ... At about 4.15 pm Captain Dyer gave the order "advance and enfilade the enemy." I climbed over the bank and through a wire fence and with about six men I joined the attack. I was joined by Captain Dyer and together we made about 3 advances in rushes in the face of very heavy rifle and machine gun fire ...Captain Massy and Captain Joliffe ... quickly fell severely wounded. During the rushes Captain Dyer was wounded in the heel but together we continued to advance employing rapid fire against the Germans at a range of approx 250–300 [yards]. Captain Dyer then ordered a retirement as our casualties were severe.*'[57]

Miraculously both Dyer and Matterson managed to return to the 1/Cheshires' line with a handful of men leaving the more severely wounded behind, but as the Cheshires' history said, 'the forlorn hope had failed'. Matterson's account tells us that on their return they and the remaining men were ordered to 'stand up and cease firing' by the senior officer present.

The senior officer present was Major Chetwynd-Stapylton and it was he who gave the command to surrender at about 6.30 pm. Every possible line of retreat had been sealed and conscious that further resistance would be pointless, he gave the order that ended the Cheshires' resistance. Only 40 of the survivors, according to the Cheshires' history, were unwounded. What was remarkable about the stand of 1/Cheshires was that many of them chose to fight it out rather than surrender. We will never know exactly why they chose this option but we do know that several small groups of men with their officers fought to the last until they were either killed or captured. Of the little band of 6 men who were with Captain Ernest Jones when they were surrounded southwest of Wihéries, Jones, 19-year-old Drummer Edward Hogan and Private Frederick Garrad were shot down after refusing to surrender; the already wounded Corporal Walter Crookes collapsed and was taken prisoner whilst Sergeant Arthur Raynor and Private Blake escaped only to be rounded up later. Another officer, Lieutenant Kingdon Frost, a Special Reserve officer with No. 9 Platoon of C Company, was seen by a wounded officer of 4/Dragoons, 'fighting like a demon, having refused to surrender.' There is no record of the fate of 24-year-old Lieutenant Charles Campbell, who died near the small bridge over the railway line from Audregnies to Dour after being sent to make contact with Shore and B Company.

Of the 26 officers and 933 other ranks who had gone into action that morning, only 199 men, 6 officers and a Warrant Officer answered their names in the early hours of 25 August at Bavai.[58] 3 officers and 54 NCOs and men were killed in action. The remaining 788, including Colonel Boger, were taken prisoner, many of them later succumbing to wounds or disease. Captain Shore, along with Captain William Rich and Lieutenant Groves, managed to evade capture and, collecting scattered groups of Cheshires and Norfolks on the way, eventually rejoined the brigade south of Athis.[59] At the time it was thought that most of the battalion's officers had been killed, General Gleichen's diary recorded his initial shock when they were reunited with the remnants of the rearguard he had left at Audregnies:

'Just beyond Athis we found the Norfolks, who had been at Elouges all the morning, and then we came across the sad remainder of the Cheshires ... It was horrible to hear of this appalling loss. Shore was the only captain left [sic] and he was in command with two or three subalterns only ... Tahourdin, Stapylton, Dyer, Dugmore, and lots more were reported killed. Shore was in a terrible state of mind.'[60]

As Shore and the men with him would have unquestionably testified, one of the more distressing aspects of a fighting withdrawal for the soldier on the ground is leaving the severely wounded behind in the knowledge they will surely fall into enemy hands. The experience of those wounded who were captured at Audregnies was one of mixed fortune. Captain Joliffe who was wounded in both legs was found by a party of Cheshires detailed to collect the wounded by their captors. He lay where he fell during Captain Dyer's charge and an RAMC doctor managed to splint one leg before he was evacuated to Audregnies Convent which had been turned into a hospital by the Germans after the battle. He was fortunate, many of the wounded lay where they had fallen for up to a week before they were brought in. Private Curran was left in the open for 'about a week' before he was found by two Belgians and brought to the convent hospital, an experience shared by Private John Sherring who was found after 5 days by men from the German Cycle Corps.

At Audregnies the whole of the ground floor of the convent was taken up with the wounded and many of the severely wounded men like Private Albert Brock spent several months in the care of the sisters before being shipped off to Germany. Both Curran and Sherring were later transferred to the civil hospital at Mons where Curran says civilians were turned out by the Germans to make room for them. Trooper Thomas Grassick, who was one of the 4/Hussars wounded, also found himself at Mons having spent the night immobile on the battlefield but to his dismay he was moved to Germany within days. The German medical authorities were quick to remove any of the wounded who, in their opinion, were deemed fit to travel to camps in Germany. One of these was Private Frank Palmer of the Norfolks who was part of a large group who were moved to Sennelager after only a few days treatment. Palmer was clearly not fit to travel and as a result of a gruelling journey, spent several months in hospital in Germany before being repatriated.

The *Official History* gives BEF casualties for the whole of 24 August as roughly 2,600 officers and men killed, wounded and missing, of those 1,650 were from the 5th Division. The casualty figures for the eleven German infantry regiments and one of artillery that were in action against the BEF on 24 August are given as 1,288.[61] Of those units which were engaged at Audregnies, IR 93 reported 14 killed and 77 wounded, IR 72 had 34 killed and 218 wounded and IR 26 22 killed and 126 wounded and missing. The artillery batteries of Field Artillery Regiment 74 (FAR 74) recorded only 9 men killed and 49 wounded.

After the cavalry charge at Audregnies General de Lisle issued a special order to the men of 2 Cavalry Brigade expressing his thanks and pride in the conduct of his men and passing on Sir Charles Fergusson's thanks for 'saving his division.' Fergusson had apparently told de Lisle that, 'but for the Cavalry Brigade the [5th] Division would have been destroyed to the last man.' A statement that is hard to treat with any degree of seriousness. What's more, it is unlikely that many cavalrymen would have had sight of de Lisle's order, or even agreed with it, as they were now scattered far and wide. The 4/Dragoons had lost over 300 thoroughbred horses and at a roll call later that evening over 400 of their number were missing, it was a similar story with Colonel Campbell's 9/Lancers. Although many of these eventually rejoined their respective regiments, the process took days and significantly reduced the effectiveness of 2 Cavalry Brigade in covering the retreat over the next 72 hours. It is said that when Campbell was informed by de Lisle that he was being recommended for a Victoria Cross – which was not awarded – his reply was to the effect that he wanted his squadrons back, not medals.

If anyone had 'saved' Fergusson's division it was the combined efforts of the artillery batteries and the infantry. What had begun as a rearguard action to delay the advancing German IV Corps rapidly developed into a full-scale battle that concluded with the sacrifice of nearly a whole battalion. Von Armin's corps had indeed been delayed and fortunately for the retreating II Corps he chose not to pursue Fergusson but to remain that evening bivouacked on the Elouges-Baisieux line. The last troops of the, by now, footsore and exhausted 5th Division finally reached their overnight positions sometime after midnight where they joined Haig's two divisions of I Corps. Von Kluck's plan to throw the BEF back against Maubeuge had failed.

Chapter 6

25 August – I Corps Join the Fight

At 9.00 pm on the evening of 23 August Lieutenant Edward Spears had been summoned to GHQ by Sir John French's Chief of Staff, Archie Murray. Spears was told that the BEF would continue its retreat the next day as the threat to its left was still apparent and as the main body of Lanrezac's Fifth Army was a day's march ahead of the British right, the BEF had no choice but to keep pace. Spears dutifully relayed the message to Lanrezac's HQ at Aubenton at 10.00 pm only to receive the news that the whole of the French Fifth Army was to retire south of Le Cateau the next morning to a new line running through La Capell-Hirson-Mezières.

Operational Order No. 7 giving details of the retirement on Le Cateau had given Murray and the staff at GHQ some anxiety as they had debated the difficulties of passing the 35 square miles of the Forêt de Mormal that stood between Bavai and Le Cateau. Just why there had not been a preliminary reconnaissance to ascertain whether any of the roads that ran through the forest were practical for marching infantry and their transports is another indication as to the sense of hesitation which existed at GHQ on 24 August. There appears to have been plenty of time for this reconnaissance to have taken place and the men of A Squadron, North Irish Horse, serving as GHQ attached cavalry, were the ideal troops to carry it out. Admittedly the scattering of de Lisle's cavalry brigade had forced half the squadron to be deployed with the recently arrived 4th Division, but it would only have required a single troop of cavalry on what should have been considered a vital reconnaissance.[62] Murray's report to Haig later on the 24th stating that the roads through the forest were unsuitable was apparently based on evidence from maps and would have possibly suggested to Haig that a proper reconnaissance had been carried out. Even so he did not order any reconnaissance of his own and in so doing he, and GHQ, left a large 35 square mile question mark unanswered.

Having taken the decision to avoid the forest GHQ effectively split the two corps of the BEF and although Sir John French intended that Le Cateau would be the point at which they would reassemble, it would be a further 8 days and

90 more miles of retreat before Haig's and Smith-Dorrien's commands would be reunited. Thus in the circumstances there was only one sensible plan if I Corps was to avoid a lengthy flank march across the advancing enemy's front and further widen the gap between the BEF and Lanrezac's retreating army. Consequently, GHQ determined that Haig's I Corps would retire east of the forest in two columns: The 1st Division to cross the Sambre River at Hautmont and thence to Dompierre and 2nd Division to cross at Pont sur Sambre and Berlaimont, and to march via Leval and Landrecies to Le Cateau. On the opposite side of the forest, II Corps would use two main routes, the direct Roman road that ran through Englefontaine and the more westerly road through Solesmes. Archie Murray, writing after the war, was adamant that in issuing the retirement orders he emphasised to Douglas Haig the importance of maintaining contact with II Corps.

A late start by I Corps on the morning of 25 August was not helped by having to share the roads with retiring French forces and the inevitable trail of civilian refugees with their belongings piled high on carts of all descriptions. Major Lord Bernard Gordon Lennox was marching with the 2nd Battalion Grenadier Guards (2/Grenadiers) and recorded in his diary 'a long and very hot march with continual gunning going on in our rear' noting further that 'they seem pushing devils these Germans.'[63] The march was not made any easier by two French reserve divisions using the same route as I Corps and General Sordet's French Cavalry Corps moving across their path at right angles from Avesnes en route to Cambrai. Haig must have decided early on that he was going to halt before he reached Le Cateau, thus having motored down from Bavai and with Le Cateau still 7 miles away, he established his overnight HQ at the small town of Landrecies on the southern extremity of the Forêt de Mormal. During the late afternoon and early evening the two divisions of I Corps halted in and around the town and further east at Maroilles and Avesnes, the last troops arriving by 6.00 pm.

Bernard Gordon Lennox and the Grenadiers marched into Landrecies at 3.30 pm curious to know why they had passed no outposts on their way into the town. Continuing over the railway and on towards the square in perfect march order, Major Ma Jeffreys who was at the head of the battalion recognised the lanky form of the Brigade Major, Gerry Ruthven who was standing by a street corner. Jefferies first question to Ruthven was blunt and to the point.

"What about the outposts?" He said there were to be no outposts, as we were covered by other bodies of troops, and by the great Forêt de Mormal, through which there were no roads that could be used by troops.'[64]

Jefferies was right to be troubled, it was an omission that would have grated uncomfortably with any professional soldier but after a long and weary route march his primary concern for the moment was his men and he took Ruthven at his word. Fortunately for all concerned, when a false alarm was sounded at 4.00 pm by 'a French cavalryman who rode into town in a wild state of excitement' claiming the Germans were close behind him, the Coldstream Guards established an outpost line on the Le Quesnoy road just north of the railway station. Captain Robert Whitbread and his company of the 3rd Battalion Coldstream Guards (3/Cold stream) had been in the town since 1.00 pm and both officers and men were anticipating a good meal and a few hours undisturbed sleep, particularly as a dawn start had been ordered for the next morning:

'About 4pm there was an alarm that the town was full of Germans, and we stood to arms for half an hour. About 7.45 pm ... No 1 Company were ordered to fall in, and the officers of the company regretfully left an unfinished dinner to which they had just sat down. We marched out of the town across the railway, and met a cavalry patrol coming into the town, who told us there were no Germans within ten miles. We went about 600 yards past the station, here we met Monck [Captain C H S Monck] and some of his company (No 3) with the machine guns, under Bingham, [Lieutenant D C Bingham] in position across the main road at a point where two roads met in a V pointing toward the town.'[65]

Dismissing the French cavalryman as a 'harmless lunatic', Bernard Gordon Lennox and the Grenadier officers of No. 2 Company quickly settled into a comfortable billet and even found someone to cook their evening meal for them. It was to be a dinner they too would leave unfinished:

'... we rushed out to hear heavy firing – musketry – going on just outside our end of the town. Everyone fell in hurriedly, there was a good deal of skurry but no disorder, when word came down the Coldstream Guards outposts were being driven back.'[66]

They had not quite been driven back but there was a moment or two when German troops disguised as French and Belgian soldiers nearly achieved their objective, Robert Whitbread was in conversation with Charlie Monck when the attack began:

'We heard the noise of a large body of troops approaching, and also heard the noise of wheels. Then we thought we could hear German being talked when the leading men came to a strand of barbed wire which had been tied across the road 75 yards from the machine gun.'[67]

Monck was not taken in by the bogus Frenchmen and gave the order to open fire. However, before his order could be executed the enemy rushed the outpost line, knocked Monck down and killed Private Thomas Robson who was working one of the machine guns, carrying it away with them. The gun was soon retrieved but it swiftly became very clear that the attack was the vanguard of a much larger force:

> 'We lay down in the road in readiness for a rush, we next heard some words of command in German and dimly saw a mass approaching, apparently slowly and without noise. When this mass was about fifty yards off we let them have five rounds rapid and a burst of machine gun fire…the same thing was repeated several times, each rush being stopped by our fire. The din of rifles and machine gun fire drowned any sound of their advance and the flashes from rifles prevented us from seeing even dimly what had happened to the Germans.'[68]

With the increasing noise of battle up ahead the Grenadiers doubled up towards the firing line in the pouring rain to safeguard the other entrances to the town whilst the Irish Guards were employed putting the town in a state of defence. Gordon Lennox's company deployed on the right by the railway station, his men breaking into the empty houses to establish fields of fire down the streets that ran parallel to the station. Major Hamilton and No. 1 Company held the side roads on the left behind the station.

Charlie Monck's company had thwarted an attempt by units of IR 27 to gain access to the town; they were probably as surprised as the British at the encounter on the Le Quesnoy road and had fully expected to take the Sambre road bridge at the southern end of the town without opposition and even find comfortable billets for the night. Now, thrown into confusion by the ferocity of the Coldstream defence, the commanding officer of IR 27 sent his adjutant back for reinforcements which arrived in the form of two companies from IR 165 and a couple of artillery pieces.

In spite of the gathering mass of German infantry to their front, Whitbread and two companies of Coldstream Guards were managing to prevent any serious attack from developing until a field gun began firing at them over open sights:

> 'We swept the hedges and surrounding ground with fire at intervals to stop them working their way under cover of the hedges to our flanks. Eventually the enemy worked up the road on our left and partially enfiladed the right half of our little line across the road, our line was moved back six yards but then, unluckily for us, the roof of a barn on our left was set on fire and our position on the road was lit up as if it were daylight. This enabled the enemy to bring up a gun on to the main road and they shelled our position at point blank range … it was certainly very unpleasant to see their shells come all the way from the gun, the sparks accompanying each shell showed its passage in the darkness. Every time the enemy fired their gun they knocked out men all round me and I think they fired five shells

when ... BIFF, I next remember finding myself tumbling about in a field with a wound in my head. I got out my field dressing but dropped it so held some wet grass to my head to stop the bleeding and called for help.'[69]

From the Grenadiers' positions at the railway station they could see the gun being fired by the light of the burning stack until it was knocked out by one of the two British guns which had been brought up in reply. But what they didn't witness was 28-year-old Lance Corporal George Wyatt run out under fire on two separate occasions to extinguish the blazing stack which was revealing the Coldstream positions. It was a very brave act from an individual who had been walking the beat as a Barnsley policeman before he was called up on 5 August. His subsequent Victoria Cross was presented by the king at Buckingham Palace in March 1916.[70]

Any further German advance was now out of the question; the darkness together with hedges and wire fences prevented any thoughts of overwhelming the Guards who in reality were never seriously threatened. 'So the night wore on with bursts of rapid fire at intervals, one of the longest nights I have ever spent' wrote Bernard Gordon Lennox. At first light it became obvious the Germans had withdrawn and soon after came the order for the Guards to begin evacuating the town. The place was in a mess and the last of the civilian population had long gone:

'The streets had been barricaded through the night with every conceivable sort of thing, carts, wagons and faggots and all available paraphernalia. Unfortunately we had no time to get our kits, the men having turned out in such a hurry, and they had to be left behind.'[71]

The Irish Guards had been responsible for the barricades and Lieutenant Aubrey Herbert, although still the Member of Parliament for Yeovil, had managed to wangle himself a commission in the Irish Guards and leave for France as the official interpreter with the 1st Battalion. Although the time he gives is probably incorrect, he describes the confusion in the town as 4 (Guards) Brigade was preparing to leave:

'About 2.30, in my sleep I heard my name, and found Desmond [Captain Lord Desmond FitzGerald, the battalion Adjutant] *calling me loudly in the street outside. He said: "We have lost two young officers ... Come out and find them at once.*

The Germans are coming into the town, and we shall have to clear out instantly." I said to him: "I don't know either [of them] *by sight, and if I did it is far too dark to see them." "Well", he said, "you must do your best." I went out and walked about the town, which was still being shelled, but I was far more afraid of being run over in the darkness than of being hit. Troops were pouring out in great confusion – foot, artillery, transport mixed – and there were great holes in the road made by the German shells.'*[72]

The two officers in question were Second Lieutenants Woodroffe and Livingstone-Learmonth both of whom were not located by Herbert in his rather half-hearted attempt to find them. They were, in fact, still sleeping having failed to hear the call to arms and were completely oblivious of what had taken place during the night. They eventually woke in daylight with the battalion long gone and the Germans in the town. Fortunately they fell into the hands of one of the captured RAMC officers who, by chance knew the whereabouts of a horse abandoned by one of the British battalions. Seizing their opportunity, the two young officers mounted the steed and managed to escape across country. I would have loved to have eavesdropped on the subsequent interview they had with Lieutenant Colonel George Morris on their return to the battalion! Second Lieutenant Neville Woodroffe later wrote home about the incident:

'My personal billet was away from my own platoon as I and another officer had managed to find a room in another part of the village in which to sleep... However when the alarm went we did not hear it and the two men detailed to warn us never came so eventually when the remainder had managed to get out of the place we were left asleep in our room. We woke up at 7 o'clock and found the town surrounded by Germans and the village partly blown down. The house next to ours was completely shattered and all windows and roofs of the neighbouring houses were smashed and the streets torn up. We collected our kit and made out as quickly as possible.'[73]

Marching with the Guards Brigade away from Landrecies went 2 officers and 70 other ranks of 19/Field Ambulance. The remaining sections of 19/Field Ambulance who had marched into Landrecies at 5.00 pm the previous day now set about transferring the less severely wounded to the waiting ambulance train. One of those was Robert Whitbread:

'Hawarden [Lieutenant R C Hawarden] was in the next bed to me and was quite cheerful in spite of very bad wounds. He afterwards died I regret to say. I should think it was a bout 8am on the 26th when one of the medical officers came round telling all who could walk or hobble to go outside as a fresh lot of wounded had just been brought in. I got into an ambulance and with a lot of other ambulances went to Guise.'[74]

Whitbread was one of the more fortunate wounded who was evacuated before the Germans arrived. Not so for the men of 4/Field Ambulance who now resigned themselves to the inevitable and began the task of treating the wounded and burying the dead. They had been directed to Landrecies with I Corps having spent much of the day treating exhausted men in the wake of the main columns. They arrived just east of the town soon after the action began and sensibly halted in an orchard along with several stragglers from 13/Field Ambulance. When the Germans entered the town some hours later, 4/Field Ambulance and two sections of 19/Field Ambulance were taken prisoner. It is interesting to note that the casualty figures reported by IR 27 – 37 killed and 88 wounded – concurs with the evidence of two of the captured RAMC officers who found only 30 new German graves. Of the British casualties, the greater number were from the Coldstream Guards who left 12 dead and 7 missing when they retired. Evidence from Private Joseph Taylor, who was captured with one of the field ambulances, suggests only 30 of the 105 wounded were left behind at Landrecies. The Grenadiers lost Second Lieutenant Robert Vereker who was killed fighting with Bernard Gordon Lennox's company together with 6 NCOs and men wounded.[75]

Although he remained at Landrecies until 11.30 pm that evening, Douglas Haig soon moved his HQ to the nearby village of Le Grand Fayt under the impression his I Corps was in grave danger of being overrun. If we are to accept his own account, he and Johnnie Gough place much of the blame for what he describes as the 'penetration' of the town's defences on the 'sleepy' Guards and his diary gives the impression he personally directed operations until he left for the security of 3 Brigade HQ at Le Grand Fayt.[76] Haig was clearly rattled by this surprise attack and his report to GHQ, now at St Quentin, that he was under assault by four German divisions caused some consternation amongst an already anxious staff. Even at 3.50 am on the 26th, when he was 6 miles away from the fighting, he requested further assistance from Smith-Dorrien, suggesting troops at Le Cateau should advance immediately to Landrecies. As we shall see later, the II Corps Commander had other things on his mind on 26 August.

To be fair though, in defence of Haig's apparent panic it could be argued that the quite disproportionate amount of firing which was kept up until daybreak at Landrecies and the uncertainty of the number of the enemy that might be hidden in the Forêt de Mormal was reason enough for Haig's alarm. Nevertheless, more importantly, from the troops' point of view, it had the unfortunate result of keeping the Guards Brigade under arms all night and depriving the weary troops of their much required rest.

With Haig assuming the worst and GHQ taking him at his word that I Corps was under a sustained attack, questions were being asked as to why Haig had decided to halt on the Landrecies line and not east of Le Cateau as ordered. While Haig claims he received the approval of GHQ, Henry Wilson appears to refute this and was of the opinion that Haig should be 'made to go onto Le

Cateau' otherwise there would 'be an awkward gap'. Whether Haig and his increasing distrust of Sir John French's ability to support I Corps decided to beat his own course and ignore GHQ's directives is anyone's guess, but the fact remains that he did choose to ignore an order directing him to rejoin II Corps the next day at Busigny, some 7 miles south west of Le Cateau.

* * *

The attack on Landrecies was made by the advance guard of the German 7th Division, which had marched along the western side of the forest quite unaware that the town was occupied by the British. The attack on Maroilles was made under similar circumstances by the advance guard of the 5th Division, which had marched through the forest. In the space of 9 days the inhabitants of both towns had witnessed the BEF marching north in expectation of victory and then returning in disarray with the Germans in hot pursuit. Maroilles on the evening of 25 August was an entirely different place to that experienced earlier in the month by Cyril Helm, the medical officer attached to 2/KOYLI. When he had first arrived on 16 August the battalion had spent 'two happy days' billeted on local farms and people 'gave them as much butter and milk as they wanted.' Now the single main street of the small town was choked with refugees and military transport causing some consternation to Lieutenant Alan Hanbury-Sparrow, the transport officer of 1st Battalion Royal Berkshire Regiment (1/Royal Berks), who had just turned up with the battalion after a 14 mile march from Bavai along some extremely congested roads:

> *'Wherever you look you can see wagons, carts and pedestrians making for the road you are on. The whole countryside is emptying itself onto it. The little groups you behold are rivulets hastening to join the main stream on the road, which soon becomes a spate of refugees, pouring along like a highland torrent.'*[77]

1/Royal Berks and the rest of 6 Infantry Brigade had spent the previous night in a cornfield and had been detailed as brigade rearguard on 25 August. Being the last to arrive, the battalion was, in typically soldierly fashion, looking forward to getting something to eat and a place to get their heads down for a couple of hours. B Squadron, 15/Hussars had been with the battalion on and off for most of the day with several small detachments patrolling the numerous rides which criss-crossed the forest. Leaving the Berkshires at Pont sur Sambre the squadron trotted on to Noyelles where it was to be billeted. No sooner had the men dismounted and loosened the girths of their weary horses when orders arrived to occupy the bridges at Maroilles and remain in position until relieved by the infantry.

Captain the Hon William Nugent arrived at the bridge northwest of Maroilles just as it was getting dark.[78] The forest came almost down to the banks of the Sambre at this point and there was very little the hussars could do to fortify the crossing apart from defend the approach road between the railway crossing and the river and put a troop on the bridge itself. The second, smaller, bridge was further down the canal to the east of Maroilles and Nugent chose to send the troop under Lieutenant Guy Straker there. With the sounds of heavy firing coming from the direction of Landrecies, Nugent realised he would probably soon be under attack himself. He was not wrong. At 8.00 pm the first units of the German III Army Corps attacked Nugent's bridge, bringing up artillery to fire directly at the besieged cavalrymen. They hung on grimly until the sheer weight of fire forced them to abandon the bridge to the enemy. Realising Lieutenant Straker's bridge was now in danger Private William Price slipped into the canal and swam down to Straker, warning him of the danger. Straker was able to withdraw his troop before he was surrounded and Price was awarded the DCM for his bravery.

As soon as the attack on the bridge began Nugent sent a galloper to Maroilles with a request for help; halfway there the cavalry trooper met a company of the 1/Royal Berks en route to the bridge. Major Alexander Turner and B Company had been ordered to relieve the cavalry and were doubling up the road. The last mile or so was on a raised, unmetalled causeway which was little more than a farm track across a low-lying marshy area intersected with deep drainage ditches. Forced to keep to the causeway in the darkness, Turner and his men discovered from the hussars they had been driven off the bridge which was now occupied by German infantry.

Several sources provide accounts of the engagement that followed Turner's arrival, yet despite this there is still a degree of uncertainty as to what exactly took place. The *Official History* tells us that B Company 'took post by the Rue des Juifs about a mile to the south east of the bridge.' Turner was then enticed forward by some troops on the bridge which the Royal Berks thought were French. In the ensuing confused encounter Turner was wounded and taken prisoner. Quite why this encounter took place when the hussars had already pulled back from the bridge under fire is a mystery but two accounts of the death of Captain Henry Shott found in his service record do throw a little more light on what took place after Turner's capture.

Henry Hammond Shott was highly regarded by his men and considered to be one of the bravest officers in the battalion. The fact that he began his military career in South Africa as a trooper in Bethune's Mounted Infantry doubtless endeared him to the men under his command. He was commissioned in 1900 and his award of the DSO was announced in the *London Gazette* in 1902. Promotion to captain came in 1911, followed three years later by his marriage to

Hazel Brown, the American daughter of a Yonkers businessman, 5 weeks before he left for France. She was never to see her husband again.

According to evidence given by Sergeant John Frogley, when the company was advancing to take the bridge:

> *'Captain Shott went to the left of the bridge and swam the River Sambre, returned and collected some men, including myself, returned again to the river, a fierce fire fight being opened upon us. Captain Shott again entered the river. On orders to retire from the position Captain Shott had not returned.'*[79]

Rather frustratingly Frogley's account does not go onto say what happened next. If this took place after Turner had been captured, which I assume it did, Shott was either attempting a rescue bid or trying to establish a presence on the northern end of the bridge. This is borne out to some extent by Private Watts, who states in his evidence that B Company was holding the bridge at the time of Shott's death. Turner's own account of what occurred after his capture speaks of a 'fusillade [of shots] that broke out from our side of the river (it must have been the battalion attacking the bridgehead) and several bullets passing through the wall of the stable,' where he was being held. Was this in reality Captain Shott's attempt at rescue? We will never know. Thus the situation when the remainder of the battalion arrived was: B Company, less two of its senior officers, in shaky possession of the causeway and one end of the bridge and the Germans holding the remainder.

The arrival of two further companies of 1/Royal Berks and a charge across the bridge led by Lieutenant Charles Fulbrook-Legatt and Major Herbert Finch secured the southern end of the bridge after some close-quarters fighting resulting in many of the wounded falling down the steep river banks and drowning. Drummer Henry Savage was one of those who was floundering in deep water and was rescued by Corporal Walter Brindle.[80] Brindle rescued a number of men from a watery grave before he was killed by a shell.

The 1/Royal Berks war diary for 25 August records the action at the bridge with ten short lines but it does state that the 'bridge was taken about 1.30 after a night attack by B, D and C Companies.' This is unlikely given the weight of opposition and the presence of a German artillery piece positioned to fire directly along the length of the bridge. However, Private Wright, who was fighting with C Company, is sure they retook the bridge. His account, although a little garbled, does point to more than one attempt to retake it:

> *'Then came the most exciting part of the evening, namely the charging and retaking of the bridge. I don't think any of us who took part will ever forget that. For my part I seem to have gone mad. My ears ringing with the noise of the firing and cheering. I did find myself on the bridge in the second charge, there wasn't*

many of us, about 40 of us, no more until the work was finished, then many more.'[81]

But whatever happened on that wet and dark night, by holding the bridge until the 1st Battalion Kings Royal Rifle Corps (1/KRRC) arrived to relieve them, the Royal Berks prevented the enemy advancing on Maroilles and allowed the overcrowded and congested main street in the town to clear itself, much to the relief of Lieutenant Hanbury-Sparrow.

There were numerous other isolated actions on 25 August, mainly involving cavalry as they covered the retreating infantry brigades. At Mecquignies, a small village on the northern extremity of the Forêt de Mormal, Lieutenant Richard Moore and his troop of 12/Lancers were ordered to reinforce C Squadron which was heavily engaged with a battalion of Jägers:

'Just as I reached my position in the firing line I received a bullet through the right ankle. The troops on my left were ordered to retire and I naturally had to hold on as long as possible to allow them to get back to their horses, some 200 yards in the rear ...I emptied my revolver at the charging Germans at close range. In consequence I was, very naturally clubbed on the head with the butt of the rifle of the first German to reach me.'[82]

The young officer recovered to find a German soldier with a fixed bayonet standing over him shouting '*Schweinhund Englander*' and clearly intending to finish him off. Fortunately an officer materialized in the nick of time and sent the man away. It had been a close call. That evening Moore and ten of the wounded lancers were taken to a nearby farm house where one of the wounded died, the following morning a German ambulance section picked them up. Moore and his men spent the rest of the war as prisoners.[83]

Sharing the roads with the retiring French had not only caused innumerable problems on the march but added to the general confusion in the towns and villages earmarked for overnight billets. When Captain John Savage and the 1/Northants turned up at Monceau they found one of the French territorial divisions had got there first, forcing them to continue onto Marbaix.[84] To make matters worse it rained hard all the way and the whole battalion was soaked through before they even set foot in the village:

'Found the most awful chaos, the whole brigade (2 Brigade) being billeted in a few houses. Streets full of transports etc. Arrived about 8.30 pm and tried to find our billets, heard heavy firing all round the village. When we were in the village heavy fire was opened on us down the main street. My Company (D) was in front. A lot of the transport stampeded and there was general chaos for a few minutes. Everyone thinking the Germans were on us and the darkness made it worse.

Eventually we found out that is was one of our own picquets who fired on a French cavalry patrol thinking they were Germans …one man of B Company was killed and one man from D Company wounded.'[85]

Drummer George Whittington, also en route to Marbaix with B Company of 2/Royal Sussex, missed all the excitement. His battalion arrived half-an-hour after the shooting had ceased, but the stories of the 'attack' had already begun to circulate, exaggerating wildly what had taken place. He was billeted that night in an empty house where they were 'one on top of another' nevertheless he found time to complete his diary before he got his head down.[86] 'There was an attack just before we arrived', he wrote, 'which led to a stampede, five men were killed.'

Further to the west, Jim Pennyman, had arrived at Le Cateau after a long and weary 23-mile march down the west side of the Forêt de Mormal. 'Eep Eep Ouray' the pony had performed very well, pulling the farm cart containing the battalion's machine guns and as Pennyman prepared food on his primus stove before snatching an hour or two of sleep he was under the impression that the retirement would continue at dawn.

Chapter 7

26 August – Accidental Rearguard

The twelve battalions of the 4th Division under the command of Major General Thomas D'Oyly Snow arrived at Le Cateau on 24 August from England. It was, however, far from being complete as it had no divisional cavalry or any of its auxiliary units such as engineers, field ambulances or signals. For some unexplained reason GHQ had kept these units at St Quentin, a decision that was presumably prompted by the need to keep the roads clear but may have unintentionally contributed to the high level of casualties later experienced by the division during the Battle of Le Cateau. General Snow's first orders were to move at once to Solesmes to assist the withdrawal of II Corps. To the casual observer Solesmes is an insignificant little town hidden away in a hollow with nothing very special to recommend it but unfortunately for the retiring troops, it was also situated at the junction of four main roads and as such became the focus of an almighty tangle of columns of British and French cavalry, infantry, guns and wagons.

Some of the wagons belonged to 9/Field Ambulance and apart from the wounded being conveyed in their horse-drawn ambulance wagons, the medics had stopped on numerous occasions during the day to deal with footsore and exhausted men and now found themselves caught up in the confusion at Solesmes. Captain Arthur Habgood, a Special Reserve officer in command of C Section, had been a little taken aback that there were not more motorized ambulances available to the BEF when he had first reported for duty at Southsea, A great many more wounded, he felt, could have been dealt with far more efficiently with more of the faster motor ambulances. Ten days previously he had been in general medical practice at Wroxham in Norfolk, and now, as he ruefully remarked in his diary, was at Solesmes in the pouring rain and cold:

'Trenches were being dug on each side of the road for rearguard action, the country was very hilly and uninteresting. As we entered the town, masses of cavalry and guns could be seen on the hills to the northeast. The town was in a panic, shrapnel could be seen bursting over the wooded country north west, batteries on the

northeast were engaging the enemy as we slipped out of the town by the Solesmes – Le Cateau road to the south. Guns, cavalry and straggling infantry were mixed up with us, units of the 3rd and 5th Divisions owing to the lack of roads and the rapidity of the retirement.[87]

The trenches Habgood had observed were intended for 1/Wiltshires and 2/South Lancs from Brigadier General Frederick McCracken's 7 Brigade which was forming the rearguard.[88] Captain Robert Partridge and C Squadron of 5/Dragoon Guards, had also been detailed to cover the retirement of the infantry through Solesmes.[89] Tasked with intercepting enemy cavalry intent on probing the British defences – a demanding enough job in broad daylight – but in the darkness and rain on the high ground above Solesmes it was proving almost impossible to maintain contact between the four troops of the squadron. Lieutenant Robert Egerton was none too impressed when his mounted troop of engineers 'got under shrapnel fire owing to some lunatics in the 5th DGs showing themselves on the skyline.'

Nonetheless, even with the 'lunatics' attracting fire, the advance units of IR 153 were held off until after dark by the rearguard. It was late in the evening when Partridge finally disengaged C Squadron from a skirmish with the German 9th Dragoon Regiment and led his men back across country to rejoin the regiment at Inchy, only to discover they were without Lieutenant Ronald Lechmere and his troop of signallers, who at some point during the night had become separated from the squadron. He and his men eventually rejoined the regiment a week later near Compiégne.

It was not until after 9.00 pm that Solesmes was reported clear and the rearguard troops withdrawn from the town which was then occupied by the Germans. The 4th Division, which had been posted south of Solesmes, received orders to march at once to the extreme left of the line at Le Cateau. 12 Brigade moved soon after 9.00 pm followed by 11 Brigade an hour later but the unfortunate 10 Brigade was not able to march until midnight owing to the congested state of the roads and did not arrive at its destination until 6.00 am on the morning of the 26th after a wearying march of 12 miles in torrents of rain.

Lieutenant Cyril Helm had already had a close shave at Wasmes when retrieving his battalion's Maltese cart under heavy shell fire. The two wheeled cart was the standard equipment for regimental medical officers and contained all the necessary medical supplies required to establish a battlefield aid station. Now, on the seemingly endless Roman road that ran down the western edge of the Forêt de Mormal, the contents of the cart alleviated the suffering feet of many of the 2/KOYLI reservists:

'My task was hard that day, encouraging the men who were falling out from sore feet. One knew perfectly well that once they were left behind they would never return as they were certain to fall into the hands of the Germans within a few hours. It was a wearying task, trying to cheer up some and cursing others, anything to get the poor devils along.'[90]

The battalion reached Montay in the late afternoon where it was held up temporarily as six regiments and a cyclist battalion of General Sordet's cavalry corps crossed over the bridge en route for Cambrai and the British left flank.

The hint of panic that accompanied Douglas Haig's request for II Corps to advance on Landrecies didn't exactly fall on deaf ears, but as darkness fell over Le Cateau the problems faced by Smith-Dorrien at his Bertry HQ during the night and early morning of 25/26 August were considerably greater than those being experienced by his opposite number. Whereas the majority of I Corps had been in billets by 9.00 pm on the night of 25 August, at Le Cateau, as we know some units of II Corps did not arrive until the early hours of the next day. Certainly the exhausted state of his men was on Smith-Dorrien's mind that evening and any doubts that he had about their ability to continue the retirement the next day was brought into sharp focus by Allenby's arrival at Bertry just after 2.00 am.

'Bull' Allenby was not a man to beat about the bush, he came straight to the point: with three of his four brigades of cavalry scattered far and wide, and with only one brigade effectively still under his control, he could not guarantee to cover the retirement of II Corps. Furthermore, it was his opinion that if II Corps did not get away at once they would be forced to fight at daylight. It was quite an admission for Allenby; in effect he was calling attention to poor cavalry staff work and the individualist nature of his cavalry commanders that had resulted in a breakdown of communication and control. By and large the cavalry's performance over the preceding two days had not been exemplary and Allenby must have been painfully aware of that.

Conferring with his old friend, Major General Hubert Hamilton, on the condition of his division only served to further convince Smith-Dorrien that II Corps was unable to continue the retreat. Hamilton's estimation that 3rd Division could not move before 9.00 am and the certainty that Fergusson's 5th Division would be in the same condition led to the only conclusion Smith-Dorrien could possibly have come to – he would have to stand and fight. To continue the retreat as ordered by GHQ would have turned retirement into a rout, Smith-Dorrien's only chance now lay in facing von Kluck and giving him enough of a 'stopping blow' to allow as much of II Corps as possible time to get away. The atmosphere at the Bertry HQ must have been electric as Smith-Dorrien stood at his map table considering his options with Allenby and his

Chief of Staff John Vaughan together with Hubert Hamilton looking on in anticipation:

> 'There was a moment of dead silence while Sir Horace reviewed the information which had just come in. He then asked Allenby, who was not under the II Corps, whether he would accept orders. Without hesitation Allenby agreed to do so. Sir Horace said: "Very well, gentlemen, we will fight and I will ask General Snow to act under me as well."[91]

Smith-Dorrien was quite aware he was disobeying the orders of Sir John French and when his telegram arrived at St Quentin at 5.00 am informing GHQ of his decision it apparently had a devastating impact upon the already fragile and gloomy outlook that prevailed amongst the staff. Already downcast about the attack at Landrecies, French and Wilson were convinced that Smith-Dorrien's stance at Le Cateau would end in total disaster. It seems that after failing to convince Sir John to order II Corps to fall back from the Le Cateau line, Wilson fell into a fit of depression and Archie Murray is said to have fainted from shock when he heard. So much for having faith in one's commanders! Smith-Dorrien had of course anticipated Haig joining him on his right flank and it was not until 3.50 am on 26 August that he heard news to the contrary. Whether Haig was aware of the difficulty facing II Corps or not, it does appear that he was more concerned with the plight of I Corps and thus, as Edward Bulfin candidly remarked in his diary, Haig left II Corps 'to face the Germans alone.'[92]

* * *

At Le Cateau there were two outstanding 'accidental' rearguard actions that came about because the orders to retire were not received by commanding officers. In similar circumstances to the Cheshires at Audregnies two days earlier, two infantry battalions fought a desperate and brutal rearguard battle until the majority were either overwhelmed or killed. There were of course other rearguard actions during the course of the battle; the 2nd Dublin Fusiliers (2/Dublin Fusiliers) and 1st Royal Warwicks (1/Warwicks) fought a costly rearguard at Haucourt, whilst the Royal Irish and the indomitable Major Zulu St Leger covered the retirement from Caudry and Audencourt. Men from all three of these battalions were left behind enemy lines and made epic journeys through occupied territory to return to British lines, their stories will be looked at in more detail in Chapter 14. Nevertheless, it was the self- sacrifice and resolve of the 5th Division which stood its ground just west of Le Cateau that provided one of the finest episodes of the retreat and witnessed acts which led to the award of five Victoria Crosses.

Major Cecil de Sausmarez, the battery commander with the 108 Heavy Battery guns at Reumont, was convinced that the 'inspired' order to stand and fight saved II Corps from pursuit.[93] Had it not been made clear there was to be no retirement, argued Sausmarez, it would have been understood that the 'main object was to retreat and not to fight, and the blow given to the Germans would have been trifling compared to that which was actually struck'. Whether we consider the order to have been 'inspired' or not, stand and fight is exactly what 2/Suffolks and 2/KOYLI did from their positions either side of the crossroads on the main Cambrai road. Both commanding officers appear to have accepted that as no orders had been received to the contrary, their battalions would not retire despite the fact that others were retiring around them. Whether, as Sausmarez suggests, the order not to retire and the subsequent stand by the two battalions contributed to von Kluck's failure to follow up his victory at Le Cateau or not is debatable, but the fact remains that he did not and his delay enabled II Corps to open some crucial distance between themselves and their pursuers.

With the exception of the action involving the 1/DCLI and two companies of 1/East Surrey on the high ground to the east of the town, the battle was fought along a 10 mile front running west towards Cambrai with the centre at Caudry. The right flank was held by Fergusson's 5th Division – crowded into an arc that straddled the Roman road south of the crossroads with the modern day N43 – while the remainder of II Corps held a line that ran more or less parallel and south of the N43. Hamilton's 3rd Division was holding the centre from Troisvilles to Caudry whilst the 4th Division took up the left flank, its positions bending obliquely to face northwest from Fontaine-au-Pire to Esnes, roughly following the course of the Warnelle Ravine.

What most concerned Smith-Dorrien was the state of his two flanks. While he was reasonably confident that the French would appear on his left, it was his right flank – just as it was at Mons – which was the weakest point in his rather fragile line. What tends to be overlooked in accounts of the fighting at Le Cateau is the vital part that Sordet's cavalry and General d'Amade's territorial divisions played on the British left flank. The 61st and 62nd French Reserve Divisions along with the 84th Territorial Division that had fought on the BEF flank at Mons were heavily engaged near Cambrai with the German II Infantry Corps. Smith-Dorrien knew only too well that without them 'it is almost certain we should have had another Corps against us on the 26th' and that would have been disasterous. In the event it was the French that gave Snow's 4th Division the opportunity to get away without pursuit.

* * *

Jim Pennyman and 2/KOSB stood to arms at 3.00 am on the morning of 26 August. The battalion transport was sent off and they were told to hold on as long as they could and then fight a rearguard action. About dawn there was a change of plan:

> 'The CO and Adjutant galloped round the trenches and said we had to stay on ad lib and not retire under any circumstances. I had been told to choose my own trench and selected one near Harvey's platoon [Second Lieutenant Henry Harvey]. I had an excellent field of fire for about 800 yards and we thought we would anyhow do some damage before we were all put out of action. To our right front was Le Cateau Church and crossroads and straight to our front was a poplar-lined road running NW from Le Cateau to Cambrai.'[94]

The orders to stand and fight arrived at battalion level about the same time as the first ranging shots from the German batteries opened fire on the II Corps positions and it wasn't long before units of German infantry made contact with British troops on both flanks. We know from Pennyman's account that 13 Brigade only got its orders at dawn having already sent the battalion

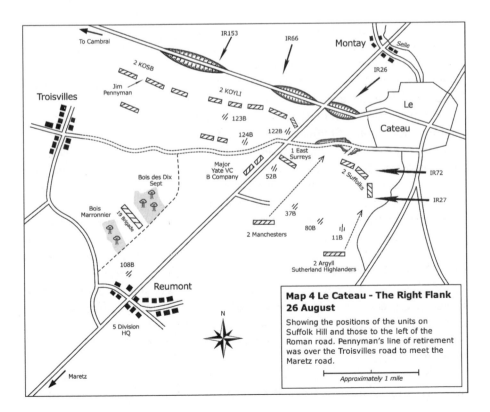

Map 4 Le Cateau - The Right Flank 26 August

Showing the positions of the units on Suffolk Hill and those to the left of the Roman road. Pennyman's line of retirement was over the Troisvilles road to meet the Maretz road.

Approximately 1 mile

transports south. Other units received no orders at all and were in the process of continuing their retirement when the battle opened in Le Cateau, surprising the unfortunate DCLI.

The 1/DCLI, having spent a very sodden and uncomfortable night in Le Cateau, were formed up by the railway bridge in the Faubourg de Landrecies ready to continue their retirement when they came under assault from the forward platoons of IR 72 which had occupied some of the houses on the eastern outskirts of the town. The initial blow fell on 14 Brigade Signals Section and amongst the casualties was Captain John Dennis, the brigade machine-gun officer who was attached to Brigade HQ.[95] IR 72 was very much in advance of the main body of the German 8th Infantry Division which was probably why they did not pursue the retreating Duke of Cornwalls and East Surreys with too much vigour. But the damage was done. The flank was now wide open, the consequences of which in due course would contribute to the destruction of two infantry battalions.

Recovering from the initial surprise, the column fought its way down the valley to rejoin 14 Brigade at Honnechy aided by some very effective fire from L Battery RHA. Nevertheless, they suffered around 200 casualties at the hands of IR 72. Not everyone went south; the battalion transport fled east towards Bazuel under the command of 27-year-old Lieutenant Ion Benn the battalion machine-gun officer. He eventually rejoined the battalion at Crépy-en-Valois 6 days later having crossed the Sambre Canal at Catillon and headed south via Oisy after attaching himself to the cavalry. His story is typical of many small detachments that became separated from their units and headed south independently until they were finally reunited with their regiments.

The officers and men of 2/Suffolks had dug themselves in on the Sentier de Reumont, the hump of high ground on the Montay spur to the southwest of Le Cateau – a place now known as 'Suffolk Hill'. The battalion was particularly badly placed with a limited field of fire and concealed ground on every side capable of concealing attacking troops. But the die had already been cast with the demise of the DCLI and the absence of I Corps on the right flank: however stubbornly the Suffolks were prepared to defend their 'hill' they were powerless to prevent the German troops of IR 72 moving through Le Cateau on their right. The Suffolk's first contact with the enemy came shortly after 6.00 am when Second Lieutenant Edward Myddelton's Number 15 Platoon opened fire on an Uhlan cavalry patrol, killing an officer. It was shortly after this that Brigadier General Stuart Rolt arrived and, according to the regimental history, said – presumably to Lieutenant Colonel Charles Brett the commanding officer – 'You understand; there is to be no thought of retirement.' From that moment their fate was sealed.

A similar directive in the form of a written order from General Cuthbert had been given to Lieutenant Colonel Reginald Bond and 2/KOYLI west of the crossroads: 'Orders have now been changed. There will be no retirement for the fighting troops. Fill up your trenches as far as possible with water, food and ammunition.' A little later a staff officer rode up and repeated the order verbally. Colonel Bond's right flank was strengthened a little after 5.00 am by Major Harold Tew and two companies of 1/East Surrey who had become separated from the battalion after their action on the canal at les Herbières on 23 August. Bond suggested the East Surreys should dig in along a front of some 200 yards on the right of the Roman road behind and to the left of the Suffolks, both men unaware that the remaining half of 1/East Surrey was on the other side of Le Cateau.

The 2/KOYLI battalion war diary recorded that the first German shell fell a little before 6.00 am, although Cyril Helm thought it was nearer 7.00 am when the barrage intensified. The three artillery batteries of XXVIII Brigade were deployed amongst the KOYLI with 122 Battery partly dug in just north of the Troisvilles road, whereas the 5th Division heavy artillery – the 108 Heavy Battery commanded by Major Sausmarez – was in place north of Reumont near the Bois Marronnier, close to 19 Brigade which was being held in reserve. On the other side of the Roman road three batteries of XV Brigade and 37 Battery from VIII Brigade were clustered behind and around the Suffolks' trenches.

And what poor trenches they were – barely providing cover from rifle fire, let alone the close attentions of shrapnel and high explosive artillery rounds. When the first enemy salvo struck home, one shell landed in the trenches occupied by Lieutenant Myddelton and his platoon, killing the 21- year-old special reserve officer and his platoon sergeant instantly.[96] As the British guns to their rear opened fire in retaliation the noise must have been deafening as the battle for the right flank opened with a vengeance. It was not long after this that the Suffolks lost their commanding officer, Lieutenant Colonel Brett. Charles Brett had been a soldier for nearly 30 years and had won a DSO at Colenso in South Africa; his death was a tragic loss to the battalion, one which Major Edward Doughty would have felt keenly when he assumed command.

Lieutenant Pennycuick and the 59/Field Company were digging trenches with 1/Middlesex just north of the farm at des Essarts on the Montay spur. Major Walker, who commanded the company, witnessed the artillery battle get underway:

'It was the finest pyrotechnic display I have ever seen. The German shells were bursting all about. They came from all directions except the rear, and the bursts were of all colours, white, black and white, black and pink and yellow. We could see little of the infantry, but could see the yellow bursts of our Lyddite shells in the enemy's lines. It was a lovely day, brilliant sun and no wind'.[97]

The men on Suffolk Hill would have taken no consolation from the sunshine as they took cover in their scrape holes under the rain of shrapnel and high explosive that was now descending on both them and the 13 Brigade battalions on the other side of the Roman road. Jim Pennyman thought it would only be a matter of time before the infantry of IR 153 put in an appearance and they would be 'in for a big thing':

> '*Soon their shells began to come and battery after battery opened upon us – searching the whole place. It was very frightening, but no-one in my trench was actually hit. Our artillery replied, but it was obvious that they were hopelessly outnumbered. They seemed to give attention most to the German infantry, which was by this time massed behind cover at 1,500 to 2,000 yards. We imagined these infantry were getting it pretty hot as they shewed no inclination to come on, but their artillery fire had got more and more severe and our gunners suffered.*'[98]

Cyril Helm established his regimental aid post in a shed close to the Reumont road after sending the Maltese cart back with the remainder of the 2/KOYLI transport. From his shed he had a 'splendid position' and could see everything:

> '*The Germans had no difficulty in spotting our guns, one of their observing officers being in the tower of the Hotel de Ville in Le Cateau, which overlooked the whole of our position. Why our sixty-pounders did not blow this tower to hell was a mystery to all of us … It was a ghastly sight, seeing our guns silenced one after the other. From one battery only one man escaped, all the officers being killed. As soon as the enemy had silenced most of the field guns, they began on the trenches and the infantry tried to advance.*'[99]

In fact it wasn't until after 10.00 am that IR 153 and IR 66, supported by machine guns established on the main Cambria road, began to advance and by so doing to offer the British riflemen a target. The Suffolks' firing line had been reinforced on the right by 2/Argyll and Sutherland Highlanders and 1/Middlesex just 15 minutes earlier; both battalions digging in just behind them. Their much needed fire power was soon required as the German battalions began to press against the British right flank.

The massed German infantry seen by Jim Pennyman were now advancing on a 2 mile front and for a while the combined firepower of the British artillery batteries checked the advance but small groups of German infantry managed to establish firing positions in the cutting on the Cambrai road, despite the efforts of the 2/KOYLI machine guns sweeping the Montay spur. German machine-gun fire from this sheltered location could not be silenced and was soon brought to bear on the 14 Brigade positions cutting down many of the 2/Manchesters and remaining Argylls who attempted to move forward in support of the Suffolks. By noon the situation had become desperate. The Suffolks were running short of ammunition and it was proving difficult to get fresh supplies forward. During one attempt to replenish Lieutenant Nigel Bittleston's machine guns with ammunition Major Doughty was badly wounded – handing over command to Major Arthur Peebles. Peebles was another seasoned soldier who had seen action in South Africa and, like Doughty, realized that with German infantry now attacking their right flank their position was fast becoming untenable.

It was a conclusion that General Fergusson had also come to from his vantage point at Reumont. It was time to begin withdrawing the 5th Division and at 1.20 pm he gave the order to disengage and to begin retiring – orders that did not reach Colonel Bond and Major Peebles. For the guns of 15 Brigade General Fergusson's orders were easier said than done. On the understanding that there was to be no retirement, Lieutenant Colonel Charles Stevens had manoeuvred the XV Brigade guns in as close to the infantry firing line as possible; the guns of 80 Battery being manhandled to within 100 yards of the Suffolks' trenches. Extracting those guns that remained intact under the hail of fire from an enemy in close proximity would be, as a gunner subaltern in XVIII Brigade put it, 'absolute slaughter.' And 'slaughter' it was.

Galloping in under fire, horses and men were subjected to a murderous barrage but incredibly the gun teams of 11 Battery got four of the battery's guns limbered up and away before those attempting to retrieve the fifth and sixth were all shot down. 80 Battery, which had only two guns left intact, was assisted by some of the Suffolks and managed to limber up five of its guns which was one more than 37 Battery which only recovered four of its guns. But for 52 Battery, which had sited its six guns next to the East Surreys and close to the Roman road, the furious deluge of fire prevented recovery. Surrounded by the dead and wounded of the battery and with typical gunner resolve, Captain William Barber-Starkey and Sergeant Jesse Woolger remained firing the one serviceable gun until the ammunition ran out. Woolger was killed at his post and Barber-Starkey later died of his wounds.[100]

There were three gunner VCs awarded for actions which took place on the slopes of Suffolk Hill. Captain Douglas Reynolds, having left two of 37 Battery's guns behind, now called for volunteers to return and rescue the remaining weapons. German infantry were little more than 200 yards away when the two teams galloped into view and began to limber up. The first team in – Drivers Job Drain, Ben Cobey and 18-year-old Frederick Luke successfully limbered up their gun and managed to get away despite losing the 19-year-old Cobey.[101] Grabbing Cobey's whip, Reynolds guided the two centre horses as the limber bounced and lurched over the rough ground. The second team was less fortunate; led by Lieutenants Earle and Morgan, the horses were shot down before they could get the gun away. Reynolds, Drain and Luke were awarded the Victoria Cross and Earle the DSO for this brave and audacious recovery under enemy fire. Many felt Ben Cobey was hard done by in receiving no official recognition for his gallantry which surely deserved a posthumous VC – as did the actions of Baber-Starkey and Woolger of 52 Battery. It had been a costly day for the gunners, of the thirty-six guns lost by the Royal Artillery at Le Cateau, twenty-seven were lost supporting the two brigades of Fergusson's 5th Division.

Anxious to know how the battle was developing GHQ asked for an air reconnaissance flight which was duly provided by 3 Squadron in the shape of Second Lieutenant Vivian Wadham and Lieutenant Dermott Allen. Criss-crossing the airspace above the battlefield for more than an hour they watched the withdrawal of some of the British guns amidst salvoes of bursting shellfire. Allen found it a 'sickening sight, when the smoke cleared, to see groups of wounded horses struggling panic-stricken on the ground'. The subsequent report from Wadham and Allen that II Corps was retiring only served to reinforce the view at GHQ that II Corps was in the process of being all but annihilated.

By the time Reynolds and his men had brought their last gun out of action, units of IR 72 and IR 27 had worked so far round the right flank that the Suffolks and Argylls were practically surrounded on three sides. The end came for the Suffolks, according to the Regimental History, between 2.30 pm and 2.45. For 9 hours they had been under fire from artillery, machine guns and rifles; they had stood their ground as ordered and 'fought to the very last, covering themselves in glory'. However, the price of glory had been severe: although many of the missing had been taken prisoner, the Suffolks' casualties in killed, wounded and missing amounted to over 700 of all ranks. 4 officers had been killed and 10 wounded with all but Lieutenant Oakes and 111 men avoiding capture.

The retirement of the remnants of General Rolt's 14 Brigade now exposed the flank of Cuthbert's 13 Brigade. 2/KOYLI and 1/East Surrey had been in action since the first German infantry had begun pushing forward at 10.00 am, now fire from Suffolk Hill raked their positions and those of the three batteries of XVIII Brigade. Attempts to recover the brigade's guns were largely unsuccessful; Second Lieutenant Clarrie Hodgson was serving with 122 Battery:

> *'We were in position, doing what we could, although we were practically cut off by the Hun and realized our position was hopeless. Our colonel, the adjutant and two battery commanders had been killed and the place was a shambles. Then to our intense relief, came the order – every man for himself, destroy the guns.'*[102]

Only two of the 122 Battery guns were got away, the remainder were abandoned after the breech blocks had been removed and the sights smashed. 'It was an extraordinary sight' said the *Official History*, 'a short wild scene of galloping horses, then four guns standing derelict, a few limbers lying about, one on the skyline with its pole vertical, and dead men and dead horses everywhere.'

Although it is not clear exactly which of the XVIII Brigade guns it was, the first of the two KOYLI Victoria Crosses which were won at Le Cateau was awarded to 24-year-old Lance Corporal Frederick Holmes for assisting in the recovery of one of the gun teams – in all probability one of those belonging to 122 Battery.[103] Holmes, a reservist in A Company, having been ordered to retire across ground that was swept with machine-gun fire, came across a badly wounded comrade. Picking the man up, he carried him to safety on his back for 2 miles until he deposited the wounded man with some stretcher bearers. He then assisted in bringing one of the XVIII Brigade guns to safety by taking the place of a driver who had been wounded.

Lieutenant Tom Butt took matters into his own hands when his platoon was enfiladed on both flanks about 3.30 pm, 'which added considerably to our other difficulties, viz that since midday our guns had almost ceased, owing to a lack of shells, whilst our rifle ammunition was rapidly coming to an end'. Realizing it was only a matter of time before they would be completely surrounded Butt gave orders for his platoon to retire but was hit in the knee almost immediately afterwards. Crawling forwards some 300 yards he propped himself up against a corn stook and waited. He didn't have to wait long before lines of German infantry began sweeping up over and through the KOYLI positions. Fortunately a passing German officer stopped and bound up his leg which was bleeding freely, appearing 'utterly oblivious of the fact that thousands of bullets were finding a dusty resting place all around him'.[104]

At about 2.00 pm German infantry had got round the right flank of the KOSB and were making life very uncomfortable for Jim Pennyman. Moving his machine guns to meet the new threat he was joined by Henry Harvey who remarked that:

> '...*everybody on our right and left had gone, so we decided there was nothing for it but for us to go too. We dismounted the guns and I distributed the ammunition boxed amongst Harvey's men, as the men in my section were carrying two or three boxes each. I pointed out a place behind which to rendezvous and at the word "go" we just ran like rabbits bolting out of a burrow... We found some more fellows lined up at the place I had pointed out and began to dig ourselves in. To my horror I found that we had exactly one box of ammunition left, all the men having run so hard that those who started with boxes arrived without them. I had done the same thing myself so I hadn't much to say about it.*'[105]

Harvey's platoon and Pennyman's machine gunners were fortunate they retired when they did; the remaining three platoons of C Company were surrounded and taken prisoner before long. Still with both his machine guns intact,

Pennyman and Private Charles Harding returned to retrieve as many ammunition boxes as possible:

> 'We went back quite a long way, but couldn't see any of the boxes and the whole place was alive with shell fire … When we got back the others had gone; we found one gun and a tripod being carried along and I told the men to get it onto an artillery limber and get away the best they could.'

The retirement was now well under way with men streaming down the Reumont road. Pennyman got his second machine gun aboard an artillery limber and as he later commented in his diary, 'I cleared off with them sitting astride a gun and got my breeches very dirty'. He also observed Colonel Stephenson 'knocked silly by being too close to a bursting shell'.

Cyril Helm's diary indicates that he retired when he saw the East Surreys moving. With as many wounded as he could take with him he made his way to Maurois where 14/Field Ambulance was based in the school:

> 'The road was in a most indescribable state of confusion; infantry, cavalry, guns, limbers, wagons, ambulances, staff cars and every conceivable form of vehicle, all going as hard as they could and all mixed up together'.

It was a view shared at 3.00 pm by Kenneth Godsell and his section of 17/Field Company sappers; his main concern was that the German cavalry would soon appear in pursuit:

> 'One could see the infantry on the left streaming back across fields under a hot shell fire … it looked like a perfect debacle and every moment we expected to see the Bosche cavalry appear over the crest.'[106]

But there was to be no cavalry pursuit and any thought that the German infantry might have had of getting too close to the Roman road and cutting the line of retreat was discouraged by two companies of the Argylls at Reumont together with the 108 Battery guns which tore great gaps in any infantry bold enough to get too near.

But even as Kenneth Godsell and Jim Pennyman were heading southwest along the Roman road towards Maretz, the final VC of the day was being won in the KOYLI trenches held by B Company and 42-year-old Major Charles Yate. Dug in just south of the Troisvilles road, Yate had seen the Suffolks overwhelmed and as 'no order cancelling that of 6am had been received' retirement was, as far as Colonel Bond was concerned, still out of the question. By that stage retirement may well have been impossible, German infantry were now appearing in force from the direction of Suffolk Hill as well as to his front and rear but despite being offered several opportunities to surrender, Charles Yate, who was commanding the remaining firing line, chose instead to fight to the end.

With the artillery out of action and abandoned and the West Kents and the KOSB retiring to the south, Yate must have realized that the battalion – or at least what was left of it – was surrounded on three sides and there was little hope of escape, yet he and his men continued to defend their ground. Those who have been in the position where there is apparently little hope of survival will recognize the self-control and composure that often pervades once the inevitability of death in action has sunk in. When the final rush came Charles Yate gave the order to the nineteen survivors to greet it with a bayonet charge and those that could met their enemy defiantly – led by the indefatigable Charles Yate.[107] Less than a month later, having survived Le Cateau, Yate died in captivity, his VC was awarded posthumously.

A small group of the KOYLI did manage to escape, Cyril Helm found them late that evening in the corner of a field near Joncourt and was horrified to find that 'we mustered seven officers and about 150 men'. It had begun raining at 5.00 pm and they spent a miserable night wet through and shocked but 'luckily the cooker had arrived so we managed to get plenty of hot tea'. Other men lay dotted around that night, utterly exhausted but, for all that, still in the fight. Kenneth Godsell spent the night under a haycock at Estrées in a wet, ploughed field alongside Pennycuick and the 59th, whilst Pennyman and the small group of men he and Lieutenants Gilbert Amos and Hamilton-Dalrymple had managed to collect, spent the night on the kitchen floor of a farmhouse at Serain.

Chapter 8

26 August – Le Grand Fayt

L e Cateau was the most costly of the BEF's encounters with the Germans
during the retreat. There has long been discussion and disagreement
over the number of casualties inflicted on both sides and in the light of
more recent evidence we should assume the *Official History* figure of 7,800
British casualties is somewhat inaccurate. Recent works on the battle have
argued that a more realistic figure is more likely to be in the region of 5,000.[108]
Of this figure at least 50 per cent were taken prisoner and only some 500 were
actually battlefield fatalities. German casualties were in the region of 2,000
killed and wounded. Very few, if any, prisoners would have been taken by the
retreating British.

As had happened on the battlefield at Audregnies, the more seriously
wounded were either left where they fell – along with their dead comrades – or,
if they were fortunate, moved by field ambulance units out of the battle zone.
Those that remained fell into German hands. Up on Suffolk Hill, Major Arthur
Peebles, the only senior officer left unwounded, was escorted from the field at
about 5.00 pm and taken to the nearby Château du Mérinos on the Rue du Bois
in Le Cateau. The château was the family home of the Le Cateau textile
merchant, André Seydoux.[109] Here and in a neighbouring building Peebles
found an RAMC doctor, Captain Robert Cahill, attending over 100 wounded
without any medical supplies or instruments. Peebles found several other
officers at the château who had been involved in the action on Suffolk Hill,
amongst them Major Eustace Jones the commander of 37 Battery who had been
wounded at 7.00 am by a high explosive shell. Jones recounted that the shell had
killed the telephonist who was sitting next to him and left him with shell
splinters in his back. The battery had been surrounded just after Reynolds and
his gun teams had left and their capture had all been 'very civilized'; a German
officer giving Jones a flask filled with coffee before he was escorted into Le
Cateau.

One of the more badly wounded was Captain Cecil Morley who had been
fighting with 2/Manchesters near the sunken lane on Suffolk Hill when he had

been hit by machine-gun fire during the attempt to support the Suffolk firing line. Wounded in the lung, stomach and left shoulder, the stretcher bearers had been unable to reach him in the hail of fire that swept the position but one of his men had managed to roll him into the lane where he had lapsed into unconsciousness. After the surrender he had been carried off the battlefield by men of his own regiment and thence to the Château du Mérinos. After a preliminary examination by a German doctor who had clearly decided he was beyond repair, he had been left in the hands of Eustace Jones and Arthur Peebles who, under the medical direction of Cahill, nursed him back to recovery. Many of the wounded at the Seydoux château owed a great deal to Peebles and Jones, who along with another Suffolk officer, Captain Lawrence Hepworth, looked after the more serious cases day and night.

Major Edward Doughty who had been badly wounded early on in the Suffolk Hill encounter, was only found during the night by German soldiers. Wet through and close to death he was carried to a nearby farm building where the Suffolks' Adjutant, Captain Arthur Cutbill, and Lieutenant James Morgan had been taken earlier in the day. The next day these officers were found by Arthur Peebles who had finally been granted permission to search for the wounded of his battalion. His insistence and determination to find his men, in the face of initial blank refusal, without doubt saved the life of Doughty who was moved to the hospital at Cambrai with Morley a few days later. Another Manchesters officer badly wounded during the advance to the Suffolk firing line was Captain Reginald Miller. He was hit by the same traversing machine gun that brought Morley down and he lay in the sunken lane for nearly 4 hours. Finally, when the position was overrun, two German soldiers splinted his leg with bayonets and a puttee, but it was another 11 hours before he was brought off the battlefield, by which time he was in a very poor state. Arriving at the Château du Mérinos he was taken into the care of Peebles and Cahill. 'Those who could not get out of bed' he wrote later, 'depended entirely on [Peebles and others] for help and food'. Miller was also moved to Cambrai hospital and eventually, on 18 September, transported to Germany with Doughty and Morley. All three men spent the war in captivity and survived.

Large numbers of the 5th Division wounded were brought into Le Cateau and housed in private houses and the school building or at the convent hospital. Tom Butt with his company commander, Captain Charlie Luther, was eventually taken to the convent hospital where they were treated kindly by the sisters. Butt was eventually shipped off to Cambrai and thence to captivity in Germany. One of those taken to the school house was Private Charles Brash, an Argyll and Sutherland Highlander captured on Suffolk Hill. As his company was surrounded and overwhelmed he had witnessed his company officer bayoneted through the chest in the final fraught moments of the battle as they stood up to surrender. He and another 70 of his regiment were eventually marched to Cambrai on 31 August and entrained for Germany. With that group went Arthur Peebles, a man whom many would remember as more than just a soldier long after the events in which they were involved at Le Cateau.

Was Le Cateau a German victory? If it is agreed that it is the victor who holds the ground at the conclusion of a battle then of course it was but there was more to Le Cateau than raw casualty figures and the taking of ground. The German advance had been disrupted and there is no doubt that the severity of the blow delivered by II Corps left the Germans wondering if this was indeed the same army they had 'beaten' at Mons. Like the British, von Kluck's forces were exhausted but their failure to pursue the disorganized and scattered II Corps was due largely to faulty intelligence. Von Kluck was under the false impression that the BEF was based upon Calais. Accordingly, he moved southwest towards Péronne in the belief that he would prevent the British from connecting with their supply line further north. His error would give II Corps the opportunity to break away and march south towards St Quentin.

The fallout from the Battle of Le Cateau would smoulder on long after the fighting there had concluded. Despite the glowing testimonial bestowed upon Smith-Dorrien by Sir John French in his first official despatch published in the *London Gazette* in September 1914, he privately allowed his true feelings towards Smith-Dorrien to feed the flames of the growing animosity between the two. Sir Horace had now fought two major battles in the space of four days and granted that he had been assisted both by the failure of German intelligence to grasp the implications of the real situation that had faced them at Mons and Le Cateau and a good helping of luck, nevertheless, historians agree that he had been absolutely correct in making his stand just south of the Cambrai road. Had he continued the retirement as GHQ had ordered, the eventual outcome for the BEF would have been significantly worse.

* * *

I Corps, which we left retreating from the relatively minor actions at Landrecies and Maroilles, was also marching south but on a parallel course to Smith-Dorrien and further east towards Guise. Its route would widen the gap between the two commands and bring it into further contact with von Bülow's Second Army. Over the next 48 hours that contact would strike two heavy blows, the first of which would be centred on the village of Le Grand Fayt, whence Douglas Haig had fled in the early hours of 26 August after the Landrecies attack. Dubbed the 'Rearguard Affair of Le Grand Fayt' in the *Official History*, it serves to illustrate the penalties of poor command and control which resulted in many of Haig's men being scattered far and wide and condemned many more to weeks and even months of hiding behind enemy lines – sometimes with fatal results.

In order to fully appreciate what happened at Le Grand Fayt it is necessary to return to 25 August. Readers will recall that Douglas Haig had moved his headquarters to Le Grand Fayt after the Landrecies attack to join Brigadier General Herman Landon and 3 Brigade which had been in billets there since 6.30 pm that evening. The 3 Brigade war diaries for 25 August provide us with an impression of the bedlam that greeted the men as they arrived in that hitherto small and tranquil settlement:

> *'There are crowds of wretched people on foot and in carts, going south all over the place. Brigade left Marbaix, except Queen's* [Queen's Royal West Surrey Regiment] *who had preceded it, and reached Le Grand Fayt. Here, what with the "Convoie Administrative" of the 53rd Division de Reserve, the Heavy Battery and Divisional Ammunition column of the 2nd Division all coming in the opposite direction to assemble, there was a pretty good muddle'.*

Contributing to the muddle was the 1st Battalion Gloucestershire Regiment (1/Gloucesters). Even by today's standards, given the size of the village, quite where everyone was accommodated in 1914 is a mystery but at least C Company of 1/Gloucesters passed a relatively undisturbed night on outpost duties on the outskirts of the village listening to the machine gun and rifle fire coming from the Landrecies and Maroilles actions. A little before midnight Douglas Haig's motor cavalcade had driven into the crowded village announcing his arrival and that of his staff; an event which hopefully did not catch the outpost commander off guard. Having conferred with General Landon, and still convinced he had a large force of German infantry hot on his heels, Haig ordered the 1st Division to move immediately and take up a position near Favil to cover the withdrawal of the 2nd Division.

Haig's fresh orders for the next day's retirement took some time to percolate down to the 2nd Division's brigade commanders who, in turn, had to send word to their subordinates in command of battalions. It was, therefore, not until sometime after 4.00 am on 26 August that Brigadier General Richard Haking, the officer commanding 5 Brigade, was able to get a message to Lieutenant Colonel Alexander Abercrombie and the 2nd Battalion Connaught Rangers (2/Connaught Rangers) who were at Noyelles, directing him to act as rearguard to the brigade. Haking's brigade was at the most northerly extremity of I Corps and thus, in effect, the Connaught Rangers would be acting as rearguard to the entire division.

1/Gloucesters marched out of Le Grand Fayt at 5.00 am – almost exactly an hour later than Abercrombie's Connaught Rangers who left their billets at Noyelles some 5 miles further north at 4.00 am. Marching southwest across country the Gloucesters soon reached Favil and sent a patrol from A Company out towards Landrecies whilst the remainder of the battalion positioned itself as rearguard across the main Landrecies road close to two guns of 54 Battery. These guns, under section commander Lieutenant Ralph Blewitt, came into action shortly after noon when a German column was seen on the western bank of the Sambre Canal. German artillery responded with alacrity and although the majority of shells fell short, several men in C Company were wounded. German shooting was very much improved after an aeroplane in French colours – which later transpired to be German – flew low over the Gloucesters' trenches. Soon after the aircraft had passed over them, a German infantry attack developed from the direction of Landrecies, forcing the Gloucesters to withdraw B Company from its advanced position 200 yards up the road. The first two fatalities of the war to be suffered by the battalion were inflicted during this withdrawal, one of which was Private James Lander. Lander was seriously wounded when he was caught up in some close-quarters fighting during the forced withdrawal of his company. The 35-year-old reservist died of his wounds the next day at Landrecies and was buried by a party of 4/Field Ambulance which had remained behind with the wounded of the Guards Brigade.[110] Lander's company commander, Captain Guy Shipway, was hit by sniper fire in the same action and later died of his wounds at Etreux.[111] By 5.00 pm the excitement was all but over. German forces not wishing to get too enmeshed with troops of 3 Brigade withdrew giving the Gloucesters time to disengage and get clear.

In the intervening period a semblance of composure had returned to Le Grand Fayt and apart from the occasional troop of French cavalry passing through, the village was left relatively undisturbed. Unfortunately this proved to be the calm before the storm. A few miles to the north the march of the Connaught Rangers from Noyelles had been uninterrupted and on arriving at Taisnières – en -Thiérache, B Company moved to the crossroads south of the village whilst the remaining three companies followed the main column to Marbaix, where, it will be remembered, Drummer Whittington had spent the previous night in billets. Just south of Marbaix, where the road crosses the main Maroilles–Avesnes road, the brigade transport was held up by a large French force of territorials moving east. Anticipating a long wait Colonel Abercrombie ordered A Company to remain with the transport and sent C and D Companies to the crossroads south of Taisnières where they were briefly reunited with B Company.

At the crossroads they met detachments of French cavalry which informed them there were no Germans in the vicinity. Accordingly Abercrombie sent word to brigade HQ that he would remain in position until 3.00 pm and then march to Le Grand Fayt. A view of the situation from the ranks is provided by Sergeant John McIlwain, a reservist who had been called up in early August and was then serving as a platoon sergeant in D Company. His account gives an insight into the very slow progress made by the battalion that morning. They had been on the march for several hours but McIlwain apparently had no idea what they were supposed to be doing:

> *'Told to keep a sharp lookout for Uhlans. We appeared to be on some covering movement. No rations this day. Seemed to be cut off from supplies. Slept again for an hour or so on a sloping road until 11am.'*[112]

The battalion war diary does not indicate the time the battalion arrived at the crossroads but from all accounts it must have been there for some time if John McIlwain's diary is anywhere near accurate. 'We retired to a field, were told we could drum-up as we had tea. I went to a nearby village to get bread. None to be had, but got a fine drink of milk and some pears.'

At 3.00 pm Captain Ernest Hamilton and A Company entered Le Grand Fayt and, according to Hamilton's account, set about organizing billets for the battalion at the request of Colonel Abercrombie. Back at the crossroads at 3.15 firing was heard coming from the direction of Marbaix quickly followed by French cavalry galloping helter-skelter up the road and shouting that 200 Germans with a machine gun were close by. Reacting to this threat personally, Abercrombie led about 100 men from C and D Companies up the road towards Marbaix where they almost immediately came under heavy enemy fire, forcing them to seek cover on the high ground to the south. It appears the colonel left no orders with Major William Alexander and Captain O'Sullivan who remained at the crossroads with the remainder of the two companies. Marbaix was now unmistakably occupied by the Germans who captured 9 men of the rear party of the Royal Sussex still in the village along with the transport containing all the battalion's greatcoats; a grievous loss which the men would regret a few weeks later on the Aisne when the autumn weather set in.

Shortly after Abercrombie had moved off towards Marbaix, the crossroads became the focus of German shell fire as did the village of Le Grand Fayt. Fortunately 5 Brigade transport had passed through but as Ernest Hamilton observed, 'in five minutes what had appeared to be a peaceful hamlet became a positive inferno'. Expecting an imminent infantry attack, Hamilton tried to reach Abercrombie but found the road blocked by German troops. He then took the only sensible option open to him and marched south west towards Etreux arriving there at 11.00 pm. Hamilton had vivid memories of that night march which he later described in the regimental history:

> *'I could not ride my horse as I fell asleep the moment I got up. I even fell asleep walking – to be awakened by bumping into the men in front of me, most of whom were also half asleep. Some of them fell out and lay down in the road – it exhausted all one's vocabulary of entreaty and abuse, and even called for a liberal use of the boot to get them up again. Even so, in spite of our efforts, I am afraid some half dozen were left behind'.*

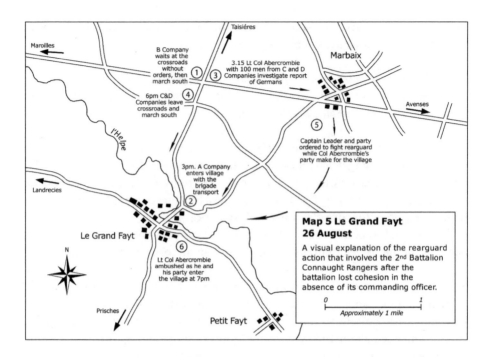

Maroilles

Taisiéres

B Company
waits at the
crossroads
without
orders, then
march south

① ③ 3.15 Lt Col Abercrombie
with 100 men from C and D
Companies investigate report
of Germans

Marbaix

6pm C&D
Companies leave ④
crossroads and
march south

⑤

Avenses

l'Helpe

Captain Leader and party
ordered to fight rearguard
while Col Abercrombie's
party make for the village

3pm. A Company
enters village
with the
brigade
transport

Landrecies

②

Le Grand Fayt

N

⑥

Lt Col Abercrombie
ambushed as he and
his party enter
the village at 7pm

**Map 5 Le Grand Fayt
26 August**

A visual explanation of the rearguard
action that involved the 2nd Battalion
Connaught Rangers after the
battalion lost cohesion in the
absence of its commanding officer.

0   1

Prisches

Petit Fayt

Approximately 1 mile

In the meantime Colonel Abercrombie sent Second Lieutenant Robert Benison down to the village to inform Brigade HQ that he was under attack. Benison returned with the disconcerting news that the 5 Brigade staff had left the village and it was apparently deserted and under fire.[113] The battalion was now scattered widely and none of the battalion's senior officers appeared to be in possession of their commanding officer's plan of action. Thus at this critical point in the proceedings the situation was as follows: Abercrombie with 5 officers, including the battalion second-in-command, Major William Saresfield and about 100 men, were under fire on the high ground to the north of Le Grand Fayt. A Company was marching south with the brigade transport – as was B Company with Major Hugh Hutchinson, whom, after failing to get in touch with Colonel Abercrombie, decided to follow the transport – whilst the remainder of C and D Companies were still at the crossroads just south of Taisnières.

Up at the crossroads, Major Alexander – still unsure of the whereabouts of A and B Companies – now faced a dilemma: should he wait for Abercrombie, whom he presumed was somewhere further east responding to the enemy fire, or should he proceed to Le Grand Fayt in the hope that he would find the remainder of the battalion there? Bearing in mind the crossroads was being shelled and he was taking casualties, his decision to move downhill to the by now shell-torn village was, in the event, a most reasonable one. John McIlwain provides a glimpse of the uncertainty and confusion that prevailed at the time. He was at the crossroads when he and his comrades first came under shell fire:

'Then the Germans got the range of us … and it simply rained small shells, horse artillery apparently. I followed my platoon officer, Lieutenant [Second Lieutenant Victor] Lentaigne into a turnip field. When taking cover, Private [Patrick] Sweeney, an old Indian wallah, lying beside me was wounded. Had to cut our way through a hedge to help Sweeney onto the road. Formed up under our company commander, Major Alexander. Cut off from the remainder of the battalion. Major at a loss'.[114]

Collecting as many men as they could, Alexander and O'Sullivan moved into Le Grand Fayt sometime after 6.00 pm to find French troops about to retire. The French officer in command had no idea where the Colonel Abercrombie might be, but recommended immediate retirement as they were all in danger of being overrun by a large force of German Cavalry and motorized infantry. McIlwain was part of the advance guard as they retired towards Beaurepaire:

'I with eight men do advance guard. Fixed bayonets and a sharp lookout each side of the road, but still no Germans. After sundown came up with some French troops in a village [probably Cartignies] they had retired to, chased by Germans. Germans a mile or so behind us, burning the village as they pass. The sky lit up. Then rain, rain! And I in the stress of the retreat, like so many others who were trained by Kitchener always to travel light, had thrown away my great coat'.[115]

Their march ended at Le Nouvion at midnight where, soaking wet through and exhausted, they bivouacked a mile south of the town.

So what of Colonel Abercrombie and his party? After coming under fire near Marbaix and realizing Brigade HQ was no longer at Le Grand Fayt he and his party continued their retirement downhill towards the village. The country above Le Grand Fayt is difficult to move through, thick hedges and numerous orchards – which largely remain today – made communication and movement difficult. Together with Lieutenant Gordon Barker's machine- gun section, Abercrombie deployed 33-year-old Captain Francis Leader and Second Lieutenant Charles Turner with a platoon from D Company as rearguard. Abercrombie had only just moved off towards the village when the rearguard party came under heavy attack. Captain Leader, with little choice but to hold on as long as possible, was in a poorly placed position lining the side of one of the small minor roads running down to the village from the Maroilles-Marbaix road. As the night drew on ammunition became short.

Charles Turner and four men were alongside Gordon Barker and the machine gun- section and it soon became apparent to both officers that they were up against a much larger force than first realized and that their situation was rapidly becoming indefensible. Just after dusk, outgunned and enfiladed, Captain Leader was killed. Barker fired the last round from the one remaining machine gun and took charge of the few men that remained. Ordering them to fix bayonets he led them in a last counter attack. The gallant young officer was brought down by a bullet in the thigh and Charles Turner was hit twice in the shoulder leaving him dazed and only partly conscious:

> '*I only collected my senses in time to see the forms of men looming up in front, whom I knew by their voices to be Germans. Some of them showed a declined inclination to bayonet me, but they were ordered off by a German officer who immediately knelt down beside me and asked why we were fighting against them, also various questions as to the strength of our force, to all of which I professed ignorance*'.[116]

They were fortunate that Barker spoke German fluently, which seemed to 'command our captors' respect at once.' Turner's belongings, which had been taken from him earlier, were duly returned after Barker spoke to the officer and 'appeared to dress down the enlisted German soldiers in very sharp tones.' The survivors spent the night in the field and were taken the next morning in a cart to Avenses-sur-Helpe. By rights Barker should have been decorated for his gallantry that night but he died of his injuries in England in December 1916 after being repatriated and the story of what took place above Le Grand Fayt remained forgotten until long after the war was over.[117]

Meanwhile the Connaught Rangers, led by Abercrombie, Captain Walter Roche, Major Saresfield, and Lieutenants de Stacpoole and Hardy approached the village at about 7.00 pm.[118] Told by an inhabitant that there were no German forces in the village the Rangers were ambushed minutes later by a strong force of Germans hidden on either side of the road. Pandemonium prevailed as officers and men scattered in all directions, Major Saresfied, and Robert de Stacpoole succeeded in escaping through the village with a handful of men and eventually rejoined the battalion. Colonel Abercrombie with Captain Roche and Jocelyn Hardy gathered up some 50 men and also got through the village taking up a defensive position to the west near Le Gard where they again came under fire. For some unexplained reason Abercrombie then headed northwest instead of south. Had he moved south he may have evaded capture and been reunited with the battalion.

On the word of a local man that there were still English troops at Maroilles, Abercrombie led his party in that direction and before long was met by Lieutenant Colonel Thompson, the Assistant Director of Medical Services for the 2nd Division, who was about to evacuate the town with a field ambulance convoy. He directed the Connaught Rangers to the two houses which had been used as field hospitals. English troops, he thought, were due to be back in Maroilles the next morning. Thompson then left to rejoin the field ambulance but lost his horse in the darkness; stumbling into the village of Prisches he was captured the next morning just after the *curé* had presented him with three Connaught Rangers he had found hiding in the church.

Bad luck still continued to haunt the luckless Abercrombie. Hardly had the Rangers got inside the two buildings pointed out by Thompson than German troops entered Maroilles. Remaining quiet they were undetected until the next day when Abercrombie's party was discovered early in the morning and taken into captivity. For a short while it looked as if Captain Roche's group would remain hidden but their luck ran out at 7.00 pm that evening when they were finally discovered and made prisoner.

With the loss of 6 officers and 280 other ranks in an encounter that should never really have taken place, questions inevitably arise as to the effectiveness of Lieutenant Colonel Abercrombie's handling of the situation. True, the battalion was held up by General Valabrègue's reserve divisions on the Mariolles-Marbaix road south of Taisnières which did allow the vanguard of von Richtofen's German Guard Cavalry to make contact but should Abercrombie have taken personal command of the force he sent forward in response to gunfire from the Marbaix direction? Would it perhaps not have been better to have despatched one of his company commanders to assess the situation whilst the remainder of the battalion continued on into Le Grand Fayt, rather than allow two companies to rest for several hours at the crossroads – apparently without orders? Unfortunately Abercrombie's version of the episode went with him into captivity during which he died in November 1915 and it was forever lost. Young Charles Turner was invalided first to Switzerland and then eventually to England whilst the irrepressible Jocelyn Hardy made nine escape attempts until he finally succeeded in making a home run in 1918.

At 9.00 am on the morning of 27 August – having had just 3 hours sleep – Captain Ernest Hamilton and his men began the long and weary march to Mont d'Origny. Just before reaching Guise they saw a small column of British troops moving towards them on a side road from the direction of Iron:

> *'You can imagine our joy when we discovered that it consisted of three hundred of our regiment under Major Alexander who had escaped from the débacle of the night before.'*

The 2nd Battalion of the Connaught Rangers with its proud history of tradition and service was destined to be amalgamated with the 1st Battalion in December 1914 in what was the only permanent merger of regular battalions during the entire war. While the official explanation is attributed to recruiting problems and heavy casualties, it does leave one to wonder if there were deeper and more engrained difficulties which contributed to the demise of the 2nd Battalion.

26 August was also the date of the second and last meeting between Sir John French and Charles Lanrezac which took place at St Quentin with the French

Commander-in-Chief, Joffre. Sir John, whose command of the French language was as poor as his understanding of the French psyche, relied on Henry Wilson to translate his evident, and quite understandable, irritation at the manner in which he felt the BEF had been treated, particularly by Lanrezac. Not only had the BEF been attacked by overwhelming numbers of the enemy but was constantly ahead of the Fifth Army which he felt was not taking its share of the burden. Spears,who was present at the meeting, reported that whilst Lanrezac was plainly well aware of Sir John's frustration, his body language and occasional remarks provided neither answers nor explanations of his own actions. Joffre, said Spears 'looked hard at his subordinate but said nothing ... the atmosphere was one you could cut with a knife'. Wilson continued to relay Sir John's decision to continue the retirement of the BEF until the Fifth Army stops and advances, at which point he would 'push forward with all his force'. The only practical outcome of the conference was an agreement that the left of the Fifth Army would retire on La Fère and not on St Quentin, a decision which would go some way to preventing the delays caused by British and French forces retiring along the same roads.

Smith-Dorrien was also making for St Quentin intent on making a personal report to Sir John on the Le Cateau encounter. Motoring to St Quentin where he understood GHQ was still located on the evening of 26 August, he discovered it had moved another 20 miles further south to Noyon which, in the early hours of the next morning proved exasperatingly difficult to find. Sir John and his staff were woken to hear Smith-Dorrien express himself 'quite happy about the results of the battle and the safety of the troops'. The Commander-in-Chief was plainly still very worried about II Corps and after listening to Sir Horace, instead of offering his congratulations and expressing relief at the successful retirement of II Corps, he allowed his temper to get the better of him and reprimanded the II Corps Commander for being too optimistic. What followed in private between the two men has not been recorded but it does leave one wondering whether, during that early morning meeting, Sir John's ire was raised by Sir Horace's failure to obey his orders at Le Cateau.

Any optimism that may have been present at GHQ prior to 25 August hit rock bottom after Le Cateau and Landrecies and there were a series of hasty relocations as the retreat continued on its southward course. These 'relocations' may have accounted for remarks made by Frederick Coleman, an American civilian who had volunteered his services as a driver. Coleman and his colleagues had been sponsored by the Royal Automobile Club to provide their own motor cars to act as transport for GHQ staff, but, as Coleman later wrote, 'GHQ took some watching in those days. If one turned round it was likely to disappear to the southward'.

Chapter 9

27 August – St Quentin and Etreux

When Second Lieutenant Kenneth Godsell woke under his haycock in the field at Estrées it was still dark and 17/Field Company had gone. Having failed to find him, Major Singer had assumed he was lost and left without him. Somewhat concerned at to what his commanding officer might have to say about his absence when he caught up with them again, he picked up an abandoned bicycle and pedalled furiously down the St Quentin road until he caught up with Lieutenant Valdo Pottinger who had also lost the company:

> *'It sounds as if I had a good night's rest – as a matter of fact I had not slept 3 hours. In ten minutes time I overtook Valdo who had been foraging and was carrying a basket of foodstuffs, unfortunately raw'.*[119]

At St Quentin he and Valdo Pottinger did manage to scrounge a breakfast of omelette, red wine and fresh bread and butter which they washed down with fresh coffee, their first meal for almost 36 hours. Then, discovering twelve sappers of the company wandering about in St Quentin, the two young officers and their charges headed south for Ollezy where the remainder of the company were 'all bivouacked in a field, nice and cosy' – to which note Godsell added with obvious pleasure – 'with my bed all laid out'. He was, however, destined not to sleep in it that night.

Food was also on the mind of Jim Pennyman as his party of KOSB moved off from the farm at Serain. They were still unaware that Colonel Stephenson had been captured and uncertain of who had or had not been killed, he and the 18-year-old Gilbert Amos – who had only joined the battalion a month before war was declared – wondered idly if their little group might be the only survivors. There was still a deal of confusion on the road which made marching tiring but to Pennyman's delight their numbers increased as more of the scattered battalion spotted the familiar Glengarry cap of the regiment and fell in behind their officers. Their route took them past some 'horrible looking carcasses in the mud by the roadside' which on closer examination proved to be perfectly good

British ration meat that had been dumped. Hacking off enough meat for the party they made for the village of Beaurevoir where a handy kitchen garden provided enough vegetables for the first proper meal they had had for three days.

> *'We ate our meal, some of the men had a wash and shave, and we lay down for an hour's rest. The stew was absolutely tip top, and the men said it was the best meal they had had since leaving Dublin.'*[120]

After taking a photograph of his luncheon party, Pennyman, as the senior subaltern, led his Borderers on to St Quentin, arriving tired and footsore at 4.00 pm where a less than friendly staff officer sent them onto Ham where, he said, the 5th Division was reported to be assembling. It was dark when they got to Ham only to find yet another staff directive to continue a further 3 miles to Muille and in the darkness they lost Gilbert Amos who had gone off looking for food. Continuing without him, the party marched at long last into Muille where Pennyman calculated they had done 35 miles since leaving Le Cateau.

L Battery had been on the road since 4.30 am and had trekked slowly towards St Quentin. Jack Giffard noted the road was strewn for about 5 miles 'with howitzer and gun ammunition, small arms ammunition and every description of stores, harnesses etc all abandoned' all belonging to XXXIV Brigade RFA. It was not a sight which gladdened the eyes of the horse artillery men, rivalry there may be between the horse and field artillery but this visible evidence of destruction was beyond all that. L Battery was covering the retirement of the 5th Division which was 'just about done in' and had collected numerous stragglers who were now ensconced on the battery's horse drawn wagons and limbers. Reaching St Quentin, Giffard noted it was very congested with 'every description of troops and transport' and it was with some relief they moved out to positions south of the town to cover any pursuit by the Germans.

The protective screen between St Quentin and the advancing Germans was the responsibility of the remnants of de Lisle's 2 Cavalry Brigade. The command of this scratch force fell to Major Tom Bridges of 4/Dragoon Guards who had been brought down during the cavalry charge at Audregnies and had only managed to avoid capture by jumping through the window of the cottage in which he had taken refuge. His rearguard was made up of two squadrons of his own regiment and some of 5/Lancers; their orders were to hold off the Germans long enough to allow the British to get clear of the town. As the number of stragglers coming in from the Le Cateau direction dried up, Bridges moved into St Quentin to find there were still a large number of men scattered around the town, sleeping on pavements and in gutters. Captain Arthur Osburn who was riding with Bridges' rearguard, found the Grand Place, 'thronged with British infantrymen standing in groups or wandering about in an aimless fashion, most of them without either packs or rifles.' It soon emerged that two battalion commanders from Brigadier General Aylmer Haldane's 10 Infantry Brigade, having decided their men – and perhaps themselves as well – were unable to march any further, had attempted unsuccessfully to find a train to get them away by rail.

When this failed and faced with the imminent arrival of the Germans, Lieutenant Colonels Elkington, commanding 1/Royal Warwicks, and Mainwaring, commanding 2/Dublin Fusiliers, were asked by the town's mayor to march their troops out to prevent the Germans bringing an artillery barrage down on the town. On hearing that the condition of the men prevented this, the Mayor demanded they sign a surrender document which he hoped would satisfy the German field commander as to the neutrality of the town. Incredibly both Elkington and Mainwaring agreed to the mayor's request. The young Bernard Law Montgomery was a lieutenant in the Warwicks at the time but had become separated from the battalion during its withdrawal from Le Cateau and consequently was not present during this episode. It is interesting to speculate whether the future field marshal would have complied with his commanding officer's orders at St Quentin and surrendered. Somehow I think not.

It was a scandalous decision on the part of the two battalion commanders and one that Bridges very bravely set about to rectify. With the contentious surrender document in his possession he gave the large body of men at the railway station an hour's grace during which time he promised carts would be found for those who were unable to walk. His ultimatum that he would leave no British soldier alive in St Quentin appeared to galvanize the men into action and they left the station. The men in the Grand Place however, were in no mood to be ordered about, particularly by a 'bloody cavalry officer'. Bridges' first entreaties fell on very deaf ears and Arthur Osburn watched as one soldier raised a rifle at Bridges. Sill refusing to entertain the thought of so many men to falling captive, however, Bridges had a moment of inspiration – if only he had a band the men might yet get up and move. Providentially, luck was on his side in the shape of a nearby toy shop in which he and his squadron trumpeter purchased a toy drum and a penny whistle:

'We marched round and round the fountain where the men were lying like the dead playing 'The British Grenadiers' and 'Tipperary' and beating the drum like mad. They sat up and began to laugh and even cheer. I stopped playing and made them a short exhortation and told them I was going to take them back to their regiments. They began to stand up and fall in, and eventually we moved off slowly into the night to the music of our improvised band, now reinforced by a couple of mouth-organs.'[121]

Tom Bridges led his tattered band out of the town just after midnight, the Germans were slow in advancing and the rearguard was left unmolested, it looked, commented Bridges later, 'as if 'more haste, less speed' might well have been the description of this part of the retreat.' Today the fountain is no longer a feature of the Grand Place at St Quentin but the image of Bridges and his trumpeter, marching in time to the music generated by their toy drum and tin whistle, is conjured up every time I sit in the square – and it has absolutely nothing to do with the local beer!

* * *

To the northeast of St Quentin the retirement of I Corps on 27 August was taking it through Etreux towards the high ground south of Guise. The rearguard for the day was the responsibility of Brigadier General Ivor Maxse's 1 (Guards) Brigade, which, on hearing that practically the whole of Haig's Corps was to use the same highway to Guise, realized the day 'promised to be critical'. I Corps was underway by 4.00 am with the 1st Division remaining in a covering position until the three brigades of Monro's 2nd Division had moved off. By 7.00 am Maxse had moved his brigade HQ from Fesmy to the canal bridge at Petit Cambresis where he was visited by his divisional commander, Major General Lomax, who made it clear that it was vital to hold the Fesmy-Wassigny line until the two divisions of I Corps had passed through Etreux. Not only were they passing through, reiterated Lomax, but they were being resupplied in the town and thus it was essential that this took place unhindered. Accordingly, Maxse issued his orders: the first to 23/Field Company and Lieutenant Colonel Adrian Grant-Duff of 1/Black Watch to reconnoitre and prepare a fall-back rearguard position just north of Etreux. His second batch of orders was issued to the three rearguard units:

> 'Those orders were read out to mounted officers (sent from units to Headquarters) at about 12 noon, and they (including Major Day, Royal Munster Fusiliers) returned to their battalions to explain the retirement orders to COs.'[122]

Once I Corps was clear of Etreux, Maxse explained to the assembled officers, he would instruct the rearguard to withdraw.

The rearguard consisted of the 2nd Battalion Royal Munster Fusiliers (2/Munsters) with the addition of C Squadron 15/Hussars under Major Frederick Pilkington and two guns from 118 Battery, XXVI Brigade, in the charge of Major Abingdon Bayly. Commanding the Munsters was Major Paul Alfred Charrier, a man fluent in French and very much a Francophile – he and Henry Wilson would have had much in common. Known in the battalion as an individualist, the 45-year-old Charrier was easy to spot on the march in his brown tropical issue pith helmet with its green and white hackle of Munster, a nostalgic reminder perhaps for those with an eye for the history of the regiment's origins under Clive of India in 1756. With the demise of Lieutenant Colonel O'Meagher soon after landing in France, Charrier had been officially in command of the battalion since 20 August 1914, the announcement of his promotion to lieutenant colonel appearing in the *London Gazette* six years after his death!

Having been handed his orders by Major Day, Paul Charrier took stock of what was required of him: He was to hold his ground until forced back but only to retire on receipt of orders from General Maxse, using a route which would take him directly south through the village of Boué. Turning his attentions to the job in hand, he prepared his defensive positions on the crossroads at Chapeau Rouge – a mile to the north of Fesmy – and also around the crossroads at Bergues to the southeast, with the guns of 118 Battery facing northeast and sited north of Fesmy just opposite the minor road that led to Le Sart.

Contact with German forces on the morning of 27 August had begun well before Maxse issued his orders for the day. Shortly after dawn 15/Hussars found themselves deployed right across the brigade frontage, a strong detachment was at Chapeau Rouge, another with the Munsters at Fesmy and a third operating on the flank between the 1st Division and the French. It was from this troop of Hussars that the first worrying piece of information came in. The French territorials on this flank had vanished south leaving the right flank of the brigade unprotected. Reserve troops of the Hussars and cyclists were sent out to reinforce both flanks and soon became engaged with German cavalry patrols in advance of General Otto von Emmich's X Army Corps. German forces were evidently moving quickly.

As the tail end of the long and weary column of men and equipment passed through 2/RMF's lines on their way south, the 1st Battalion Coldstream Guards (1/Coldstream) left two of their companies on the left of the main Landrecies road to defend the bridge over the Sambre Canal just north of Petit Cambresis. Captain John Gibbs, commanding Number 3 Company, was already a little uneasy as he was unable to get in touch with the Munsters at Fesmy even now lightly engaged with the enemy. Thus even at this early stage in the day there was a hint of what was to follow.

By 10.00 am, with the sky darkening to the north and threatening rain, most of the 15/Hussars patrols had been forced back and thick lines infantry of the German X Corps, many of whom had been brought forward in motor lorries, were advancing across the fields on both flanks. Those German units which had come up against Charrier's entrenched positions had waited until they were in enough strength to penetrate Fesmy where a counter attack by Captain Claud Rawlinson's C Company cleared the village and restored the status quo for the time being. Further north at the Chapeau Rouge crossroads B and D Companies were engaged in a furious fire fight at close quarters which caught their attackers by surprise. In the confusion which followed – aided by the rain which was now sheeting down in torrents – the Munsters withdrew down the Bergues road to Fesmy. It was now 1.00 pm.

The message from General Maxse, which went out at 12.46 pm ordering all rearguard units to retire, did not reach Charrier at his battalion HQ in a small estaminet close to the guns of 118 Battery. The cyclist carrying those orders came under fire north of Petit Cambresis and was unable to reach the Munsters, instead he delivered them to Major Day who attempted to get through to Charrier on horseback from brigade HQ – but he too was unsuccessful. However, the orders did get through to John Gibbs and the two 1/Coldstream companies which withdrew to the bridge and continued their march south through Etreux. At 2.30 pm Charrier was in the process of pulling back towards Oisy when he got word that German cavalry had been seen to the south, although they were soon dispersed by 29-year-old Lieutenant Challoner Chute and his machine guns, it was another ominous sign that the enemy was closing in.

Ivor Maxse had also read the signs and realized – just as Charrier must have done – that the battalion was in great danger of envelopment, particularly as German infantry had been reported in the wooded area south of Boué. In conference with Major Pilkington he raised the question of the practicality of mounting a rescue bid to recover the beleaguered 2/Munsters whilst the remainder of the brigade continued south. Pilkington knew that Fesmy was practically surrounded but his intelligence suggested there was still a gap at Bergues that might just allow A Company to get away. The 'greater part of the squadron therefore dashed for this gap and a fierce fight now ensued at the outskirts of Bergues'. Pilkington's men attacked with such determination that the Germans were caught a little off guard and in the ensuing mêlée over 170 men of 2/Munsters retired under the covering fire of the Hussars. It was a gallant action but it was not without cost. In enabling the Munsters to get away relatively unscathed Private William Wilkes was killed in action and Lance Corporal John Stent died of his wounds six months later in captivity at Guise.[123] The only officer to fall in the action was Lieutenant the Hon Edward Charles Hardinge who was wounded in both arms and later died of his wounds in England.[124]

At 5.30 pm the main body of the Munsters was at the crossroads west of Oisy but without Captain George Simms and B Company. Charrier sent runners and cyclists out to find them but it was nearly an hour before they appeared, an hour of inactivity which was to prove fatal. Moving through Oisy, Captain Rawlinson's C Company brought up the rear of the battalion and almost immediately came under attack from General Karl von Plettenberg's 2nd Guard Division from which it was only just able to escape thanks to the covering fire

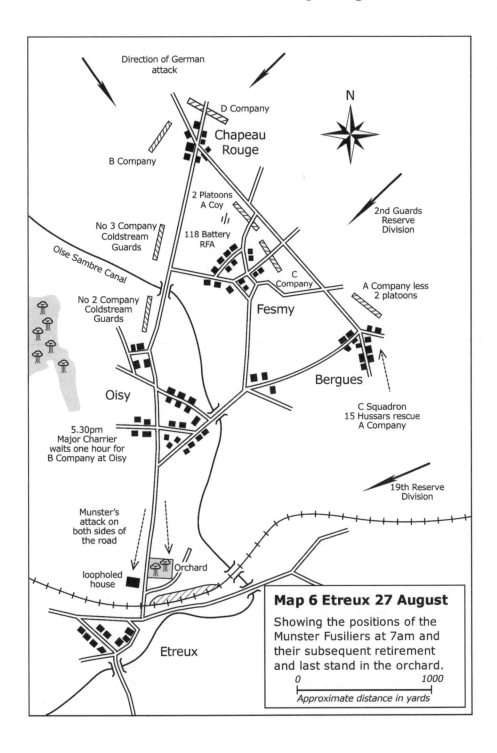

Direction of German attack

D Company

Chapeau Rouge

B Company

N

2 Platoons A Coy

2nd Guards Reserve Division

No 3 Company Coldstream Guards

118 Battery RFA

Oise Sambre Canal

C Company

A Company less 2 platoons

No 2 Company Coldstream Guards

Fesmy

Oisy

Bergues

C Squadron 15 Hussars rescue A Company

5.30pm Major Charrier waits one hour for B Company at Oisy

19th Reserve Division

Munster's attack on both sides of the road

loopholed house

Orchard

Map 6 Etreux 27 August

Etreux

Showing the positions of the Munster Fusiliers at 7am and their subsequent retirement and last stand in the orchard.

0   1000

Approximate distance in yards

from the two platoons of Lieutenant Deane Drake and Sergeant Foley. But now the consequence of the delay caused by B Company was beginning to manifest itself; further east the German advance was continuing as planned, General von Barfeldt's 19th Reserve Infantry Division was heading towards Guise when the heavy firing to the north sent his reconnaissance patrols scurrying towards Fesmy. With signs of battle evident everywhere and rifle and artillery fire continuing through the afternoon, Barfeldt swung his division towards Etreux. The door was closing fast and it would be the German 19th Division which finally slammed it shut.

Moving onto the Oisy-Landrecies road and covered by Lieutenant Chute's machine-gun section, 2/Munsters approached Etreux only to see enemy infantry crossing the road ahead of them. Before Charrier had time to deploy his men a heavy fire was opened up on them from the houses on the edge of the town and a field battery from the direction of Le Gard. Almost before the 118 Battery guns were unlimbered one was destroyed with a direct hit; the other was hastily prepared for action but having already fired over 300 rounds, ammunition was in very short supply and the number of gunners left alive or unwounded was diminishing fast. Undeterred, Charrier moved forward to discover that the enemy had occupied positions created by their own countrymen – trenches dug that morning by 1/Black Watch and a house which 23/Field Company had loopholed just off the road on the right. It was a twist of irony that would not have been lost on Major Paul Charrier; an irony which would prove to be the final straw in a rearguard action destined to catapult his battalion into British military legend.

Dividing into two, the battalion attacked to the left and right of the road. Struggling to bring the remaining gun to bear on the loopholed house, the gunners, including Major Bayly who was wounded, were shot down in a hail of fire that came from both sides of the road even before the breech could be opened. Charrier led three charges against the loopholed house, Captain Douglas Wise, the battalion adjutant, actually getting close enough to fire his revolver through a window, only – according to the regimental history – to fall stunned by falling masonry. It was now 7.00 pm and the end was very near. Although held up by the loopholed house on the right, the attack on the left of the main road initially made progress. Lieutenant Erasmus Gower was with A Company:

> '*Ordered to push on half went* [and] *pushed on* [the] *left of the road (East) other half on right – I went to* [the] *left. We pushed on through some orchards and a brickfield to a sunken lane near Etreux railway station – held up there. Captains Hall, Barratt, Lieutenants Sullivan, Crozier and self, supported by* [our] *fire, a charge* [made by] *Jervis' company. Only Jervis and three men got to the hedge, where* [they were] *taken prisoner.*'[125]

Still the Irishmen fought on, refusing to give in to a force that by now completely surrounded and outgunned them. In the final act of the day in the gathering dusk, Captain Charles Hall and some 200 of the Munsters fell back to a small orchard near the main road – but not before they had lost Captain Phillip Barrett and Second Lieutenant James Crozier. Gower's account again:

> *'When we got to the orchard I went to report to Major Charrier. I found him by the gun* [which was] *deserted as all the team of men were killed or wounded. Charrier* [was] *killed almost while* [I was] *talking to him, Rawlinson wounded at the same time.'*[126]

Returning to the orchard Gower passed Captain George Simms lying dead and reported the death of Charrier to Captain Hall. In his absence 20-year-old Second Lieutenant Phillip Sullivan had been mortally wounded and young Challoner Chute killed next to his remaining machine gun. A last desperate bayonet charge to push the enemy out of the nearby lane resulted in Hall being badly wounded and command falling to Lieutenant Gower. It appears from Gower's account that the remaining men on the right side of the road attempted to break through at around 8.00 pm but were unsuccessful. Lining the four sides of the orchard Gower's dwindling band of Munsters continued to keep the enemy at bay until it became obvious that further resistance was pointless. Gower then took what is probably one of the hardest decisions a professional soldier has to make:

> *'Fresh enemy coming up from* [the] *north so surrendered at 9.12 pm – very little ammunition left … I could hear no other firing to show any relief coming and was only losing men and doing no good. Also, fresh machine guns* [were] *getting into position. I surrendered with 3 officers and 256 men.'*[127]

They had been fighting for nearly 12 hours against a considerable force of von Bülow's X Corps in a rearguard action that enabled the main body of I Corps to put 12 miles between it and its pursuers. The Munsters' action gained them membership of that exclusive but tragic list of battalions that had remained 'faithful unto death'.[128]

It was said at the time that after the surrender the German soldiers applauded the Munster's bravery; that may have been so but none of the surviving accounts appear to support this generous plaudit. Many of the Irish wounded remained where they had fallen for some considerable time. Lieutenant Thomas was wounded in the last hour of the battle with a bullet through the throat and shrapnel wounds in his left arm and lay for some time in the ditch at the side of the road listening to the repeated attempts to neutralize the fire from the loopholed house. Finally, when Lieutenant Gower's men in the orchard had surrendered, the gunfire fell silent and German infantry with fixed bayonets appeared through a gap in the hedge where he was lying:

> 'They were very angry and excited, and I distinctly saw them bayoneting several wounded men. There was an angry crowd of them around Captain Rawlinson and myself and I believe they would have also bayoneted us but for an officer who came up just in time to stop them. Then I heard this officer say in English. "You are our prisoners, and if another shot is fired we will kill you all." I saw German soldiers pulling about the dead bodies in a most brutal manner to make sure they were really dead or not.'[129]

All the wounded who could walk were separated and shut up in a barn close to the entrance to the town whilst the others were marched off to a nearby factory building. Thomas remained all night and most of the next day in the barn, his breathing becoming more and more difficult as the wound in his throat restricted his breathing. Finally a German doctor performed a tracheotomy without anaesthetic, a procedure that Thomas fortunately remembered little of. Writing to his mother from Etreux, he described his situation:

> 'My throat, of course, is bad and very troublesome. They put in a tube so as to allow me to breathe, and I can eat and drink but I can't speak. All the officers were sent off to Germany yesterday, and the men who were able to travel, so I am alone among the Germans, except for three men who are very bad. This town ... is just one big hospital; every house is full of wounded, and flies and smells are awful.'[130]

One of the three men left with Thomas may have been Private John Lenihan who was wounded early in the action – probably at Fesmes – and lay drifting in and out of consciousness for most of the day. He woke to find a group of German soldiers standing around him, the sergeant in charge asked if he was an Englander and being unable to speak Lenihan nodded, only to be bayoneted in the thigh. His clothing was then stripped from him and he was kicked and abused before the Germans moved on. He realized afterwards that if he had been able to tell them he was an Irishman he may have been treated a little more sympathetically.

John Lenihan's experience was perhaps not typical but his encounter with the enemy as a wounded man lying on the field of battle was an appalling episode. In September he had his arm removed in Germany by an Italian doctor and soon after was repatriated home. Private John Power had a different experience, after lying out in the open for two days he was eventually picked up and taken to what he describes as a bicycle shop where his wounds were dressed by German field ambulance staff. He was then moved to another house where he was left with others without food or water for three days. His plight was discovered by Colonel Thompson – whom readers will remember was captured at Prisches – Thompson found a German doctor to attend to him and ensured the men in the house were fed regularly. After his capture the RAMC colonel had been allowed to work with the 47th German Field *Lazarett* based at the Mairie at Etreux and in so doing directed German medical teams to many of the wounded Munsters. Another badly wounded man in the same house as Power was Private Martin O'Rourke, He remained at Etreux for 3 days in the care of Thompson before being sent on to hospital at Wesel in Germany where he remained for some 6 months. Like many of the badly wounded he was eventually repatriated and came home to be discharged as unfit for further service.

Of a battalion which landed in France with 1,008 officers and men, only 201 of 2/Munsters were present at a roll call on 29 August and these were largely made up from the survivors of A Company. Whilst initial estimates of the number killed at Etreux have been shown to be incorrect, the current figure of 108 officers and men is probably the most accurate. It is clear, however, that a fairly large body of men did evade capture after the battle and went into hiding in the local area, exactly how many is unclear but recent estimates suggest that between 50 and 120 Munsters were still on the run a week after the battle. Some of these were able to get away with the help of escape organizations such as that organized by Edith Cavell and the Croys, others tragically fell victim to German reprisals and were captured and shot.

On reading the quite lengthy report of the action sent in by Maxse, Douglas Haig was very critical of the manner in which the rearguard had been handled, 'I consider that Brigadier-General Maxse committed an error in not withdrawing the Munsters before they were surrounded' wrote Haig, 'The whole rearguard seems to have been placed in jeopardy owing to the large gap which existed between it and the main body before General Maxse commenced to withdraw from his first position.'

Despite the sometimes less than sympathetic attitude towards the Irish wounded, the German authorities did allow the surviving men of the Munsters to bury their dead in the orchard. Two mass graves were dug, one for the officers and another for the NCOs and enlisted men. After the war when the Imperial War Graves Commission assumed responsibility for the upkeep of the cemetery, two other burials from nearby Bergues and Boué were added to the 126 casualties who are commemorated there.

* * *

We last left Kenneth Godsell looking longingly at his bed after he and Valdo Pottinger trekked – Godsell still with his borrowed bicycle – wearily into the 17/Field Company bivouac at Ollezy. Little sleep was to be had that night, divisional orders had decreed three bridges spanning the Somme were to be prepared for demolition and he and Gerald Smyth were sent off with their sections to set the charges. Godsell was sure his section had been included in the nocturnal excursion because he had still been 'in the arms of Morpheus' when the company left that morning and Major Singer, he felt, was making a point. He may well have been right but orders were orders and the two sections of sappers headed for their respective tasks. Gerald Smyth's bridge was at St Simon, the charges had already been laid two days earlier by Major Howard, commanding 57/Field Company, all Smyth had to do was check all was still in place, wait for orders from Divisional HQ and blow the bridge. Whilst his sappers checked over the charges at St Simon, Smyth found a second bridge upstream not connected with any road but strong enough to carry troops and equipment. Sending a galloper to secure the necessary permission, he set two separate charges to deal with the five girders of the bridge. Back at divisional HQ at Ollezy they heard two distinctive explosions and assumed – incorrectly – that the bridge at St Simon had been destroyed prematurely, leaving the cavalry on the wrong side of the river. When irate staff officers appeared at St Simon to find 'that blasted Irishman who had blown the bridge' they found a very relaxed and rather surprised Gerald Smyth sitting with one of the local inhabitants enjoying a glass of wine.

Edward Gleichen had only eaten a couple of apples and a piece of bread all day and would dearly have loved to have washed it down with a glass of wine. His brigade had already marched 24 miles during the night and was looking forward to its bivouac when he was ordered to take and hold the bridge at Ollezy – another 9 miles south. Given the urgency of the orders Gleichen naturally assumed there was going to be some fighting involved and it was with some relief that he found the bridge deserted and intact.

The last 10 miles or so from St Quentin had been littered with the human debris of fatigue, Major Herbert Stewart, en route for Ham, found the road, 'lined with hundreds who had dropped out of the ranks too exhausted to continue the march'. Gleichen found it a depressing sight and wondered how some units would come together again, noting in his diary that, all things considered, his own 15 Brigade appeared to be relatively intact. Still expecting the German cavalry to appear at any moment he took the precaution of leaving a rearguard at the bridge and he and the brigade continued over the river towards Eaucourt where they finally collapsed exhausted for the night. As for Kenneth Godsell:

'I went down and prepared the bridge with Corporals Geraghty and Taylor – we saw a moving star and lost our way in the swamp. It was love's labour's lost as the bridge was left labelled but not demolished.'[131]

After all the urgency, HQ decreed the two remaining bridges were to be blown by the cavalry field troop once it was across, but as the cavalry crossed the Somme at Ham further west, the night's work was, according to a rather disgruntled sapper officer, 'a rather pointless exercise'.

The big complaint from sapper officers during the retreat was that they felt they were always being sent back towards the enemy to reconnoitre and prepare demolitions. It appeared to them that the staff never considered them as tactical operations:

> *'They seemed to say to themselves when they crossed something: "By God! Here's a bridge, let's blow it up! Where's a Sapper?" all their arrangements were very confusing – orders, counter-orders, disorder. The transmission of orders was bad too; it was of necessity slow, but the order writer seemed to think that when an order had been written the deed was done, even if that site was 10 miles away. Aggravating to all and dangerous to some.'*[132]

There was certainly some justification in this allegation. When I Corps crossed the Oise at Guise there appears to have been some alarming uncertainty as to whether the bridges were to be destroyed or left intact. The 23rd and 26th Field Companies prepared several bridges for demolition but in the event none was actually destroyed. Arrangements had been made to destroy the two bridges over the Sambre at Oisy after the Coldstream Guards had crossed but at the last minute these orders were cancelled by General Maxse. At Etreux Major Harry Pritchard, commanding 26/Field Company, had been told to prepare the bridges over the Oise, his report that there were actually five – all within three quarters of a mile of each other –resulted in an order not to destroy them – presumably from General Maxse. What impact these demolitions might have had on the fate of the Munsters is impossible to say but the destruction of the road and rail bridges at Le Gard may have temporarily held up the German 19th Division as might the demolition of the road bridge over the Oise at Petit Cambresis have delayed the German X Corps.

Despite the rearguard action to the north of Etreux, the fighting continued for Maxse's brigade all the way down the straight length of the road from Etreux to La Maison Rouge until well after dark. What was correctly assumed to be dismounted cavalry and German horse artillery was kept largely at bay by the four remaining batteries from XXVI Brigade which came into action at Jerusalem Farm and La Maison Rouge. In his report to 1st Division Headquarters Maxse drew attention to the brisk rearguard action that was executed with steadiness by the three arms in cooperation during the retirement and recommended 7 officers for special mention, Lieutenant Charles Hardinge was included in the list but not one of the others was a Royal Munster Fusilier.

That night Drummer George Whittington and the Royal Sussex, having marched the 16 miles from Petit Cambresis through Etreux to Hautville, learned not only of the loss of the Munsters but also of the missing greatcoats and the rear party they had left behind at Marbaix. Thankful it was not his battalion on rearguard duty that day, George Whittington was too tired to worry very much about either event, being 'properly done up' and it was not long before he was sound asleep.

Chapter 10

28 August – Cavalry Capers

The repeated disappearing act which GHQ managed to sustain over the course of the retreat did little to enable it to recover control of the army and the confidence of the two corps commanders. Despite the escape of II Corps from Le Cateau, GHQ continued to view events through hazy panes of gloom and doom, an atmosphere which must only have been intensified on 27 August with the loss of the Munsters at Etreux. In a directive sent out that evening – which clearly illustrated GHQ's failure to recognize the tactical realities facing the BEF and did little to bolster the morale of the retreating troops – Henry Wilson ordered all unnecessary baggage and ammunition to be abandoned in order that exhausted troops could be carried on the transports. The sight of eleven wagon loads of personal kit belonging to units of the 4th Division burning in great piles by the roadside was too much to bear for Brigadier General Hunter Weston, commanding 11 Brigade, and he complained bitterly to Smith-Dorrien about the 'damping effect' it was having on his troops. Smith-Dorrien immediately countermanded the order and in so doing found himself on the sharp end of Sir John French's tongue, being accused once more of being over optimistic.

That said, the physical state of the troops of II Corps after fighting two major engagements was very different to that exhibited by their counterparts of I Corps. Arthur Habgood and his medical team – still with the main body of the 3rd Division – thought that 'officers and men were dirty and unshaven; units were a scratch lot with infantrymen on the wagons and limbers and stragglers all over the place'. Yet despite this poorly presented exterior, he saw no signs of 'grousing and despondency'. The contrast between the two corps was plain to Captain Jacques Helbronner, one of the French staff liaison officers with the Fifth Army. He watched the British 1st Division march past him near Mont D'Origny early on the morning of 28 August and noted, 'its excellent appearance'. The men were tired and suffering from the extreme heat but marched in perfect order. Later, on his way to see Smith-Dorrien, he encountered some of the II Corps regiments who in contrast 'looked harassed

...there was some disorder and some units were intermingled'. GHQ staff officers had also returned reports of the poor state of II Corps which may have contributed to the rather startling instruction issued by Henry Wilson to the Chief Royal Engineers Officer to reconnoitre and report on the bridges that would have to be destroyed if the BEF retreated to La Rochelle – 250 miles southwest of Paris![133] It took a visit from Lord Kitchener on 1 September to steady the nerves of a panic-stricken GHQ.

If GHQ harboured thoughts that the BEF was a beaten army it wasn't an observation shared by Frederick Coleman who had, 'no hallucination about the army being a beaten one' and, like Arthur Habgood, felt that 'the spirit of the men alone made it impossible to describe them as beaten'. From the comfort of his motor car this was perhaps an easy remark to make but nevertheless he had seen a large number of the II Corps units over the preceding few days and certainly more of them than the fleeting glimpses afforded the occasional staff officer venturing forth from GHQ. However, from the perspective of Kenneth Godsell and his two corporals who had remained at the Ollezy bridge all night, all they could think about was how long the day's march would be and where their next meal was coming from:

> 'At 9am the outposts were withdrawn and we followed them. Then we walked – Corporal Geraghty, Corporal Taylor and myself plus a punctured bicycle – as the Company had gone on earlier. After about half an hour we went into a cottage and breakfasted off new bread and butter and vile white wine. Refreshed, we continued the trek'.[134]

Cyril Helm and his party of 2/KOYLI had rejoined 13 Brigade soon after leaving Joncourt and as darkness fell on 27 August they found themselves on the other side of the River Somme at Ham and for the moment – they hoped – safe from the German cavalry which Helm fully expected to materialize at some point. The battalion was now reorganized into two companies under the overall command of Major Herbert Trevor. Helm was by now the only medical officer left in the entire brigade, and consequently was attending to the, sick, lame and weary of four different battalions. A note made in his diary on 28 August hinted at his own tiredness, 'often, having just settled down for a few hours sleep I was hauled out to see some poor devil. It was my job and I had to make the best of it.' At Ham, to Helm's amazement, their first mail from home caught up with them and they were lucky enough to find a hay barn in which to get a couple of hours sleep.

Cyril Helm was not alone in wondering where the German cavalry was. As the BEF retired south of the Somme on 28 August, the distance between Smith-Dorrien and Haig increased to an unhealthy 15 miles and for the first time since Le Cateau, German cavalry found the gap between the two corps south of

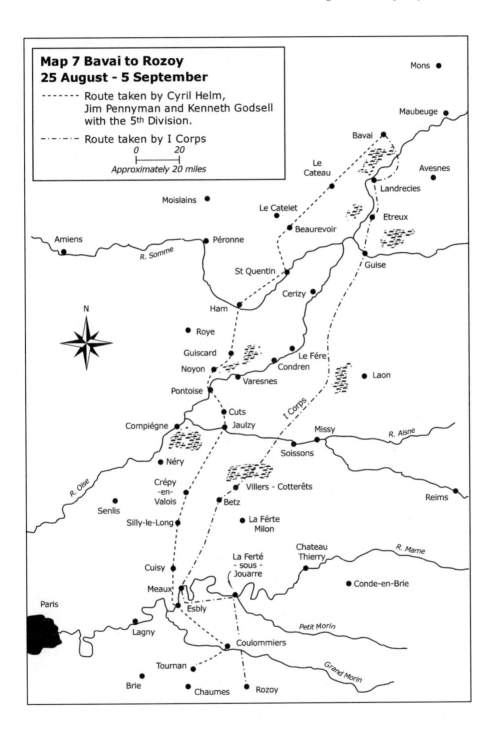

Map 7 Bavai to Rozoy
25 August - 5 September

------- Route taken by Cyril Helm,
Jim Pennyman and Kenneth Godsell
with the 5th Division.

--·---·- Route taken by I Corps

0   20

Approximately 20 miles

Mons

Maubeuge

Bavai

Avesnes

Le
Cateau

Landrecies

Moislains

Le Catelet

Etreux

Beaurevoir

Amiens

Péronne

R. Somme

Guise

St Quentin

Cerizy

Ham

Roye

Guiscard

Le Fére

Noyon

Condren

Varesnes

Laon

Pontoise

Cuts

Compiégne

Jaulzy

Missy

R. Aisne

I Corps

Néry

Soissons

Crépy
-en-
Valois

Villers - Cotterêts

Reims

Betz

Senlis

La Férte
Milon

Silly-le-Long

Chateau
Thierry

R. Marne

Cuisy

La Ferté
- sous -
Jouarre

Meaux

Conde-en-Brie

Paris

Esbly

Lagny

Petit Morin

Tournan

Coulommiers

Grand Morin

Brie

Chaumes

Rozoy

St Quentin. The threat manifested itself in the form of two columns of von Richthofen's 1st Cavalry Corps which now looked as though it was in the perfect position to exploit the weakness. The only British cavalry units available to cover the gap were the three regiments of Gough's 3 Brigade in the west and Chetwode's 5 Brigade which had already crossed the Oise and had taken up positions to the east.

The progress of the most westerly of the German cavalry columns was successfully scuppered by 4/Hussars and the guns of E Battery RHA. Ordered to retire on Benay, one troop of 4/Hussars, under the command of 32-year-old Captain John Gatacre, was thrown out to the right to join up with 5 Cavalry Brigade.[135] Having spotted a troop of enemy cavalry from his vantage point on top of a haystack, he gave the order to mount up and led his troop over the crest of a small rise to take the German cavalrymen completely by surprise. He later recounted to his brigade commander, Brigadier General Gough, the moment they made contact with the enemy:

> *[We] 'gave one wild yell and every horse burst from a steady canter into a full gallop, the Germans also broke into a gallop, but their horses were too slow, our men were soon among them and eight or ten were run through by the swordsmen'.*[136]

Gatacre is credited with killing and wounding three of the enemy himself, Lieutenant James Bibby and Second Lieutenant Falkner were wounded along with Lance Corporal McVann, and two private soldiers – Privates William Morphy and Thomas Munns. The enemy troop was screening the main column of the Guard Cavalry Division which was attempting to outflank 3 Cavalry Brigade on its eastern side. The guns of E Battery were quickly brought into action – putting paid to any further thoughts of offensive action by the German cavalrymen.

The eastern column – led by the German 2nd Dragoon Guards – put up more of a fight. Moving down the main St Quentin-La Fère road towards the hamlet of la Guinguette they occupied La Folie Farm at about 11.30 am seeing off Lieutenant William Callendar's troop of Royal Scots Greys which had been posted to cover the main road. A mile further south Major Foster Swetenham and C Squadron of the Greys were holding a narrow wood to the north of la Guingette, the remaining squadrons of the Greys were concealed amongst the undulating folds in the ground south of the Moÿ-la Guingette road. 20/Hussars were on the high ground near Cerizy, a vantage point which gave them an uninterrupted view to east and west and in reserve were 12/Lancers, who had, by the late afternoon, taken full advantage of the comfortable surroundings and fruit orchards of the nearby 12th century château at Moÿ–de-l'Aisne.

For the next 2 hours the German cavalrymen used La Folie Farm as a forward base from which to push southwards. Although they made a little headway against the rifle and machine-gun fire from the Scots Greys who were well concealed in hedges and small copses, they signally failed to get a clear picture of the strength of the forces opposing them. Little effort was put into any flanking reconnaissance or to gather intelligence as to what forces might be held in reserve. Thus when they eventually launched their attack against what they assumed was weak enemy infantry, they came into contact – much to their surprise – with a British cavalry brigade which, according to the Hon Captain John Darling, 'were longing for a smack at the enemy.'[137]

The attack came shortly after 2.00 pm when a strong German force of two squadrons galloped straight down the slope towards Swetenham's position in the wooded area at la Guingette with the clear intention of testing the strength of the British positions. Allowing the German cavalrymen to get to within 100 yards or so Swetenham's men opened fire with devastating effect, the shock of that initial volley was followed by two guns of J Battery's Number 3 firing over open sights into the mass of disorganized cavalrymen. Those that were not killed or wounded bravely dismounted and returned fire.

Two miles away at Moÿ, Lieutenant Colonel Frank Wormald and 12/Lancers heard shots being fired from the château park.[138] The regiment had 'off saddled' and turned the horses out to graze; the hot August weather prompting both officers and men to cool off in the château lake. Wormald immediately gave orders to saddle up and with his adjutant, Lieutenant Charles Bryant, galloped off in the direction of the firing, closely followed by Captain John Michell with C Squadron. Not wanting to be left out of a fight, Lieutenant William Styles and his machine-gun troop abandoned what they were doing and followed their commanding officer towards the open country north west of the village. Catching sight of the two squadrons of German cavalry which were engaged with the Greys, Wormald's men dismounted and joined the Greys in pouring fire into the German cavalrymen who were still on the forward slope of the hill completely devoid of cover. To make matters worse the Germans' horses stampeded leaving the beleaguered horsemen little choice but to surrender or attempt to retire dismounted back up the hill.

A and B Squadrons of the Lancers had now appeared and were directed by Wormald to move to the enemy's eastern flank and establish a dismounted firing line, the remaining guns of J Battery came into action behind C Squadron and opened fire:

'At this juncture Chetwode returned from a conference with Haig to witness the enemy in a thoroughly unhappy situation. The German cavalrymen were being pounded in front by J Battery, two machine guns and the rapid fire of C Squadron of the 12th Lancers, while being assailed in the flank by that of A and B Squadrons'.[139]

Chetwode was delighted and seizing the opportunity of delivering the final *coup de grace* he took stock of the situation: German cavalrymen were still maintaining a brisk fire from the crest of the ridge to which they had retired and a German battery had come into action to the north. His next move was provided by Charles Bryant who had reconnoitred the ground between C Squadron and the German positions to find it would be possible to approach unseen to within 50 yards of them. Bryant reported to Colonel Wormald 'the wonderful opportunity for a charge' and Wormald in turn informed Chetwode.

There was not a moment to lose, Wormald directed C Squadron to mount up and move at a walk up the steep ridge in line of troop columns. Just before the crest of the ridge was reached the squadron formed line as they topped the ridge, Lieutenant Harold Charrington later recalled the moment:

> '*With a ringing cheer, the squadron charged in perfect line across the fifty yards which now separated them from the enemy, with the Commanding Officer, his Adjutant, the Trumpet Major and two orderlies some twenty yards in front of them*'.[140]

John Michell was killed almost immediately as his horse went over the ridge, Trumpet Major Tompkins was badly wounded in the thigh and one of Wormald's orderlies was killed, the other unhorsed. The German position, wrote Charrington, was completely overrun 'hardly a man escaped, over 70 killed and wounded being counted on the ground afterwards'. Whilst most of the Germans rose to their feet to fight it out they instinctively knew a bloody encounter was about to take place, dismounted men caught in this manner by charging cavalry armed with swords and lances held no advantage. 'Our lances did great work,' wrote Second Lieutenant John Leche, 'though they didn't go in as far as one would think – about a foot in most cases'.[141]

As Michell went down at the head of the squadron, Colonel Wormald, using one of the new pattern Wilkinson thrusting swords, was dismayed to see it 'buckle like an S' as it skewered an unfortunate German. Charles Bryant had retained the old cutting sword and, well sharpened, it accounted for at least 5 of the enemy, 'going in and out like a pat of butter'. As soon as the squadron had ridden through the German position they were rallied by Lieutenant the Hon Richard Wyndham-Quin and charged back through the carnage of dead and dying before being rallied for the last time to dispose of any of the enemy who still had enough fight in them to stand firm. There were none. Indeed by the time the two squadrons of the Greys arrived on the scene the 12/Lancers had done their job so thoroughly that only unwounded prisoners were left to round up.

In the meantime, B and C Squadrons of 20/Hussars had been sent up the St Quentin road by General Chetwode in a bid to get round the western flank of the enemy. As they breasted the rise they came under fire from two guns of the German horse artillery. Lieutenant Colonel Graham Edwards immediately decided to attack the guns, fortunately a charge was out of the question as numerous wire fences were seen in the vicinity. In response the three troops of Captain Cecil Mangles' C Squadron dismounted some 400 yards from the enemy guns and began to put down heavy fire onto the German battery, an action which appeared to have the desired effect as much of the battery's fire was then tuned upon Mangles and his men who had, at least, achieved their aim of distracting the attentions of the German gunners from the main attack to the east. Lieutenant Sparrow's troop which had been directed by Colonel Edwards to cover the right flank, took the opportunity to join in with the main attack and, wrote John Darling, 'had the satisfaction of getting home with their swords against some dismounted Germans' as did the regiment's French interpreter 'Chirby' Landier who, 'achieved the ambition of every Frenchman by killing a Bosche'.

As 12/Lancers crested the ridge at the charge, J Battery concentrated its fire on whatever might be behind the dismounted German cavalry. Number 1 Section joined the two guns of 3 Section and together the four 13-pounders lengthened their range to sweep the hollows and copses to the north with shrapnel – fire which 'proved to be very effective against formed general troops … throwing them into confusion'. The general troops referred to in the battery war diary were in fact infantry of the Guard Rifles who were assembling in a wood near La Folie presumably in preparation for a counter attack – which, had it gone ahead, might very well have put a different slant on the day. Chetwode in recognizing the potential seriousness of this threat, acknowledged J Battery's accurate and timely fire on the Guard Rifles in front of the whole 5 Cavalry Brigade at Autreville, without which he said, 'things might have gone badly for the brigade'.

Fortunately for the wounded, the wagons of 5 Cavalry Field Ambulance were quickly on the scene with their escort of lancers and under the fire from German carbines recovered the wounded of both sides. Apart from John Michell who died at the head of his squadron, Foster Swetenham had also been killed directing fire early in the engagement by the wood at la Guingette. Privates Hugh Nolan, Coote, Hunt and Corporal Gore of C Squadron, 12/Lancers, were also killed during the charge and 31-year-old Trumpet Major Edward Tompkins died from the wounds to his thigh later in the day. The 20/Hussars lost only one man, Lance Corporal William Ryan who died the next day from his wounds.

The highly successful rearguard action at Cerizy – mulishly referred to as the Battle of Moÿ by 12/Lancers – was in direct contrast to the débâcle at Audregnies. At Cerizy Chetwode's brigade had early information of the enemy's movements and the troops which were in position were well concealed from the enemy. The charge – when it came – was a total surprise and in the 30 seconds it took for 12/Lancers to gallop into the mass of dismounted German

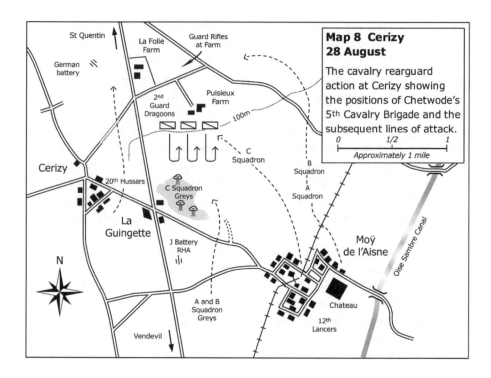

St Quentin
La Folie
Farm
Guard Rifles
at Farm

German
battery

2nd
Guard
Dragoons
Puisieux
Farm
100m

Cerizy

C
Squadron

B
Squadron

20th Hussars

C Squadron
Greys

A
Squadron

La
Guingette

J Battery
RHA

Moÿ
de l'Aisne

N

A and B
Squadron
Greys

Chateau

12th
Lancers

Vendevil

Oise Sambre Canal

**Map 8 Cerizy
28 August**

The cavalry rearguard
action at Cerizy showing
the positions of Chetwode's
5th Cavalry Brigade and the
subsequent lines of attack.

0   1/2   1

Approximately 1 mile

cavalrymen after cresting the ridge, there was little time for the enemy to respond. Crucially, where mounted action was not possible, the dismounted firing lines were highly effective. It was, Charles Darling felt, 'an excellent example of one way in which cavalry can fight a rearguard action'.

If the cavalry felt their day had been one filled with interest and excitement it turned out to be anything but for the sappers. Early on 28 August Major Denis de Vitry, commanding 11/Field Company, was told to reconnoitre three bridges over the Oise for demolition, the first being at one at Beautor and two further east at Condren. Lieutenant Kevin Martin and Number 2 Section was despatched to make the calculations which were checked and sent on to divisional HQ. They heard no more about it until the next day. At Ham the men of 57/Field Company were up at dawn reconnoitring two bridges over the Somme. Both bridges passed close to lock gates on the canalized section of the Somme and whilst Captain Henderson had little difficulty with his, Lieutenant Percy Boulnois – the officer who had cycled up and down the towpath at Mons – had some difficulty in attaching the charges to the three girders which spanned the canal. He was in the process of commandeering a nearby barge to use as a platform for his sappers when the cavalry clattered across above them. 'No hurry', shouted the troop commander, 'no Germans for miles'. The job completed, Boulnois waited for orders to detonate his explosives – an order that

Mons – where it all began. The Grand Place today is still very much as it was on 22 August 1914 when it was full of British troops.

Mons – 23 August 1914: Men of D Company 2nd Battalion KOSB in action along the canal at Les Herbières. The picture was taken by Lieutenant James Pennyman from the window of the white house which housed his machine-gun section. German infantry were on the opposite bank.

Mons - St Symphorien Military Cemetery. Men of the 4th Battalion Middlesex Regiment remain together in death nearly a century later.

Mons – The Nimy bridges. The modern road bridge on the site of the swing bridge and the railway bridge where Lieutenant Dease and Private Godley won the Victoria Cross. Inset: the plaque under the railway bridge commemorating the event.

TO THE GLORIOUS MEMORY OF
THE OFFICERS, N.C.O.s AND MEN OF
THE 4TH BN. ROYAL FUSILIERS
WHO HELD THIS SECTOR OF THE
BRITISH FRONT IN THE DEFENCE
OF THE TOWN OF MONS
AUGUST 23RD 1914.

THIS MEMORIAL
MARKS THE M.G. POSITION WHERE
THE FIRST V.C.s AWARDED DURING
THE WAR 1914-18, WERE GAINED BY
LT M. J. DEASE. V.C.
AND
PTE S. F. GODLEY. V.C.

Lieutenant James 'Jim' Worsley Pennyman in the uniform of the King's Own Scottish Borderers, taken after his promotion to captain. His diary, which he began on 4 August 1914 after the battalion was mobilized, gives a detailed and sometimes quite humorous account of the 2nd Battalion's part in the retreat from Mons. After Le Cateau he found himself in command of a group of Borderers whom he kept together until they were reunited with the battalion at Noyon. He was seriously wounded in September 1914.

Jim Pennyman's luncheon party at Beaurevoir after the Le Cateau retirement on 27 August. Most of the Borderers have still got their weapons and some have picked up non-regulation headwear. Very few of these men would survive beyond 1914.

Cuesmes, 23 August: Men of the 1st Battalion Lincolnshire Regiment barricade the streets. It was here that Gerald Kempthorne and his medical team patched up the Middlesex walking wounded after they had retired.

Hyon, 23 August: Looking north over the narrow bridge at Hyon towards the Bois la Haut. Lieutenant Tandy and the survivors of A Company of the Royal Irish Regiment lined the road here as the Middlesex retired over the bridge towards Cuesmes.

Charles Allix Lavington Yate VC. He commanded B Company of the 2nd KOYLI at Le Cateau. Taken prisoner, he was killed whilst escaping.

Lieutenant Vivian Hugh Wadham, Royal Flying Corps. Killed in action in 1916 near Ypres.

Captain Lionel Evelyn Charlton, Royal Flying Corps. He landed, along with Wadham, close to a large body of German troops on 22 August.

The Blériot gained immortality on 25 July 1909, when Louis Blériot successfully crossed the English Channel. The Royal Flying Corps received its first Blériots in 1912, it was this type of aircraft which was flown by Wadham and Charlton from the RFC aerodrome at Maubeuge on 22 August. Although both officers were qualified pilots, on this occasion Vivian Wadham was flying the machine.

Above: Lieutenant Cyril Helm (seated right) strikes a serious pose with comrades – two of which sport club blazers – during exercises at an unknown location prior to August 1914. Helm joined the 2nd Battalion of the King's Own Yorkshire Light Infantry as medical officer in Ireland before the battalion sailed for France in August 1914. The covered horse-drawn ambulance wagon in the back-ground gives an indication of the equipment being used by RAMC units during the retreat.

Right: Cyril Helm – now sporting a moustache – as a captain, taken in late 1915.

Above Left: Field Marshal Sir John French, C-in-C British Expeditionary Force 1914.
Above Right: Lieutenant General Sir Douglas Haig, GOC I Corps.
Below Left: Lieutenant General Sir Horace Smith-Dorrien, GOC II Corps.
Below Right: Major General Henry Wilson, 'a devious intriguer upon whom Sir John French relied heavily for advice'.

Above: The bridge at Maroilles – scene of the Royal Berkshires' attack on 25 August.

Right: Captain Henry Hammond Shott – killed during the attack on the bridge.

Below: The Communal Cemetery at Maroilles with the private memorial to Henry Shott, erected and paid for by his wife Hazel, to the left of the larger memorial stone.

Etreux Military Cemetery. The mass graves of the Munsters are contained within the walls of the former orchard where the battalion fought its last stand on 27 August.

Lieutenant Colonel Alexander Abercrombie of the Connaught Rangers who was taken prisoner after the rearguard action at Le Grand Fayt.

Major Paul Charrier – Royal Munster Fusiliers.

The road bridge at Compiègne which was blown by Lieutenant Bernard Young on 31 August. *'I cannot describe the feeling of relief with which I saw the bridge go'* he wrote.

Looking north over the Sambre bridge at Landrecies. Number 4 Company of 2nd Grenadier Guards held the bridge on the night of 26 August whilst the remainder of 4 Guards Brigade were engaged at the end of the main street by the railway station.

The estaminet at Vaucelles where George Tailby and his cavalry patrol discovered the German cavalry cloak.

Left: Second Lieutenant George Tailby.

Below: The farmhouse on the Rue des Peupliers, Néry, owned by the Meignen family. It was here that General Briggs established Brigade HQ on the night of 31 August. One of the first German shells is said to have crashed through the roof.

The image of Number 6 Gun, L Battery in action at Néry by the war artist Matania is said to be the most authentic depiction of what took place on the morning of 1 September 1914.

The farmhouse owned by the Debuire family at Néry where the 5th Dragoon Guards officers were billeted. The photo, taken in 1915, shows Madame Marie-Amélie Debuire in the courtyard with French soldiers. The house is still occupied by the family today.

The Chateau at Cuts, which housed General Smith-Dorrien on the night of 28 August, has changed very little over the last 97 years. In August 1914 the surrounding fields would have been full of bivouacking troops and divisional transport units.

The modern road bridge at Pontoise. On 30 August 1914, Lieutenants James Pennycuick and Roger West returned on West's motorcycle to complete the demolition of the partly destroyed suspension bridge.

Alexander Gallaher, 4th Dragoon Guards. He and Sergeant Frederick Hynes successfully escaped from captivity in August 1914. Gallaher was a member of the well known Gallaher tobacco family.

Edward Spears, the British liaison officer with the French Fifth Army.

Lieutenant Jocelyn Hardy. Captured at Le Grand Fayt, he escaped from his POW Camp on his ninth attempt.

Lieutenant Gerald Smyth 17th Field Company RE. The photo was taken in 1916 after he had lost his left arm at Givenchy.

Looking west towards the Ronde de la Reine. It was on the left of this ride that the Grenadier Guards deployed on 1 September.

Kenneth Bruce Godsell taken sometime in 1916 after his award of the Military Cross, the ribbon of which can be seen above his left breast pocket. He was awarded the DSO a year later. Godsell's diary of the retreat and his work as a sapper officer with 17th Field Company provides us with a wonderful account of the trials and tribulations of a young subaltern in the first few weeks of the Great War. He died in 1959.

The memorial to the missing of the Marne at La Ferté-sous-Jouarre. The memorial commemorates nearly 4,000 officers and men of the British Expeditionary Force who died in August, September and the early part of October 1914 and who have no known grave.

Lieutenant Jack Giffard in the dress uniform of the Royal Horse Artillery. Giffard was badly wounded at Néry on 1 September 1914 and evacuated to England after a short period of captivity at Baron. His wounds were such that he did not return to active duty again.

was countermanded a short time later with instructions to withdraw the charges and leave the bridge intact. His language was only surpassed by that of his sappers as they retrieved the charges, which was just as well as shortly afterwards it was used by a French cavalry brigade to cross the canal on their way south.

Kenneth Godsell and his two corporals followed the direction 17/Field Company had taken to Pontoise where Godsell – and presumably Valdo Pottinger as well – got a lift in a car. Corporal Taylor rode the bicycle, now repaired, and Corporal Geraghty was put on an ambulance 'as he had gone lame'. All three met up later at the company bivouac where they had a good meal, a wash and a shave, 'and the first night' rest since the show began'. Pontoise was also the rendezvous for Jim Pennyman and his growing party of Scottish Borderers and it is highly likely that the two officers and their men would have been sharing the route through Ollezy and Guiscard, perhaps within sight of each other. Just before reaching Guiscard they were told by staff officers that 13 Brigade was behind them:

> *'We stopped at Guiscard, and went into an hotel, where we bought and dished out, two cups of coffee, two boiled eggs, and some smokes for each man. Then we all sat outside and watched the troops go by till our brigade appeared, but the Borderers had been on outpost duty and were behind. We didn't wait … At 3pm we got to Noyon and waited for the regiment. During the day we picked up a lot of KOSB stragglers, some of them in motor lorries, and by the time the regiment came up we were quite an imposing party'.*[142]

With the regiment was a smiling Gilbert Amos whom, having got lost at Ham the previous day, had eventually found the second party of Borderers at Ollezy. At Pontoise they were moved further down the road to Pommeraye where they learned that the 3rd Division had had a day's rest before them. After a good meal, wrote Pennyman, 'not a man stirred until 9am the next day'.

59/Field Company had been on the march since 4.00 am and had experienced delay after delay caused by ammunition columns and field ambulance units, a state of affairs not improved at Noyon where they had some difficulty getting through the gridlocked town and over the Canal Lateral to Pontoise. If confusion was apparent on the roads it was certainly noticeable in the minds of some staff officers. Major Walker, who had been ahead of the 59th for most of the day, later recounted his meeting in Noyon with a staff officer who told him that they were all to be put on trains and taken away for a rest. Dismissing the conversation as ridiculous he was somewhat pleasantly surprised on arrival at Pontoise to find not a train, but notice that the next day would indeed be one of rest. 'Heavens how we slept', he wrote, 'and the luxury of a shave!' A few miles further down the road Smith-Dorrien and his staff were surrounded by the 15th century splendour of the château at Cuts, with its pointed gables and terraced walks. He had spent the day talking to his troops and his diary tells us of the pride he felt watching them on the march; 'I was particularly struck', he wrote, 'by the splendid march discipline of the artillery ... they made a brave show as they marched along the road'.

28 August was also a day that was remembered at the French Fifth Army HQ at Marle. Still with Lanrezac's staff as liaison officer, Lieutenant Spears recalled how, 'a large figure which took up the entire breadth of the balcony', suddenly appeared. It was General Joffre himself. This was his first visit to Fifth Army Headquarters and one that Charles Lanrezac would have cause to bring to mind for some time afterwards. In the subsequent interview between the two men Joffre apparently exploded with anger at his subordinate's reluctance to engage the enemy and made it clear that unless Lanrezac counter attacked immediately the Fifth Army would have a new commander. 'Joffre's Olympian anger bore fruit' observed Spears, 'Lanrezac pulled himself together, and on that day at least a wave of energy vibrated down the nerves of the Army such as it had not known since it marched into Belgium.'

The 13 columns of the French Fifth Army had been marching south on a front of about 18 miles, this body of troops was now ordered to about turn and face northwest along a much narrower front. It was to put it mildly, a Herculean task but one that was achieved just in time for the attack to begin at dawn on 29 August. In the hope that Haig would assist him, Lanrezac sent Captain Jacques Helbronner to test the waters of cooperation. Haig was found near Mont D'Origny and to Lanrezac's obvious delight expressed his willingness to support the Fifth Army. Haig's only reservation was that his participation in the attack should be agreed by GHQ. Spears was very apprehensive about this, 'I hoped and prayed that Sir Douglas's views would prevail with Sir John but felt terribly uncertain'.

His apprehension was not unfounded; Sir John French refused point blank to cooperate and used as his justification the poor state of his troops – a further indication of the misapprehension that prevailed at the altogether too distant GHQ. The British I Corps was perfectly placed and well able to assist the French. The complaint that Lanrezac's refusal to fight was putting too great a pressure on the BEF – which Sir John had taken to the St Quentin conference two days earlier – had now backfired.

With the French turning to face the German Second Army at Guise, it appeared that Sir John was now getting his own back by rather petulantly refusing to support the French. Spears was horrified. The animosity created between the two army commanders at their first meeting at Rethel had come home to roost. For the first time since the war began the young lieutenant felt the British were in the wrong.

Chapter 11

29 to 31 August – Blowing Bridges In Our Sleep

While the BEF rested the Battle of Guise opened at dawn with French Fifth Army units pushing northwest towards St Quentin. Hardly had the opening shots been fired when Joffre made another unannounced appearance at Fifth Army HQ which had now moved to the hilltop city of Laon. The French fought well and under the eye of his chief, Charles Lanrezac directed his units with a decisiveness and skill that belied his earlier reluctance to turn and fight. Although the ground they took from von Bülow was only temporary, the sight of Germans being forced to retreat for the first time was a tonic in itself. Reeling from the shock of the French advance, von Bülow initially called on von Kluck for help, a call which, although unnecessary, was in itself was not entirely responsible for the German First Army changing its direction of march. Von Kluck's change of direction the next day, when he swung the German First Army through 90 degrees in a south easterly direction, was driven by two factors: the realization that he no longer had the men and material to continue his right flanking movement to the west of Paris and the opportunity that now presented itself to bear down on Lanrezac's flank and deliver what he considered would be the *coup de grace* to the Fifth Army.

Unquestionably Guise was a French victory in that it stopped von Bülow in his tracks for 36 hours, broke the solidarity and integrity of the German right hook and, incidentally, put the final nail into the coffin of the Schlieffen Plan. Perhaps more importantly in the long run, it took the pressure off General Michel-Joseph Maunoury's Sixth Army enabling Joffre to move Maunoury to a position where he would play a vital part in the coming Battle of the Marne. As far as the British were concerned, von Kluck's move to the southeast brought the German First Army back into contact with the BEF, the result of which would be felt directly by both the British Army Corps on 1 September.

Not every unit of the BEF were able to rest on 29 August. That morning the German 2nd Cavalry Corps was ordered to carry out a reconnaissance towards Noyon. Crossing the Somme and Crozat Canal at Ham and St Simon – over the very two bridges that had been prepared for demolition by Gerald Smyth and Percy Boulnois and then left intact – they came into contact with 4/Hussars formed up and ready to march. In the brisk fight which ensued the Hussars managed to beat off a force of cavalry and Jägers, the adjutant, Captain Henry Evans, reporting gleefully that Corporal Fred Sharpe managed to run one of the Uhlans through with his sword. South of Ham, billeted amongst the small hamlets and farms, was most of de Lisle's now reformed 2 Brigade and Brigadier General Charles Briggs' 1 Brigade. L Battery and Jack Giffard had spent the previous night in a farmhouse at Berlancourt, a small village to the east of the main Ham-Noyon road. Up and ready to move the next morning at the usual 4.00 am they were kept waiting – kicking their heels until 11.00 am:

> *'We were suddenly attacked by a German force of Uhlans, infantry and field guns ... My section was ordered up to the north of the village and the rest of the battery retired [to] the other side'.*[143]

Barely a mile to the north at Le Plessis, 4/Dragoons were falling in on parade when the first rounds from German horse artillery fell in the village and at Jussy to the southeast of St Simon, 16/Lancers from Gough's Brigade were driven out of the village but managed to hold their own until the bridge, prepared for demolition on 26 August by Lieutenant Robert Flint and his sappers, was destroyed.

As the main body of cavalry began retiring towards Guiscard, L Battery came into action against the German cavalry, Jack Giffard reckoned his two guns 'did a bit of good and the [German] cavalry got hotted up a bit'. After an hour or so the battery retired to a small ridge to the south of the village, Major Sclater-Booth taking four guns to the west towards Beines and sending Giffard to cover any enemy advance to the east of the main road. Giffard's diary again:

> *'We did a good deal of shooting and I enjoyed several hours up in an apple tree, eating delicious apples and shelling Germans! I had a bit of open country to watch and Uhlans and infantry kept on coming down in extended lines but turned back every time when I got into them, range 2800 to 3200 feet.'*

L Battery appeared to have been fortunate in that the enemy shellfire was inaccurate and the battery's guns were able to be withdrawn to cover the cavalry's retirement. Crossing the Oise at Noyon they finally reached Bailly at 10.00 pm that evening. It had been a long day and a costly one for the cavalry; 4/Dragoon Guards losing 1 officer and 19 other ranks taken prisoner and 2 Cavalry Brigade losing a good many horses.

South of Noyon, surrounded by open fields and grazing land, the château at Cuts was the ideal bivouac for many of the II Corps units including 4/Middlesex which had marched 20 miles that day. Major Herbert Stewart and his HQ Company of the 3rd Divisional Train also spent the night of 29 August there:

'Late that night I went up to the château for orders, the lights from the windows reflected into the waters of the moat surrounding the house made it look like a fairy palace. Entering the mansion, I found several officers snatching a few hours sleep in long cane chairs on the hall. Off the hall was a large room, the sides of which a dozen or more beds without bedding were ranged. Stretched upon the mattresses on these beds were officers and orderlies, booted, and spurred, deep in slumber. In the dining room the table was spread with food and drink for those who had time to snatch it. In another room the General [Smith-Dorrien] *and a few of his staff were pouring over maps and writing orders'.*[144]

The surroundings in which Kenneth Godsell and his sappers of 17/Field Squadron awoke were not quite so well-appointed, but refreshed by their unbroken sleep, they at least got their first mail from home that morning and Godsell even received a welcome parcel of cigarettes and chocolate. However, any further thoughts the II Corps sappers had of getting their feet up were frustrated that afternoon with the arrival of orders to prepare the Oise bridges for demolition. A busy time lay ahead and for the next few days, remarked James Pennycuick, 'we were blowing bridges in our sleep'.

By the evening of 29 August the main body of II Corps was south of the Oise crossings and none of the sappers were under any illusions that destroying the seemingly endless number of bridges was going to be straightforward. Alongside and north of the Oise – which meandered its way lazily across the landscape – was the Canal Lateral, each crossing was therefore spanned by two bridges, one across the canal and a second over the river. In some places the gap between the two waterways could be anything up to a mile wide and therefore open to enemy incursion.

At 1.00 pm orders arrived for 59/Field Company to prepare the four girder bridges at Varesnes for demolition; three of these spanned the canal while the fourth crossed the Oise. James Pennycuick and the sappers of his Number 1 Section were allotted the big bridge over the Oise – 'a real big one' wrote Pennycuick, 'which made a spectacular collapse' – while 20 year-old-Second Lieutenant Arthur Carr and Lieutenant Robert Flint dealt with the others.[145] Unbeknown to the sappers a German cavalry patrol had already penetrated the ground between the two waterways and in a short fire fight wounded and captured two of Arthur Carr's sappers. The two men escaped the following morning when the German cavalry were shot up by a British rearguard.

It wasn't long before Kenneth Godsell and Gerald Smyth were loaded up with orders to prepare the two bridges on the Pontoise-Noyon road. There was little trouble with the canal bridge which was blown at dawn on 30 August as the last of the rearguard crossed the canal. The second bridge over the Oise was a different proposition; Smyth successfully placed his three slabs of guncotton on the main cables of the suspension bridge and waited for the last troops to cross. Lieutenant 'Papa' Yates of the Royal Welch Fusiliers remembered sharing his bread and jam with Gerald Smyth shortly before he fired the charges, 'the effect was only partial' he wrote 'and later we heard two sapper officers went back and completed the job'. The two inch round steel cables on either side of the bridge had absorbed the explosion and the bridge remained infuriatingly intact! A second attempt – this time with the remaining few slabs of guncotton – was equally unsuccessful as was the attempt to set fire to the wooden decking of the bridge. With no further supplies of guncotton, there was no choice left to Smyth but to inform divisional headquarters and leave the bridge intact.

James Pennycuick and the 59th had only just left their bivouac at Varesnes at first light on 30 August when Lieutenant Roger West, a motor cycle despatch rider with the Intelligence Corps, arrived with a note for Major Walker to say the Pontoise suspension bridge was still intact. Pennycuick immediately volunteered to go back and see if anything could be done to finish the structure off once and for all. Travelling the 8 miles back to Pontoise on the rather precarious pillion seat of Roger West's motorcycle – with his pockets stuffed with primers and detonators and balancing fourteen slabs of guncotton on his lap – the two officers arrived at the bridge:

> *'Climbing up the back anchorage cables proved to be unexpectedly easy. West swarmed up to the top of one of the piers while I was tearing open the box of guncotton. With so solid a bridge it seemed wisest to put all the available explosive into one charge. The slabs, except for one which we dropped into the river were heaved up and fitted perfectly into the cavity between the cables.'*[146]

Just as they were about to fire the charge a Frenchman cycled slowly across the bridge. 'We took cover behind a pier and sprang out on him with revolvers cocked. The man, encumbered with a rifle, fell off his bicycle and subsided onto his knees in prayer'. Confiscating the rifle, the unfortunate Frenchman was told to go away as Pennycuick operated the exploder. Unbelievably it failed to work. There was no time to wait the usual 20 minutes before investigating the cause; clambering back up the cables to the top of the bridge the faulty detonator and primer was replaced. This time all went to plan:

> *'The entire top of the pier was blown away, both main cables on that side were cut, with their ends twisted back over the anchorage. The bridge itself dropped drunkenly down almost to the water, one side of it hanging by a few unbroken ties from the other main cables.'*[147]

The orders for the demolition of the bridges between Pont l'Evêque and Sempigny reached 7/Field Company about noon on 29 August and work went on all night whilst the 4th Division was crossing. At the same time the sappers of 9/Field Company prepared the bridges at Ourscamp, Primprez and Bailly.

Despite all the bridges being ready just after dawn the next day, orders from Brigadier General Aylmer Haldane, commanding 10 Infantry Brigade, arrived at 5.00 am to the effect that one company of Irish Fusiliers was still north of the canal and demolition was not to go ahead until they were across. Sometime after noon the missing company turned up and all the bridges were blown with the exception of the crossing at Bailly. At Sempigny Lieutenant Kenneth Gourlay and his section were completing the job under fire from dismounted German cavalry which had crossed the canal by boat. Haldane's diary recorded the last moments before Gourlay blew the bridge:

'*The engineer officer at the bridge, whose situation was a critical one, hurriedly withdrew his men and ordered the village to be evacuated. Bullets were now falling thickly, and crashing through the windows of the houses, causing the horses of the engineer's tool cart to stampede with that vehicle. But the engineer officer was not to be diverted from his duty ... and pressed the handle down. The charge exploded instantaneously, blowing a huge gap in the bridge and causing several houses in the village to collapse*'.[148]

All but two of Gourlay's party escaped courtesy of 9/Lancers which provided some timely equine transport; unfortunately Sappers Coleman and Butler were wounded and taken prisoner.

But not everything went according to plan. Orders and counter orders had played their part in creating a confusion that had allowed the bridge at Bailly to be left and when the final and somewhat last minute order went out for the bridge to be demolished at 5.55 pm on 29 August it was already too late. When the orders to blow the Bailly bridge reached 9/Field Company they were still at Cuts and it was already nearly dark. The lot fell to Lieutenant Charles Fishbourne who started out at 9.00 pm in a lorry to find the bridge. The promised infantry escort failed to turn up prompting the commanding officer, Major John Barstow, to join the party with a couple a sappers in case of trouble. Barstow was an experienced officer having been commissioned into the Royal Engineers in 1891 and appointed commanding officer of 9/Field Company at the outbreak of war after 20 years with the Indian Army at Bangalore.

The bridge was no more than nine miles from Cuts but delays in looking for the cavalry escort and some route finding difficulties through the densely wooded area in the dark meant that they did not arrive until the early hours of 30 August. Leaving the lorry 2 miles outside Bailly on the Ollencourt road they moved cautiously on foot towards the bridge. The question as to whether the bridge was in enemy hands or not was answered by a volley of fire at close range. A cavalry patrol, under the command of Lieutenant von Berkheim of 3/Uhlans from the German Guard Cavalry Division, was in possession of the crossing. Corporal Edward Sullivan thinks the German sentry allowed the party to approach the bridge before opening fire, he saw Major Barstow struggling with one of the Germans before running back shouting for the party to take cover. Sullivan was hit by a ricochet in the eye and remembered lying next to a wounded Barstow who was groaning in pain. The remainder of the party – three of them wounded – withdrew at 5.00 am leaving a badly wounded Corporal Stone and John Barstow – whom they presumed to be dead – beside the road. Had the bridge been destroyed earlier in the day it could have been achieved without any trouble or loss of life.[149]

On the morning of 30 August GHQ was still at Compiègne and Brigadier General George Fowke, Engineering Advisor to GHQ, was told to see to the blowing of the road bridge. A wire to II Corps requesting a party of engineers with 'the necessary tools and explosives' resulted in Lieutenant Bernard Young and his section from 9/Field Company arriving at 6.00 pm. Young was staggered by the size job in front of him – this was very much a case of 'here's a bridge – find a sapper' – and was much relieved by the presence of another RE officer, Captain Stewart Newcombe, who had been put in charge of the preparations by Fowke. Young's first impression – that it looked more like Westminster Bridge – was not short of the mark, the bridge he was looking at was a very solid 18th century stone structure with three arches which initial calculations suggested required a substantial quantity of explosives to destroy it and considerably more than Young had brought with him on the section's tool cart.

With urgent messages sent to the French for explosives – which appeared with remarkable ease by train later in the day – the British sappers managed to find a French territorial officer who produced plans of the bridge and, as luck would have it, revealed the presence of demolition chambers which had been built into the structure. Young calculated that it would still require 400lbs of guncotton in each of the two chambers, a task the sappers now began by lowering the charges down to Newcombe who positioned himself in the base of each of the chambers in turn. During the afternoon the French explosives arrived and duly went down each shaft to add weight to the final detonation.

By 2.00 am on 31 August the bridge was ready. Young sent his sappers away to rejoin the main column and as soon as the last of the cavalry rearguard was safely across – Jack Giffard and L Battery was in one of these units – General Fowke gave him the order to fire. Silence! The exploder – which was later found to have a damaged contact – had failed. Young was mortified. Here he was, as he later recounted, a very junior lieutenant with the Chief RE Officer watching his every move at a crucial point in the retreat and his circuit had failed. 'I think all Sapper subalterns will appreciate my feelings at that precise moment when I say nothing happened – just absolutely nothing'. With a quick glance at Newcombe, who was signalling him to strike a match, he lit the standby safety fuse and ran for cover. 30 seconds later the two arches which spanned the river vanished in a cloud of dust into the depths of the river.

'I cannot describe the feeling of relief with which I saw the bridge go; if it had failed, I imagine I could have written finis across my future career! Anyhow, I came to, so to speak, conscious that I was holding out my hand to Newcombe and feeling rather an ass. However, Newcombe was made of sterner stuff, and I don't think had any idea that I felt like shaking hands all round, and he very prosaically, seeing my outstretched hand, passed over the key of the ill fated exploder!'[150]

Young, breathing a sigh of relief, put his bicycle into the back of Newcombe's car and headed south towards the River Aisne.

By 30 August the Cavalry Division – with the exception of Gough's 3 Brigade which was now under Haig's direction – was reunited and back under the direct command of Allenby. Up until this point in the retreat the cavalry brigades had been scattered far and wide and in some cases regiments had been composed of officers and men from several different units who, having become detached, joined up with the next mounted unit they came across. There were several instances of men from former mounted infantry units fighting alongside their cavalry contemporaries and dismounted cavalrymen fighting – and dying – with the infantry. Allenby's lack of a coherent staff structure together with the maverick nature of his cavalry commanders had not been a recipe for effective cohesion. Generally speaking the German cavalry had not got the better of their British counterparts during the retreat and the cavalry division had shown itself to be far superior in both tactics and training. There was, however, one minor cavalry clash during this period where things did not go as well as might have been wished.

The story begins with Major Herbert Stewart and his ASC supply column. On 30 August Brigadier General Shaw's 9 Infantry Brigade had passed through Morsain on their way to cross the Aisne further south. The brigade halted at Morsain and Stewart left one of his subalterns to requisition supplies while he continued with a staff officer to make arrangements for the arrival of the troops at Berny-Rivière that evening. It was not until much later in the evening that Stewart discovered the young officer was missing and no one appeared to have seen him since Morsain.[151] This was not entirely unusual; during the retreat individuals often became detached from their parent units and turned up several days later, albeit a little footsore and a little leaner!

In the meantime, towards dusk, a troop of 3/Hussars had entered Morsain and found the lone officer sitting next to his recently purchased supplies waiting to be collected. Apparently, whilst he was paying for the supplies the column had moved off and so had his horse, leaving him – so he later related to Herbert Stewart – with no idea of which way they had gone. Morsain was by this time behind enemy lines and the Hussars were forming part of the 4 Cavalry Brigade rearguard with orders to remain in the village until the next morning.

Accordingly they occupied and barricaded themselves into a large house just off the main street and awaited developments. Twice that night they beat off marauding German cavalry patrols and at dawn they left and incredibly, having no spare horses, they abandoned the young ASC officer to his fate!

At 5.00 am on 31 August Stewart received a message from Divisional HQ to say that a telephone message had been received from an anxious officer at Morsain who needed to be fetched urgently as there were 'bodies of Uhlans in the neighbourhood'. Stewart set off to collect his missing subaltern:

'We pushed the car to its best speed along the winding valley road. Every moment I expected to round a bend and find a patrol of Uhlans blocking the way. At Morsain, standing in the middle of the deserted main street, was [Stewart does not give his name], *anxiety written all over his face, which changed to relief when he recognized me. We wasted no time in turning the car, and returned as fast as we had come to Berny-Rivière'.*[152]

Whatever the reader might think with regard to the lack of initiative displayed by Stewart's subaltern – or indeed to the appalling disregard demonstrated by the hussars in leaving the poor fellow – he did redeem himself a little by finding a telephone in the by now deserted village and – to his amazement as much as mine – managed to get through to divisional headquarters. I imagine the conversation between Stewart and his subaltern on the return journey touched on the necessity of tethering one's horse securely and taking due note of the direction of the day's march.

Entering now into the last instalment of the Morsain story were the 5/Lancers. Ordered to relieve 3/Hussars – which had apparently left the village at dawn without waiting for their relief – Lieutenant George Juler and two troops from A Squadron approached Morsain – evidently after Stewart had rescued his missing subaltern – and advanced towards the high ground to the west. Here they confronted a squadron of German cavalry from 10/Uhlan Regiment and pursued them back into the village. Juler and his men, in their eagerness to get at the German horsemen, were outmanoeuvred and their retreat was quickly cut off by another body of horsemen led by Lieutenant von Seydlitz who had moved round the village from the north. In the ensuing fight Juler and Sergeant Charles Dale were killed and the remainder taken prisoner. Von Poseck in his account of the skirmish tells us a large number 'of the English were shot from their horses with the revolver or thrust through with the lance'.[153]

* * *

On 30 August the gap between Haig's I Corps and Smith Dorrien's II Corps finally closed and a day later, on 31 August 1914, III Corps came into being under the command of Major General William Pulteney comprising of the 4th

Division and the independent 19 Infantry Brigade which was later temporarily absorbed into the 6th Division when the latter landed in France on 10 September. Marching west, Pulteney's Corps moved down the western bank of the Oise and reached the neighbourhood of Verberie late that night. Haig and I Corps crossed the Aisne at Soissons, the 5th and 23rd Field Companies blowing the bridges behind them.

31 August had been another desperately hot day for the marching troops, one which had compelled Haig to break off his march short of the intended destinations. Drummer Whittington and his mate George Scutt with 2/Royal Sussex thought that 'it was so hot that the men were falling out and even dropping down in the road in dozens. It was killing'. They were also hungry, 'we have been for at least 5 days without a dinner at all', wrote Whittington rather wistfully that evening at Verte Feuille on the north eastern rim of the Forêt de Retz. Thus, with the heat of the day dispersing with the cool of the evening, I Corps had drawn up for the night on the northern edge of the Forêt de Retz along a line Laversine-St Pierre Aigle – Verte Feuille.

The heat of the day had not gone unnoticed by Jim Pennyman and the KOSB who were en route to Crépy-en-Valois with the 5th Division. The previous day had been a long and tiring one and although they had halted 10 miles east of Compiègne at 3.00 pm at what Pennyman described as a good billet, Monday 31 August was particularly difficult. It began with the long steep ascent out of the Aisne valley. It reminded him of his service in India:

> *'We carried on right through the heat of the day, which was quite Eastern in its intensity. My place was at the rear of the battalion and it was a desperate job to get the men along. The NCOs were as tired as the men and the few officers that were left had to do all the job'.*[154]

That evening the Borderers were billeted in what Pennyman described as such an 'uncomfortable farm' that they all slept out in the garden, but at least they were not on outpost duty, it was the turn of the West Kents who would be the first to encounter the German Jägers the next morning.

II Corps was now halted for the night southwest of Villers-Cotterêts at Croyolles and at Crépy-en-Valois. The astute observer looking at the map will quickly recognize that there were quite considerable gaps between the five infantry divisions of the BEF, gaps through which large bodies of German forces could pass unnoticed. The source of the problem lay almost entirely with GHQ's Operational Order Number 12 which failed to establish the boundaries for which each formation was to be responsible and left it up to each corps commander to decide how much of the area allocated to them would be used. 'To the rather amateur wording of this particular order' wrote the 11/Hussars historian, 'much of what happened on 1st September can be directly traced.'

Chapter 12

1 September – Néry, the Chance Encounter

Brigadier General Charles Briggs had been a cavalry officer since 1886. Commissioned into the 1st King's Dragoon Guards from Sandhurst, he had been in command of 1 Cavalry Brigade since 1912. In South Africa, where he had been wounded at Magersfontein during the Second Boer War, he had often demonstrated his skill as a cavalry commander, being twice mentioned in despatches whilst in command of a regiment of the Imperial Light Horse. Now he was about to have another opportunity to show his mettle as a commander in an encounter the impact of which would run far deeper than any of those who fought at the small village of Néry on that misty morning on the first day of September 1914 could ever have imagined.

Since the skirmish at Bethancourt two days earlier 1 Cavalry Brigade had had relatively little contact with the enemy. Weary through lack of sleep and constant patrolling, many of the officers and men were beginning to wonder if the retreat would ever end. On the evening of 31 August, after a day spent reconnoitring the western bank of the Oise for signs of enemy cavalry, the brigade trotted into Sarron expecting to find billets for the night. Instead they found a French cavalry brigade had beaten them to it giving them little choice but to re-cross the Oise at Verberie, to where the 4th Division had its overnight headquarters.

At Verberie Briggs was informed that Néry – although in the II Corps overnight billeting area – had not been occupied by any of Smith-Dorrien's units and could be used by his brigade. In fact II Corps was not using any of the villages west of Crépy-en-Valois, the significance of which was apparently not fully appreciated by either Briggs or General Snow. Charles Briggs, although satisfied there were no German troops west of the Oise, was now heading for a village which lay in an extensive and undefended gap between the 4th Division and II Corps at Crépy-en-Valois. It was through this gap that danger would ultimately ride in the shape of the German 4th Cavalry Division.

The task of protecting the left flank of von Kluck's First Army as it wheeled southeast was left to General Georg von der Marwitz and his II Cavalry Corps.

His orders were to move swiftly against the French Fifth Army as they retreated south after the Battle of Guise and in response von der Marwitz had been pushing his cavalry divisions hard in order to catch Lanrezac's flank. Late in the afternoon of 31 August, Marwitz was at Offemont on the eastern edge of the Forêt de Laigue, where he received word from First Army intelligence that pointed towards the presence of BEF columns near Soissons and Crépy-en-Valois. For the cavalry general it was an opportunity not to be missed; if he turned south and marched overnight he knew he could be in contact with the British early the following day.

The German 4th Cavalry Division, commanded by General Otto von Garnier, had crossed the Oise using the wooden suspension bridge at Longueil and reached Offemont at 4.00 pm where it expected to halt overnight. Von Garnier had left the division's regimental and first line transport – which included the ammunition column – at Longueil in order to shorten the column as it crossed the bridge, anticipating it would catch up later that evening. But the news that the division was to undertake a night march south almost immediately – one can almost hear the stifled groans from the German cavalrymen – meant its units would be even further separated from their ammunition and supplies. It was to be a decision that von Garnier would dearly regret the next day. That night von Garnier's division crossed the Aisne at Rethondes and continued through the darkness of the Forêt de Compiègne until, just as dawn was breaking, the small village of Béthisy St Martin hove into view through the dense early morning mist. They were a mile and a half from Néry.

11/Hussars had been acting as the advance guard for the British 1 Cavalry Brigade on 31 August. Having placed outposts around the village of Néry to cover the arrival of 5/Dragoon Guards and 2/Dragoon Guards (Queen's Bays), they moved to the east side of the village and billeted in the large enclosed farm next to the church. L Battery was the last unit to arrive and conscious of the difficulty of watering large numbers of horses so late in the day, Major Sclater-Booth had halted at Verberie to water the battery's horses there. On arrival at Néry the battery was allocated the large triangular shaped field between the village and the sugar factory along the minor road that ran to Rully. The battery officers had the use of a room in a nearby cottage and the men were billeted at the sugar factory. 5/Dragoon Guards were allocated the north end of the village and whilst the officers were accommodated in the farmhouse belonging to the Debuire family on the Rue de Chalfont, the men and horses were in the open field and farm buildings opposite the village cemetery. The Queen's Bays meanwhile had drawn up around the village crossroads close to the field occupied by L Battery and a short distance from brigade headquarters which was in a farmhouse belonging to the Meignen family on the Rue des Peupliers opposite the Mairie, Néry stands on the western edge of a deep ravine chiselled out by the River Douvre as it flows north into the larger Automme valley. The ravine – which is usually dry in the summer – is a wide, flat-bottomed feature that is at its steepest on the eastern side as it climbs up again to the high ground of Le Mont Bethizoy. Unlike today, in 1914 the ravine was almost entirely devoid of vegetation apart from the eastern side which was dotted with bushes and trees. Thus, approaching the village from the direction of Béthisy St Martin as the German Cavalry 4th Division was doing, the ravine formed a formidable natural obstacle, which, for the British Cavalry Brigade in the village, proved to be of great advantage during the coming engagement. Brigade standing orders during the retreat allowed for each unit to be responsible for the defence of its own area and in the event of a night attack to hold and fight its own ground. Briggs – rightly or wrongly – had assumed that the general outpost line to the north was covered by infantry units, an assumption that led to the decision not to extend his piquet line beyond the edge of the village and to delay sending out patrols until first light the next day.

At first light the dense mist that had greeted von Garnier's men at Béthisy St Martin also cloaked the village of Néry, it was clearly going to be another scorching hot day but for the time being the misty start delayed the departure of the British from the village. Private William Bull with L Battery recalled they had reveille at 2.30 am in preparation for moving out at 4.00 am but the thick mist resulted in orders to stand fast: 'the horses were unharnessed and fed and some of the men commenced washing themselves'. However, in spite of the mist, each of the three cavalry regiments sent out their patrols at first light.

Second Lieutenant George Tailby had been instructed to reconnoitre the high ground to the east and south east of the village for any signs of enemy movement to the north. The 19-year-old Tailby – known throughout the regiment as 'the tapeworm' on account of his height – had only been with 11/Hussars for 7 months since passing out of Sandhurst and was the most junior officer in the regiment. On account of his inexperience, Captain John Halliday, had carefully selected five men from B Squadron to accompany the young officer on his first ever patrol:

> '*I took the quickest route out of the village towards the plateau and leaving the main road, stuck off in a north easterly direction down a track in the direction of the ridge, crossed the little brook and almost immediately found the steep slopes of the plateau facing me. It was too steep to ride straight up ... when on the top I found the fog as dense as ever and decided to look round the edge of the plateau*'.[155]

Tailby's patrol had almost completed a circuit of the plateau without coming across any hostile forces when there was a slight shifting of the fog:

> '*I perceived, at about 150 yards distance to the east, a column of cavalry. By their appearance of their long cloaks and spiked helmets, I knew they could be none*

other than the much-heard-of Uhlans. They did not see us, however, for they were dismounted, in sections, and appeared to have lost their bearings'.[156]

At that moment one of his men fired at the enemy and all hell broke loose. With a slight advantage gained as the Germans mounted up and wheeled about, Tailby's patrol managed to find and begin to descend a steep track down the eastern edge of the plateau hotly pursued by the German cavalrymen. Incredibly the young officer and his horse survived a fall and continued down the slope to Vaucelles where he saw, outside the village estaminet, a German cavalryman's cloak and a Mauser carbine – proof positive of the presence of German forces in the vicinity. 'No doubt [the Germans] heard us gallop down the hill and went off in a hurry ... I picked up the cloak and galloped on' recounted Tailby.

At Néry the peace of the morning was broken by the sound of galloping horses, a laconic remark from 5/Dragoon Guards' outpost line about the dangers of galloping in thick mist was greeted by the flushed form of the young Tailby whom, on arriving back at the farmyard, jumped off his horse and presented his intelligence to his commanding officer, Lieutenant Colonel Tommy Pitman. Pitman was an almost legendary figure in the regiment – 'bow legged from a lifetime spent on horseback, as fit as a desert horseman and built more for convenience than beauty' – he was an imposing figure and did not

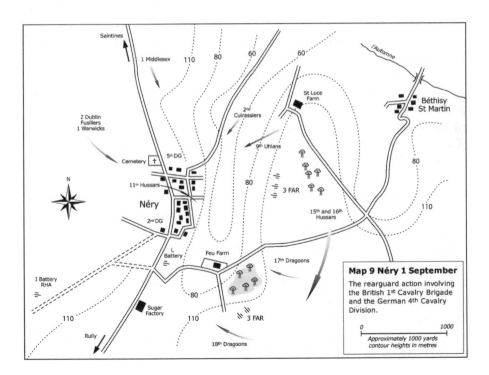

Map 9 Néry 1 September

The rearguard action involving the British 1st Cavalry Brigade and the German 4th Cavalry Division.

0   1000

Approximately 1000 yards
contour heights in metres

suffer fools gladly. Having listened to Tailby's report he dismissed the presence of German cavalry as nonsense, 'A fog is no excuse for seeing spooks, return to your patrol immediately', was Pitman's reply, 'If you saw anyone it could have only been French cavalry'. Tailby turned to one of his men who, unable to suppress a broad grin, stepped forward and handed over the grey-green German cavalry cloak for the colonel to examine. It was indisputable evidence and it sent Pitman scurrying off to report to Briggs at brigade HQ immediately.

Once von Garnier had heard from his patrols that an unsuspecting British force lay ahead of him he decided to attack at once to capitalize on the element of surprise. His plan of attack was relatively simple; he positioned eight of the twelve guns of Field Artillery Regiment 3 with machine guns on the plateau facing the eastern end of the village across the ravine and one battery of four guns to the south where they could bring a devastating enfilading fire down on the British lines. Under the cover of this fire he would then launch a mounted attack on Néry from the north and south east. What is astonishing about this plan, however, is von Garnier's failure to reconnoitre the ground ahead of him before committing his forces. He knew nothing about the length or depth of the British positions at Néry or for that matter the extent of the large gap between Néry and Crépy-en-Valois. Had he sent out flanking patrols he would have realized Briggs' force could easily have been isolated and routed. This was not the first occasion when German cavalry had failed to test the water before committing themselves, exactly the same tactical error had occurred at Cerisy four days previously.

That said von Garnier's opening bombardment, which began exactly at 5.40 am, came as a complete surprise to the British.[157] Tommy Pitman had just returned from brigade HQ when the first of hundreds of shells began to fall on the village. In the Bays' horse lines the panicking animals were killed in rows whilst other stampeded and bolted in all directions. At the northern edge of the village 5/Dragoon Guards were also subjected to shell fire and had their first glimpse of enemy cavalry from their in-lying picquet position – the same positions Tailby had galloped through minutes earlier – near the village cemetery. It was from here that Lieutenant Montague Burrows directed his machine-gun fire at the approaching cavalrymen from von Garnier's 3 Brigade.

The 11/Hussars – who had complained about being billeted in a rather smelly farmyard – now realized their good fortune and took up their positions by the church and along the eastern walls of the farm overlooking the ravine. The second-in-command of the regiment, Major Rowland Anderson, had woken that morning with a premonition of some impending doom and had made himself somewhat unpopular by deploying the regiment along its defensive line – a drill that was now speedily repeated as Anderson ordered them into their firing positions. At brigade HQ one of the first shells to land on the village was said to have crashed through the roof of the Meignen farmhouse where Briggs and his Brigade Major, John Cawley, had just received word of the presence of German cavalry from Tommy Pitman. Picking up the time fuse Briggs saw it was set for 800 metres and that it was of German origin. Immediately he sent out two motor cycle despatch riders to the nearest British units asking for assistance before leaving for 11/Hussars' lines with Cawley.

Major Walter Sclater-Booth – who was also at brigade HQ when the alarm was raised – was destined to miss the whole action. As he ran back down the road toward the battery with his bugler, Corporal Harry Goold, a bursting shell knocked him unconscious somewhere near the village crossroads. There he remained until found well after the action had concluded. A few yards further down the Rully road towards the sugar factory, where the road forms a sunken lane, Jack Giffard and Sergeant Charles Weedon were extremely fortunate not to have been killed in the opening salvo:

> '*I was trotting a horse down the road and examining his hind fetlock when suddenly a terrific burst of shrapnel and rifle and machine-gun fire was opened onto us at a range of 600 to 800 yards. No-one had the slightest idea of there being any Germans in the vicinity. The horse was killed at the first burst and I and Sgt Weedon dropped into the road and crawled along to one side of the camp.*'[158]

William Bull had been about to join his section of L Battery in their ablutions when the German attack began; he did not consider for a moment that what he was hearing was hostile gunfire. He had only just removed his equipment and stripped off his outer clothing when:

> '*We received a shell from the enemy, which at the time we thought was an ammunition wagon exploded. At the time there was a thick mist but as it lifted we could see a battery coming into action which we thought was French Artillery. Presently we were swept with a heavy gun fire and in a few moments all the horses were shot.*'[159]

The Royal Artillery historian described the next few moments as the battery recovered from its initial shock and began to deploy:

> '*At the guns, the left section was watering at the sugar factory as the first shells burst right amongst the massed horses of the rest of the battery. Captain* [Edward] *Bradbury was standing …with the subalterns* [John] *Campbell,* [Jack] *Giffard and* [Lionel] *Mundy; he shouted, "Come on, who's for the guns?" The officers and a number of the men raced towards them and began to unlimber B and D sub-sections. They were sorely hampered by the horses tied to the wheels, and the rest plunging terrified, many wounded, as the German shells crashed into the field.*

> *Eventually they freed the two guns and turned them to face twelve German guns lining the edge of the high ground some 500 yards away to the east.'*

Jack Giffard's diary account provides us with another glimpse of the holocaust of fire that was sweeping the battery positions. The noise of gunfire together with the sound of screaming horses and wounded men must have been horrendous; the fact that the battery managed to bring any guns into action at all says a great deal about the men who manned them:

> *'We rushed out and got 2 guns into action, myself on one* [the D sub-section No 5 Gun] *with half a dozen men, and Brad* [Captain Edward Bradbury], *John* [Campbell] *and Mundy & the Sgt Major* [Dorrell] *and Sgt Nelson on the other* [B sub-section No 6 Gun]. *I had only fired a few rounds when the whole of my gun crew were wiped out, so I went on until I'd finished the ammunition and then got hit through the left leg above the knee by a splinter and peppered in the right arm and back. Then a shell pitched on the gun wheel and smashed it, something getting me on the top of my head. As I could do no good there I crawled back to the stack where some of our wounded were sheltering, they were terribly knocked about. A few minutes later a shrapnel swept along our side of the track, a fragment going clean through my right leg just above the knee and out underneath near the top of my leg, just missing the main artery by 1/8 inch'.*[160]

In the midst of this chaos of death and destruction the Number 6 Gun remained firing with Lionel Mundy as section commander, John Campbell in the firing seat, Edward Bradbury as layer and Sergeant Nelson as range setter, whilst Gunner Darbyshire and Driver Osborn kept the gun fed with ammunition.

John Campbell had in fact been with Jack Giffard on the Number 5 Gun and when it was knocked out he moved across to where the other gun was firing. Sergeant David Nelson's account describes the last valiant moments of the Number 6 Gun:

> *'Lieutenant Campbell, though already wounded came to our assistance but ere long a German shell burst close to us wounding him and also fatally wounding Lieutenant Mundy and Corporal* [Thomas] *Payne, also wounding me in the right side and slightly in the right leg and piercing my cap. There were now 3 serving the gun, Captain Bradbury, Sergeant Major Dorrell (who up to now had been using a rifle under cover) and myself twice wounded. We still maintained a quick rate of deadly accurate fire until our ammunition supply began to wane and the two men carrying it to us disappeared. Captain Bradbury went to get ammunition from an adjacent wagon but he only got 4 yards from the gun when a shell from the enemy completely cut both his legs off midway between knees and body, thus leaving Sergeant Major Dorrell and myself in action. We fired the two rounds*

remaining with the gun and with them silenced the only German gun which appeared to be shooting'.[161]

Although Briggs had some idea of the composition of the forces confronting him initially he had little idea he was up against an entire German cavalry division. However, undeterred he placed Colonel Pitman's C Squadron in reserve and ordered the remaining 11/Hussars to extend their frontage to include the northern aspect of the village formally occupied by 5/Dragoon Guards which gave Lieutenant Colonel George Ansell, commanding the Dragoons, a free hand to deploy against the German right flank. Ansell sprung intro action, sending Captain Charles Blackburne with as many dismounted men as he could gather to the north of the village whilst Ansell himself took two mounted squadrons and worked up to the crest of the ridge under heavy machine gun and rifle fire. Here they dismounted and put down a heavy fire which caught the German 3 Cavalry Brigade badly, forcing it to withdraw. Unfortunately the regiment paid a heavy price for its audacity; George Ansell was killed near Luce Farm. Recalled by Briggs, the Dragoons were brought out of action by Major William Winwood, the regiment having put paid to the German attack to the north of the village with very few casualties.

Meanwhile, the two machine guns of the Bays under the command of Lieutenant Algernon Lamb had been putting down a very effective fire on the enemy gunners from their position behind L Battery in the sunken lane. They were also able to target the advancing German columns from von Garnier's 17 Cavalry Brigade which were attempting to encircle the southern end of the village. As a result of this flank attack dismounted German cavalrymen from the 18th Dragoons did manage to occupy some of the outlying buildings near the sugar factory. The Bays managed to stem any further advance temporarily in a sharp counter attack that left Lieutenant Champion de Crespigny dead, but they were eventually pushed back as the German dragoons finally secured the sugar factory building. This was the furthest advance into the British positions that any units of von Garnier's division made during the whole encounter. Lamb's machine guns, supported by the dismounted rifle fire of the remainder of the Bays, prevented any incursion onto the Rully road. Like the attack to the north, that to the south had so far failed. Von Garnier had one further move left to make.

Summoning Colonel von Prinz, commanding 18 Cavalry Brigade, von Garnier ordered a mounted attack on the southern end of the village. Although the mist was lifting the ground ahead was still obscured – a fact that the 16th Hussars quickly found to their cost as they reached the ravine at its steepest point near Feu Farm – men and horses fell in their attempts to descend the side of the ravine, leaving little recourse but to dismount and move forward on foot. The 15th Hussars were more fortunate, their line of attack took them further north, to the south of the German gun line, where the ravine – although still steep – was more accessible. In the valley bottom they dismounted and advanced on foot in skirmish lines but were handicapped by a singular shortage of small arms ammunition. It was now too late for von Garnier to capitalize, however, for as the mist lifted he could see British reinforcements were arriving and he was aware that ammunition was running very low. The decision taken on 31 August to proceed ahead of his ammunition column had left the division at a distinct disadvantage – the German cavalry commander had no choice but to withdraw.

* * *

The motorcyclist sent by Briggs to Allenby's HQ at St Vaast-de-Longmont took 20 minutes to make the short 3 mile journey. Allenby reacted swiftly and immediately despatched t 4 Cavalry Brigade and I Battery RHA to assist Briggs. Meeting one of Briggs' staff en route at 7.00 am – who appraised him of the situation at Néry – Allenby deployed I Battery on the Roman road to the south of the village and continued forward to meet the threat that was building at the sugar factory. I Battery had arrived at a fortuitous moment – still in possession of the sugar factory, two machine guns had been brought up by the German 18th Dragoons and were about to bring fire to bear on Lieutenant Lamb's guns – but ranging on the tall chimney of the factory, I Battery put an end to any further threat from that direction.

But the battle was not quite over; the German battery commander now turned his guns to fire on the four guns of I Battery commanded by Captain Hugh Burnyeat – now in a semi-concealed position south of the Roman road – some 2,000 yards from the German batteries.[162] By a stroke of good fortune the German battery commander was misled by an upright pole from a derelict farm implement close to the British battery. Mistaking this in the mist for an observation ladder, the German guns put down a very accurate and heavy fire on the pole, leaving Burnyeat's men untouched.

At 6.00 am 1/Middlesex was about a mile northwest of Néry when the men heard heavy firing from the direction of the village and soon after 'a very excited cavalry sergeant major' rode up with the news that, 'the 1 Cavalry Brigade was being scuppered at Néry'.[163] Major Frank Rowley, who was in temporary command of the battalion, immediately rode to the village and in liaison with General Briggs deployed his men east of the village to enfilade the German gunners. By now it was becoming clear that the German gun teams were attempting to limber up their guns to get them away, but with the fog lifting and revealing their intentions the machine-gun fire from the Bays and 11/Hussars was now directed on the unfortunate gunners who were shot down in every attempt to retrieve their guns.

As the Middlesex deployed past Feu Farm, C Squadron of 11/Hussars, having been brought out of reserve by Briggs as soon as the German guns had stopped firing, were now charging down on the German gun lines. Major William Lockett's C Squadron had negotiated the steep eastern side of the ravine on foot before mounting up on the edge of the plateau. Lieutenant Guy Norrie's troop led the charge:

> *'We charged the German guns with a rousing cheer and drawn swords and captured eight guns and two machine guns. This was a comparatively simple task as the machine-gun fire, particularly of the Bays and I Battery had practically silenced the gun battery'.*[164]

The Middlesex also claim to have captured the guns, the regimental historian recording the episode thus:

> *'With bayonets fixed and a cheer, the Middlesex men rushed across the small intervening valley and captured eight of the guns which had been firing on the 1st Cavalry Brigade and L Battery. With the exception of some 12 dead or badly wounded Germans, the gun crews had fled'.*[165]

I suspect that Norrie and his squadron had already passed through the now silent guns and were gathering prisoners at the top of the ridge before both units continued to Le Plessis Châtelain – where a further 70 prisoners were taken along with two German ambulances. At any rate the Middlesex historian proudly recorded that the battalion was the first British unit to capture German guns in the war and who am I to deny them their glory?

The casualties on both sides were relatively heavy for this early period in the war. During the 3 hours or so that the engagement lasted the German 4th Cavalry Division are said to have lost about 180 men – of which 78 were taken prisoner – they also lost over 200 of their horses. Although they escaped with three of their guns, these were later found abandoned in a wood near Ermenonville and were destroyed by 1/Field Squadron on 2 September. Von Garnier's once proud division was now scattered widely and incapable of further offensive action. The British lost some 390 horses and 41 officers and men killed with another 91 wounded. Of these Captain Edward Bradbury, Sergeant David Nelson and Battery Sergeant Major George Dorrell of L Battery were awarded the Victoria Cross for their conspicuous gallantry under fire. Sadly the 33-year-old Bradbury died in the care of the field ambulance later that morning and was buried in the small communal cemetery at Néry. Corporal Walter Beer serving with 11/Field Ambulance had arrived at Néry soon after the action had finished, his diary recorded Bradbury's death and it was men of his unit which formed the burial party at the communal cemetery. 11/Field Ambulance also established a dressing station and treated some 40 wounded men from 5/Dragoon Guards and L Battery before 10 and 12/Field Ambulances took some 160 wounded – including Jack Giffard and David Nelson – to Baron, some 5 miles to the south.[166]

Although the British cavalry brigade had beaten off a much larger force and by rights should have been overwhelmed, Charles Briggs had been lucky in many respects. He could hardly claim superior generalship as both he and von Garnier clearly failed to reconnoitre the ground around Néry, but Briggs certainly displayed more flair and battlefield leadership. His deployment of 5/Dragoon Guards was a masterly stroke in halting the attack from the north and his presence in the firing line – at one point firing a machine gun himself – was a continual boost to the men of his brigade. In spite of the geography and the timely arrival of I Battery, what really swung the battle in favour of the British was the good shooting of the brigade, both with the SMLE rifle and machine gun. It may be going a little too far to suggest that this was entirely attributable to Sir Horace Smith-Dorrien, but his insistence that the cavalry be every bit as effective as the infantry with the SMLE rifle had unquestionably born fruit at Néry. In the coming months and particularly at Ypres in October and November the cavalryman's ability to fight alongside their infantry counterparts as riflemen was to be a vital part in the defensive jigsaw which prevented the channel ports from being taken.

As a result of its defeat at Néry the German 4th Cavalry Division was unable to fully take up its position on von Kluck's open right flank and as a consequence was unable to provide early intelligence of the whereabouts of Maunoury's Sixth Army. However, despite the limited cavalry screen from von Garnier's mounted troops, Maunoury's advance north of Meaux was compromised by his own poor cavalry reconnaissance. Early on 5 September he unexpectedly blundered into von Gronau's IV Reserve Corps which was protecting Kluck's flank and the element of surprise which had been hoped for was dashed. Whether the German failure at the Battle of the Marne was in some part due to a depleted German 4th Cavalry Division failing to detect the presence of Maunoury's Sixth Army is debatable. Von Kluck may have exposed his flank to the French Sixth Army, but his reaction to the threat was swift and conducted with his trade mark decisiveness. The German failure on the Marne was ultimately down to poor communication between OHL and the German field army commanders and the subsequent retirement to the Aisne Valley was precipitated by von Bülow on 9 September.[167]

Chapter 13

1 September – Still a Force to be Reckoned With

2/Grenadier Guards had been on the road since 7.15 am, marching in the blazing heat for most of the day before they finally bivouacked just north of Soucy on 31 August. It had been a suffocating day too for Thomas Wollocombe with the 4/Middlesex. Fortunately he had managed to retain his horse but 'at every halt I sort of rolled off my saddle and sat in the hedge or ditch feeling half dead. It was about all I could do to climb up into the saddle again'. But the heat – although debilitating – was not foremost on the mind of Major Bernard Gordon Lennox. His diary gives a hint of the general feeling of frustration experienced by many of the officers of 2/Grenadier Guards on what was the eighth day of the retreat: 'We now know that as soon as a gun is heard – be it five miles off or 25 miles – we shall be shortly inundated with orders to march, to be followed shortly with counter orders.' It wasn't as if it was all the fault of the brigade staff. Gerry Ruthven, the brigade major, complained on several occasions that he was given no information at all regarding the disposition of enemy troops – or for that matter where other British units were either. Lieutenant Colonel the Hon George Morris, commanding the 1st Battalion Irish Guards (1/Irish Guards), was uncharacteristically pessimistic in his assessment of the situation, reckoning that it was the old problem of Allies falling out with each other and predicting that the BEF would be embarking for England within a fortnight.

Morris was correct on one count; if the retreat was beginning to nibble at the morale of the men it was also putting a dent in Anglo–French relations. On 29 August Joffre drove to Compiègne to plead with Sir John French not to withdraw from the line altogether, French's reply was not what Joffre wanted to hear. The BEF, declared Sir John, was on its last legs and desperately needed rest and recuperation. His opinion was unchanged on 31 August when Sir John told Kitchener in no uncertain terms that the BEF could do little until it was re-equipped. It would take another highly charged meeting between Kitchener and Sir John at the British Embassy in Paris on 1 September to settle the nerves of the British Commander-in Chief. If Sir John felt he would be able to

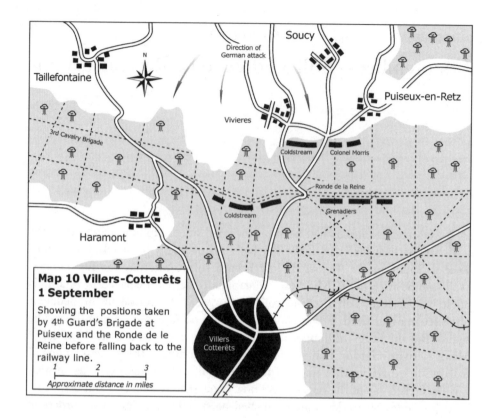

**Map 10 Villers-Cotterêts
1 September**

Showing the positions taken
by 4th Guard's Brigade at
Puiseux and the Ronde de le
Reine before falling back to the
railway line.

| 1 | 2 | 3 |
Approximate distance in miles

withdraw the BEF and refit with the intention of re-joining the conflict at a later
date he had badly misjudged the nature of what was taking place. The BEF was
committed whether he liked it or not and his five divisions were fighting for
their very existence.

I Corps was underway by 4.00 am on 1 September with the two divisions
converging on Villers-Cotterêts through the Forêt de Retz. The 2nd Division's
route took it through Vivières to the Rond de la Reine, a small forest clearing
some 3 miles north of Villers-Cotterêts. At Soucy the orders for the day woke
the commanding officers of the four Guards battalions a little after midnight
and as soon as it got light orders were issued to dig in and hold their positions
to cover the retirement of the 2nd Division. As at Néry, the morning had opened
with a thick mist and the passage of British units was almost spectral as they
moved slowly south towards the leafy cover of the forest. Lieutenant Aubrey
Herbert – ever poetic in his diary account – thought the movement of the 5 and
6 Infantry Brigades was like 'the sound of deep, slow rivers passing', the more
practical Bernard Gordon Lennox thought their hilltop position would become
a regular shell trap once the mist dispersed.

Shortly after 6.00 am the mist had lifted a little and on cue probing German cavalry patrols began to appear – only to be driven off by rifle fire. Nevertheless, Bernard Gordon Lennox's judgment of his battalion's position soon proved to be correct when a German battery opened up on them at 6.30 am, fortunately coinciding with orders to fall back onto the Rond de la Reine. As the Grenadiers retired through 1/Irish Guards and 2/Coldstream – both battalions under the overall command of George Morris – Bernard Gordon Lennox took a few minutes to chat with an old friend and former Grenadier Guards officer, Major Hubert Crichton, who was now second-in-command of the Irish battalion:

'He asked me what was going on. I told him nothing special, only the usual strategic movement to the rear. Half an hour later he was dead poor lad, and the brigade and the world are the losers.'[168]

The Irish Guards had deployed at Puiseux-en-Retz on the right of the Soucy-Villers-Cotterêts road. The first appearance of German troops advancing towards the village prompted Colonel Morris to send Aubrey Herbert with a message for Lieutenant Colonel Cecil Pereira, commanding 2/Coldstream on his left. It was an eventful ride:

'I went off at a gallop, and had got halfway there, with the wood on my left and open land on my right, when the Germans began shooting at about three-quarters of a mile. Our men were firing at them from the wood, and I felt annoyed at being between two fires and the only thing visible to amuse our men and the Germans.'[169]

As he made the return journey to the Irish lines it was becoming evident that both battalions were coming under a heavy attack from a large body of troops on what appeared to be a wide front. 4 miles further west 3 Cavalry Brigade was already engaged with the advanced guard of the German III Corps and had been since 9.00 am. At Taillefontaine, on the northwestern edge of the forest, Lieutenant Colonel Ian Hogg's 4/Hussars were under attack from cavalry and infantry advancing out of Roye St Nicholas, the small village to the north which Colonel Hogg's men had vacated only a few hours earlier. With orders to hold a line in the forest until 12.30, A and C Squadrons were gradually pushed back by sheer weight of numbers during which the 39-year-old Colonel Hogg was seriously wounded while directing C Squadron's retirement. Ian Hogg, the son of the well-known educational philanthropist, Quintin Hogg, died of his wounds the next day in the schoolhouse at Haramont.

In the meantime the two battalions of Coldstream and Irish Guards were holding their own at Puiseux and with the help of 9 Battery RFA were effectively bringing the German advance to a halt. Suspecting that the enemy had been temporarily discouraged from further offensive action, Morris sent word again to Colonel Pereira with instructions for his battalion of Coldstream Guards to fall back to the railway line north of Villers-Cotterêts. Morris was preparing to follow them when he was taken aback by a rather surprising order from brigade ordering him to stay put as the main body of the division was to halt for their lunches until 1.00 pm. The Coldstream were already past recall by this time which left the Irish Guards isolated and extremely vulnerable and in Aubrey Herbert's considered opinion, if the division took too long over their lunches the Irish Guards would probably be wiped out – a view shared by Major Jeffreys on the Ronde de la Reine with the Grenadiers. Jeffreys' astonishment at the order was only tempered by the arrival of some of Chetwode's 5 Cavalry Brigade who halted at the Rond de la Reine and dismounted:

> *'We all had a good many friends amongst the officers, we stood talking together for quite a considerable time, a risky proceeding considering how vulnerable their horses were, and that they were masking our fire should the Germans come on. As it was it was very pleasant coffee-housing in the shady ride for all the world like a big field hunting in the New Forest on a spring day.'*[170]

The respite at the Ronde de la Reine proved to be only temporary and was soon shattered by the sounds of heavy firing to the north as the Irish Guards came under attack again. Aubrey Herbert described the Germans advancing towards their front and on the left flank at about 10.45 am. 'There was a tremendous fire. The leaves, branches, etc, rained upon one. One's face was constantly fanned by the wind from their bullets'. Attacked on all sides the Irish had no choice but to fight a very costly running battle through the woods with the Germans almost on top of them. Aubrey Herbert was acting as the commanding officer's galloper and consequently remained close to George Morris during the fight, he described the retirement of the Irish Guards back to the Rond de la Reine:

> *'Men were now falling fast. I happened to see one man drop with a bayonet in his hand a few yards off, and reined in my horse to see if I could help him, but the CO called me and I followed him. The man whom I had seen was Hubert* [Major Hubert Crichton], *though I did not know it at the time. The CO ... had a charmed life. He raced from one place to another through the wood; cheering the men and chaffing them, and talking to me; smoking cigarette after cigarette.'*[171]

The Irish Guards were falling back on the line running west–east along the two rides that centred on the Rond de la Reine where the Grenadiers had established their battalion HQ. Lieutenant Colonel Noel Corry, commanding the battalion, had placed Numbers 1 and 2 Companies on the rising ground about 100 yards south of the main ride east of the Rond de la Reine and Number 4 Company along the ride to the west where they were in touch with 3/Coldstream Guards.

The Coldstream Guards were widely extended along the ride in an effort to block the enemy from using the numerous rides which ran from north to south. Altogether it was not a good spot for a fight with the dense undergrowth making communications difficult and fields of fire almost impossible.

Company by company the Irish Guards fell back onto the Ronde la Reine pursued by what Bernard Gordon Lennox described as 'the green Jaeger fellows'. At some point in their retirement Colonel Morris was killed, becoming the first ever commanding officer of the Irish Guards to fall in battle. His death was a huge loss to a battalion that had also just lost its second-in-command. A man noted for his bravery and composure under fire, not half an hour before his death, after a period of sustained shellfire which brought trees crashing down, he had called to the men: 'D'you hear that? They're doing that to frighten you.' To which someone replied 'If that's what they're after, they might as well stop. They succeeded with *me* hours ago.'

It was not long before the gaps on the left of the line were being exploited and fighting became a confused mêlée as German forces attempted to get round the left flank. Major Jeffreys:

> 'The first I heard of what was happening on my left was when Gerry Ruthven appeared leading a horse on which was the Brigadier badly wounded and obviously in great pain. He shouted to me that the enemy was held but we should shortly have to withdraw, and disappeared to the rear in the Forest.'[172]

With Scott-Kerr wounded, command of the brigade fell to the Grenadiers' commanding officer, Noel Corry. But taking over command of a brigade in these circumstances was well nigh impossible and in truth no-one was effectively in overall command as the three battalions of Guards began to fall back to the bridge over the railway line north of Villers-Cotterêts – not an easy move by any means. The Coldstream companies and Irish Guards to the west of the Rond de la Reine were forced to fall back diagonally behind the Grenadiers – a manoeuvre they carried out in characteristic parade-ground fashion as they withdrew behind the Grenadiers under a hail of fire. Bernard Gordon Lennox's company on the right of the line gave covering fire before they too began filtering back towards the railway:

> 'The firing on my left was very hot and the opposing forces were in some cases only 70 yards off each other … [then] the companies on my left were ordered off to the left to reinforce and I also sent one platoon along. Everyone was now mixed up hopelessly and officers just took command of whatever men they found. We now got the order to retire slowly on Villers-Cotterêts.'[173]

With Jeffreys now in command of the Grenadiers, the battalion eventually got over the railway bridge having successfully navigated the maze of forest rides. Fortunately the Germans were having a similar problem with the criss-cross pattern of rides and the Grenadiers were not pressed particularly heavily, nevertheless, all three Guards battalions took casualties before they finally shook off the advancing enemy. Jeffreys was left very much to his own devices:

> '*Once over the bridge I assembled the battalion ... and we marched off down the road and through Villers-Cotterêts. We had no orders. The Brigade organization had, I suppose, been upset by the Brigade Major escorting the wounded Brigadier out of action. Our CO had gone off with what remained of Brigade Headquarters, so we just followed the rest of the brigade.*'[174]

The brigade had taken some 360 casualties, many of whom had been left wounded and dying in the forest glades as the Guards fell back to Villers-Cotterêts. Some would not be discovered until it was too late; others were more fortunate and fell into the hands of German ambulance units where they received attention. One of these was Aubrey Herbert who had been shot at close range with a bullet through his side. Managing to remain on his horse he made it back to an aid station:

> '*I got off and asked them to take on my horse. Then I lay down on the ground and an RAMC man dressed me. The Red Cross men gave a loud whistle when they saw my wound, and said the bullet had gone through me. The fire was frightfully hot. The men who were helping me were crouching down, lying on the ground. While he was dressing me a horse – his, I suppose – was shot just behind us. I asked them to go, as they could do me no good and would only get killed or taken themselves*'.[175]

As the Guards retired through 6 Brigade which had established a defensive line on the southern approaches to Villers-Cotterêts, two companies of 1/Royal Berkshires – the same battalion which had fought so valiantly at Maroilles a week earlier – was instrumental in holding off the German advance which very nearly overwhelmed the six guns of 70 Battery. Rising to the occasion once more, the Royal Berks, with the help of a company of South Staffords, held off the enemy long enough for the gun teams to limber up and brings the guns out intact. This was no skirmish, the Royal Berks lost over 25 NCOs and men and 35–year-old Captain Harold Birt commanding C Company, was awarded the DSO for his part in the action.[176] Birt was killed in January 1917 when a shell hit the C Company shelter in the trenches at Festubert.

Altogether the fighting south of the town left another 160 casualties. 80 of the wounded had been picked up by Numbers 4 and 5 Field Ambulances and

Number 4 Field Ambulance – many of whose men had already been taken prisoner at Landrecies – had established a dressing station in a nearby sugar factory. It was only next morning, after the medics realized that the had been left behind, that they narrowly escaped the fate of their comrades at Landrecies. Filled to capacity with wounded, 5/Field Ambulance, moved to Betz where the Reverend Frederick Smithwick, who was attached to the unit, recalled they established a field hospital:

> '*Our Field Ambulance went to Betz and fixed up a temporary hospital in a lovely château there. Bearers went [back] towards the battlefield to bring in the wounded. All through the night the wounded were being brought in till we had about 150, including General Scott-Kerr of the Guards Brigade, Lt Desmond Fitzgerald and Captain Burton, Irish Guards. They were medically attended and put on hay in some of the large barns of the château.*'[177]

Despite being some 10 miles further south, the ambulance unit was very nearly captured the next day and only succeeded in getting the less severely wounded away with the assistance of motor lorries requisitioned by Major General Monro himself.

* * *

Jim Pennyman's experience on the night of 31 August in the 'uncomfortable farm' north of Crépy-en-Valois was not one shared by Cyril Helm and 2/KOYLI. Their billet, his diary recorded, although close by, was altogether more acceptable:

> '*My battalion was billeted in the largest and best kept farm I have ever seen. The owner was a charming man and showed me all over it, he was extremely proud of his white oxen which were indeed noble beasts. I tremble to think what probably happened to the place next day when the Huns arrived.*'

At Crepy, as at Villers-Cotterêts and Néry, the German advance guard came into contact with the British outpost lines at about 6.00 am on 1 September. The 1/West Kents and 2/Duke of Wellington's were deployed either side of the main Bethancourt road on the high ground about 2 miles north of Crepy with two batteries of XXVII Brigade guns further back around the sugar factory at Mermont. As the attack developed down the Bethancourt road 2/KOSB were brought up to strengthen the line. Jim Pennyman:

> '*About 7am we were called upon suddenly and urgently to go to their [Royal West Kents] relief. We marched out about two miles to where the action was taking*

place and lined out in two lines across turnip fields. The enemy had no artillery ... and we gathered what little artillery we had with us did tremendous execution amongst the enemy's infantry'.[178]

Unable to reply with any counter battery fire of their own German troops were at a huge disadvantage and it was Major Ernest Alexander's 119 Battery that brought the enemy advance to a standstill with its accurate shellfire. Readers will remember that it was Alexander's guns which did such good work in support of the infantry at Audregnies on 24 August and were brought out of action with the help of Francis Grenfell and 9/Lancers. Captain Josslyn Ramsden was the XXVII Brigade adjutant:

'At about 4am being again on rearguard with the 13th Infantry Brigade under General Cuthbert, we were ordered to occupy positions at once as a considerable force of Germans were advancing. The colonel, who seems to have an instinct for placing guns in splendid positions, took me forward into the advanced infantry line. We had just stopped to speak to the officer commanding the left section of the infantry line on the Bethancourt-Crepy road about 1½ miles north of Crepy, when [General] Cuthbert's horse was shot under him, the first shot – then the game began. For an hour we sat where we were till it became evident the enemy were in some force – we know now, and surmised then, that they had been sent on in large motors. The colonel now sent me back for 2 guns of the 119th which he had left behind a ridge. Mr Tenison [Lieutenant William Tenison] 119th brought up a section and we started firing into the Germans at about 1400 yards over our own infantry about 100 yards in front! I believe we did great execution with these two guns which fired a marvellous lot of ammunition. Anyhow their fire completely checked the enemy and although we withdrew about noon – battery by battery – to a new position 5 miles further south we were never attacked again'.[179]

The KOYLI were also turned out to support the right of the firing line, expecting casualties Cyril Helm turned the farm into a dressing station:

'Having arranged things to the best of my ability, I strolled off to see how the others were getting on ... almost at once our guns started firing at a wood about a mile away where cavalry had been seen. The Germans had no horse artillery with them, so could only reply with desultory rifle fire'.

The wood – in all probability the wooded area to the south of Morcourt – had been fired upon by Captain Geoffrey Masters' section of 119 Battery which discouraged any further advance from that direction for the time being with extremely accurate shrapnel fire.

About this time two motor cars with machine guns were seen driving down the Bethancourt road towards the British lines. Cyril Helm, who also witnessed the incident along with Josslyn Ramsden, was sure that the Germans driving the vehicles were unaware of the British positions. The Dukes held their fire until both cars had closed to 200 yards, Ramsden watched as the Dukes, 'opened fire and shot the driver of the first car, the second went so fast that it ran into the first and was wrecked'. One of the vehicles, wrote Helm, 'contained four German staff officers – all dead of course –and a good many bottles of looted champagne.' Lieutenant Henry O'Kelly, a platoon commander with 2/Duke of Wellington's described the events that resulted in his award of the DSO in a little more detail:

'A little later two motor-cars came spinning down the road towards our trenches. I had the greatest difficulty in keeping the men from firing until they got to close range. Other troops did open fire on them. At about 300 yards we loosed off and succeeded in stopping the motor-cars, which were armoured. Immediately we came under a veritable hail of bullets from the wood. We had not thought the enemy had infantry so near. I then noticed a man signalling from the rear motor car, so determined, as we could not make sure of them with bullets, we would have to charge them. I then sent back a message to B Company asking, them to come up and support us as I was going to charge and wanted covering fire, but they were a long time coming, so I decided not to wait and called for volunteers. We charged out with fixed bayonets and reached the motor-cars right enough. There was an old General potting at me with an automatic pistol, and I determined not to miss him, so, as I am a hopeless shot with a revolver, I shoved it in his face and pulled the trigger, nearly blowing the poor old chap's head off. The men prodded most of the others, and some had already been hit with rifle bullets. I tried to start the cars but could not get either going, so was obliged to leave everything as we were under very heavy fire from the edge of the wood. We first bust up a gun which they had mounted on the rear car. I also took all the dispatches and relieved the old general of his revolver, which I still have, and some good cigars and cigarettes. I also took a few other things, which I afterwards lost'.[180]

At 1.00 pm the British began retiring. Jim Pennyman reckoned they had got the better of the Germans and was a little annoyed at having to retire, Helm's careful preparations for the wounded were fortunately unnecessary as the battalion had only two wounded, both of whom were taken away in a bullock cart commandeered from the farm. Kenneth Godsell, whose field company had been digging some of the infantry's positions, reported that the KOSB had captured two machine guns at some point in the morning, although Pennyman does not mention this in his account. Apparently Lieutenant Valdo Pottinger, had another successful foraging expedition and 'did one of his famous local raids and returned with all sorts of gear from trench shovels to a mess blanket'.

13 Brigade passed through the constricted streets of the medieval town of Crepy – which would soon be the scene of indiscriminate looting by Germans forces – on their way south. Cyril Helm was one of the last to retire – with the bullock cart in procession behind his Maltese cart – and he was startled when a bullet whistled past his ear from one of the side streets in the town. He didn't stop to discover who the perpetrator was and was quite relieved when he eventually caught up with the battalion on the Betz road. That evening the brigade billeted in villages around Silly-le-Long, most of the inhabitants had long since left their homes shuttered and boarded up – 'like cities of the dead' – thought Cyril Helm, who could only find a few old women about who were 'for the most part weeping'. Taking full advantage of the empty buildings at Silly-le-Long, the officers of the KOSB dined in style with knives and forks to eat their bully beef and bread which they washed down with requisitioned liqueur brandy. A short distance away at Ognes 17/Field Company was billeted for the night and Kenneth Godsell, who was on guard duty, remembered a beautiful night with a full moon and heavy dew.

Accounts of the events of 1 September can give the impression that the German advance was only apparent at Néry, Villers-Cotterêts and Crépy-en-Valois but in fact British units were engaged in minor skirmishes that morning in several other localities between Néry and Villers-Cotterêts. The experience of 108 Battery RFA was probably one that was shared by other brigades on that misty September morning. On the night of 31 August, Lieutenant Eric Anderson and 108 Battery had bivouacked with 9 Brigade at Vauciennes – on the edge of the Forêt de Retz – a little to the west of Villers-Cotterêts. Detailed as rearguard the following morning, the battery took up a position close to a water tower on the main road just as reports arrived of enemy cavalry heading in its direction. Unfortunately Anderson's diary does not give us any further detail other than, 'they were easily disposed of.' The ensuing retirement through the forest was unhindered but the sounds of gunfire were apparent from the north east. Anderson felt instinctively that their skirmish had been part of a much larger attack, 'there was something funny going on though, for we were gradually merged into the main body and a sort of flank guard of main body troops took our place.'

He was, of course, correct but on arrival at Betz that evening the events of the day were set aside as the necessary task of watering the battery horses took precedence. But later, after the full implications of what had transpired became apparent, there was no doubt in anyone's mind that Tuesday 1 September had been an eventful day for the British. It had delivered some sharp reminders that the BEF was still very much a force to be reckoned with – reminders which had still not registered with von Kluck and, to some extent, with Sir John French.

* * *

At the Paris meeting which took place on 1 September Sir John suggested to the French Minister for War, Alexandre Millerand, that the Marne should be used as a line of defence to bring the German advance to a halt. His proposal was rejected by Joffre the next day on the grounds that Lanrezac's Fifth Army was too close to the Marne and would have little time to prepare defences. Late on 2 September Joffre issued his Instruction Genérale Number 4 which forecast a retreat behind the Seine! Accordingly Sir John gave orders for the Marne to be crossed by the BEF.

On 2 September 26/Field Company arrived at Meaux at 6.30 am. The company had just marched 40 miles in a little over 24 hours and were anticipating a rest. Major Pritchard had only just shut his eyes when he was roused by Brigadier General Fowke who arrived with orders for the Marne bridges to be prepared and blown. With the company still asleep, Pritchard left to reconnoitre the task ahead. The bridges allocated to 26/Field Company were but a small part of the wider operational order that was issued by GHQ later on 2 September. Operational Order Number 14 put the responsibility for ordering the destruction of the Marne bridges firmly on the three corps commanders once their units had crossed the river.

Early on 3 September the 1st Division crossed the Marne at Trilport, the 2nd and 3rd Divisions at Meaux and the 4th and 5th Divisions further west at Villenoy and Lagny respectively. Allenby's cavalry crossed at Gournay, which was practically in the Paris suburbs, serving as a sharp indication of just how close to the French capital the fighting had progressed. After crossing the Marne, I Corps turned east and marched to La Ferté-sous-Jouarre. At La Ferté, Major Pritchard had two bridges to blow; a large stone-arched bridge and a steel bridge comprising of six arched girders. With both bridges ready by 6.45 pm on 3 September, counter orders then arrived with instructions to remove the charges and leave the bridges intact. Pritchard – by now wise to the inconsistent nature of divisional orders when it came to blowing bridges – ignored the instruction to withdraw the charges and posted his men on the two bridges to await developments.

It was just as well he did – at 4.00 am on 4 September divisional HQ ordered the immediate destruction of the bridges – another case, thought Pritchard, of divisional staff writing orders without engaging the brain. Lieutenant Smith successfully blew the stone arch bridge but Lieutenant Earle Calthrop's bridge was left standing despite the girders being cut through by the charges. As Calthrop moved across the bridge to inspect the damage German cavalry arrived on the northern bank and opened fire. Fortunately two companies of 1/Coldstream Guards under the command of Major Grant had been deployed as rearguard and their rifle fire drove the enemy horsemen off, but time was running out. After a second attempt which also failed the rearguard was ordered to retire and 4 hours later – much to the disgust of the Coldstream – a German battalion crossed the Marne using the bridge.

After the 2nd Division had passed through Meaux, 5/Field Company blew the road and railway bridges successfully and 57/Field Company destroyed all the other bridges, weirs, barges and boats between Villenoy and Trilport. At Villenoy the road to the bridge on the southern bank rises steeply – any vehicle driving at speed would not realize the bridge had been destroyed until it was too late. Witnessed by two Irish Guardsmen who had been stranded on the opposite bank, a car plunged headlong through the gap in the bridge and thence into the river. It was said at the time the car was driven by a German spy attempting to return to German lines. The fate of the driver was not recorded. At Meaux Kenneth Godsell and Gerald Smyth spent a more leisurely afternoon boating on the river. The company crossed the Marne at lunchtime on 3 September and the two subalterns spent their time destroying anything that could be used by the enemy to cross the river:

'I had to take my section and work up the river for three miles and destroy all boats. This was most unpleasant, as there were a large number of rowing boats all up the river and the owners hated seeing us shove a crowbar through them. Our little motor boat was a beauty, it went to my heart to sink it'.[181]

But food was never far from the mind of the ever hungry Kenneth Godsell. That evening at Colommieres his delighted pen recorded they caught a goose and managed to find an orchard full of pears while the incorrigible Valdo Pottinger returned from yet another foraging expedition with 'a wonderful luncheon basket'. Jim Pennyman and the Borderers were also at Colommieres and once again the paths of the two young officers may have inadvertently crossed, 'We rather enjoyed our stay at the little place, as we had a charming orchard to be in' wrote Pennyman.

Had they but known it, behind the scenes the retreat was slowly grinding to a halt. On 2 September von Kluck – still pushing south in his efforts to catch the BEF – was ordered by OHL to cover the flank of the Second Army which was moving south east. Von Kluck was furious, he was already a day's march in front of von Bülow and his refusal to comply with Moltke's directive saw him continuing his advance – still under the impression the Allied retreat had degenerated into a rout. But events were now speeding towards a conclusion. By 4 September Joffre's plans for a counter-attack were falling into place – he had replaced Charles Lanrezac with General Franchet d'Esperey on 3 September – and was now in a position to deliver a blow to the German offensive that would stop them in their tracks. But would the British be part of his plan? The cooperation of the BEF on the right flank of the French Sixth Army was vital. General Maunoury was despatched to GHQ at Melun where, in Sir John's absence, Murray agreed to British involvement – subject of course to Sir John's approval.

The Melun Plan – and in reality the British had little choice – was cautiously accepted by Sir John who met Joffre the next morning to hear the details of the French Commander-in Chief's proposals. It was from all accounts a highly emotional meeting and was observed by Lieutenant Spears:

> 'The atmosphere in the room grew tenser and tenser. General Joffre was talking of the vital necessity of acting rapidly; the next twenty-four hours would be decisive … he spoke of the order he was issuing to his troops. The time for retreating was over. Those who could not advance were to die where they stood. No man was to give way even as much as a foot … Again he thanked Sir John for his decision. His plan depended entirely upon British cooperation, its success on their action'.[182]

Sir John had needed no translator, he had understood and Spears watched tears welling up in the British commander's eyes. Turning to one of his staff officers French's reply was 'Tell him that all men can do our fellows will do'. There was, wrote Spears, 'an immediate anti-climax'. It was too late to stop the BEFs final day's march south which, for some units, was already in progress, but unnecessary as it was, it was the last day before retreat became advance and heralded the next phase of four long years of war.

On Sunday 6 September, 17/Field Company began the move north. For a second time Godsell overslept and was late at the early morning stand to: 'Valdo and I both in disgrace' he wrote, 'but had a good breakfast'. Although he had only been in France a short time he – like so many others – felt it had been much longer: '3 weeks since we left Dublin – a fortnight since St Ghislain. Today we made a step in the right direction. I wonder if our retreat is really over?'

Chapter 14

Left Behind

The retreat left hundreds of men behind as it gathered pace after the Battle of Mons on 23 August. Many of these were rounded up by the Germans but considerable numbers evaded capture for long periods and were assisted by the local population to either remain undetected or to escape captivity by reaching the coast or neutral Holland. After Antwerp fell in October 1914, the Belgian Army opened sluice gates at Nieuport flooding the country to the east of the Nieuport-Dixmude line. Not only did this halt the German advance but it also effectively cut off Ostend as a destination for stranded Allied soldiers in Belgium, forcing would be escapees to head for the border with Holland. Once the permanent lines of trenches had been established from the coast to the Swiss border, Holland was the only route open, particularly for those who had escaped from German prisoner of war camps.

The German authorities were clearly very concerned at the numbers of armed men who remained at large and from early 1915 took a very hard line with anyone who sheltered or assisted Allied soldiers and those who were caught ran the risk of execution. Details of the exact number of British soldiers who were caught and shot is not available, although some sources claim at least fifty men lost their lives in this way.

However, even before the retreat began, Trooper Thomas O'Shaughnessy of 20/Hussars found himself on his own and surrounded north east of Mons on 22 August 1914. O'Shaughnessy was reconnoitring with his patrol of 20/Hussars commanded by Lieutenant Myles Thompson when the party found itslef in the middle of units of the German Second Army. In making a dash for the cover of a wooded area near Chapelle, O'Shaughnessy felt his mount stumble and moments later both horse and rider crashed to the ground. The horse had been shot down at long range, fortunately the Irish trooper was uninjured but his patrol had vanished into the distance. 'We had to leave him, as we were going at the gallop' wrote Thompson later in his diary – what O'Shaughnessy thought about that is probably unprintable but – to the amazement of all – he rejoined the regiment 5 days later having obtained civilian clothes and pretended to be deaf and dumb to avoid his Irish accent giving the game away. This was probably the first instance of a successful evasion in the whole war and it appears to have been ignored in that O'Shaughnessy did not even receive a mention in despatches for what was a quite remarkable escapade. Both O'Shaughnessy and his troop commander survived the war.

It was a different story for Sergeant Frederick Hynes. After Lieutenant Alexander Gallaher had been brought down during the cavalry charge at Audregnies on 24 August he and 41-year-old Frederick Hynes – both from 4/Dragoon Guards – were taken to the convent hospital at Audregnies. On 31 August Gallaher and Hynes managed to slip away from the convent through the nearby orchard with the intention of striking north to cross the Mons-Condé canal. With Gallaher struggling with his right leg and Hynes similarly handicapped by his injuries, the two men managed to get to St Ghislain where they were given shelter in a haystack by a Belgian farmer before attempting to swim the canal. It was only when they were both neck deep in the water that Hynes realized his injury would prevent him from swimming. Returning to the haystack they had the good fortune to encounter a Belgian woman who, that very evening, provided a guide to help them cross the railway bridge at St Ghislain. Although impassable to trains – Kenneth Godsell would have been delighted to have heard his handiwork had been effective – it was still possible to traverse the railway bridge on foot over the damaged and twisted metalwork and a few minutes later Gallaher and Hynes were heading north on the road to Tournai.

By dawn they had covered some 18 miles – an amazing achievement given the state of their injuries – but now they were exhausted. Hiding in a shed on the outskirts of Tournai they were again assisted by a local man to board a train for Bruges where they arrived only to be mistaken for German prisoners. Following a rather tense encounter with an angry crowd the mistake was rectified and the two escapees were bundled onto a train for Ostend and from there to London. Gallaher was back with the regiment by early September and in time for the battle on the Aisne but Hynes, still suffering with his injuries, was discharged in August 1915 after 28 years service with the regiment. Both men were rewarded for their exploits behind the lines; Gallaher with the Military Cross and Hynes with the Military Medal, awards that were not announced in the *London Gazette* until 1920.

Captain Ernie Taylor, 2/Duke of Wellington's, was another officer who caught a train to freedom. Wounded at Wasmes he was taken in by a Belgian family until fit enough to walk to Peruwelz where he managed to catch a train to Tournai accompanied by 29-year-old Private Albert Clarke and thence by barge along the canal to Ostend. Captain Thomas Ellis of the same regiment found himself cut off in a wood after the Wasmes action. Still in uniform he and Corporal Harold Kerman walked for 12 days, hiding during daylight hours and moving only by night, until they reached Leuze. Here they boarded a train to Ostend and were taken home in style by the Royal Navy arriving in England on 5 September. Taylor, Clarke and Ellis were killed in 1915 during the bloody encounter on Hill 60 but Harold Kerman appears to have survived the war.[183]

A lucky escape was recorded by Second Lieutenant Robert Smith-Barry who had crossed the English Channel flying with 5 Squadron RFC but crashed his BE8 en route to Maubeuge from Amiens on 18 August. His passenger, Corporal Geard was killed and Smith-Barry was badly injured. Languishing in hospital at Péronne with a broken leg he was still there when German cavalry entered the outskirts of the town. Smith-Barry – with characteristic coolness – summoned a horse-drawn cab to which hospital staff carried him on a stretcher. Ordering the driver to get him to the station he was fortunate enough to find a train going to Amiens. A day later he was crossing the channel again, but this time by hospital ship.

Following the action at Audregnies there were several groups of Cheshires still in hiding days after the war had passed on. Many of these eventually surrendered or were rounded up but Private Arthur Wood – who had fought with Captain Wilfred Dugmore in C Company – managed to avoid capture. He and several others were fortunate enough to be passed along one of the many escape lines to Brussels where the British nurse Edith Cavell arranged the last leg of their escape to Holland from her teaching hospital, the Berkendael Medical Institute. Two more of the Audregnies fugitives were Lieutenant Colonel Dudley Boger and CQMS Frank Meachin, both of whom had been wounded and captured after the battle. Managing to escape from the convent hospital at Wihéries they eventually arrived at the Berkendael Institute where Boger's wounds were treated before both men made their bid for the Dutch border. Meachin managed a home run via Flushing disguised as a fish hawker but his commanding officer was not so lucky. He was picked up on the outskirts of Brussels at Villevorde and spent the remainder of the war as a prisoner at Ruhleben. Frank Meachin returned to the front and was later awarded the Distinguished Conduct Medal. Dudley Boger returned home in 1919 and was awarded the DSO for his stand at Audregnies. He died in November 1935 aged 70.

By 1914 Edith Cavell had been matron of the Berkendael Institute for 7 years, a fluent French speaker, the plight of British soldiers trapped behind enemy lines was first brought to her attention by Herman Capaiu, a young engineer who lived at Mons and from then on she saw it as her patriotic duty to give whatever assistance she could. Capaiu also put Cavell in touch with Prince Reginald de Croy, a Belgian aristocrat who lived at the Château de Bellignies, just north of Bavai. The de Croy family headed another group assisting Allied soldiers to escape, many of whom were sheltering in and around the Forêt de Mormal and in November 1914 the two groups linked up in a collaborative effort that saw some 200 Allied soldiers evading capture before the organization was exposed and shut down by the Germans in July 1915.

Another beneficiary of the Brussels escape route was Private Harry Beaumont of the Royal West Kents. After he was wounded at Frameries on 24 August he was taken to the same temporary hospital in Wasmes as Captain Taylor and Albert Clarke. Having witnessed their successful escape from the building he and Lance Corporal Arthur Heath followed suit in late October. Sheltered initially by a friendly Belgian family Beaumont had met at the hospital, they were eventually transferred along the escape route to Brussels and the Berkendael Institute. Beaumont remembers several of the Munster Fusiliers – fugitives from Etreux – also being sheltered there and in particular a woman with a quiet cultured voice:

> *'We did not know the name of this little woman with her calm grey eyes at this time; and if we had heard it, we would have paid no heed to it then. It was enough for us to know at that time she was English and that she really intended to help us. Only later did we learn that this unassuming person was none other than the brave Nurse Edith Cavell!'*[184]

It was probably Edith Cavell's naivety in allowing the soldiers she was hiding to go out in the evenings for walks which contributed to her eventual arrest and execution in 1915. Whilst Harry Beaumont was at the Institute he was appalled when a group of the Munsters went as far as practically advertising their presence to the German authorities by getting involved in a drunken fight after which they returned to the Institute singing *Tipperary*! In the scramble to disperse the fugitives before the authorities arrived to search the premises, Heath and Beaumont were separated for the first time since their escape from the hospital at Wasmes.

Eventually on 17 May 1915 Harry Beaumont and a Munster Fusilier named Michael Cary were warned that they would be taken to the Dutch border the following night. A guide had been arranged to take them across the formidable barbed wire barrier that separated Belgium from neutral Holland, a barrier that Beaumont described as 'an iron wire cobweb at least thirty feet in depth'. Throwing their clothing over the wire they crawled naked on their stomachs emerging cut and scratched – but jubilant – on the other side. In the meantime Arthur Heath had also made a successful escape to Holland, not by crawling under the wire but hidden in a hay cart. The two comrades were reunited at Rotterdam and travelled home to England together.

Whilst Beaumont's remaining war was spent in England with the Royal Ordnance Corps Arthur Heath had an altogether more disorderly experience. By 1916 he was an acting sergeant serving with the 3rd Battalion Royal West Kents. In early 1917 he was up before a district court martial, charged with conduct likely to be prejudicial to good order and military discipline. Exactly what he did to be 'busted' back to private and awarded 84 days detention is anyone's guess but I would put money on Heath assaulting an officer. His record indicates he was removed to Wandsworth detention barracks where on 30 May 1917 his sentence was reduced and he was sent back to the front. In July 1917 he was transferred to the Labour Corps, presumably at his own request or possibly by the regiment in an attempt to give him a fresh start. He survived the war ending his 15 years service in 1920 as an acting corporal. Both Heath and Beaumont were mentioned in despatches for successfully evading capture and managing to escape back to England.

The Dutch border was the scene of another successful escape by Classon Preston – whom readers will recall commanded a section of 119 Battery's guns at Audregnies. After his section sergeant had put him in the care of the field ambulance, Preston was taken to the Bavai Red Cross hospital but managed to escape before the hospital was overrun. Heading north he was given shelter by the de Croy family at the Château de Bellignies. He could not have fallen into safer hands. In late October 1914 Preston – by now a captain – and the Princess Marie de Croy made contact with a large group of British soldiers hiding in the Forêt de Mormal, a group which was led by an officer of 2/Dragoon Guards, Lieutenant Claude Bushell. The Queen's Bays officer had found himself on the wrong side of the line after the retirement from Le Cateau and had been on the run ever since. Bushell's men were a collection from several different regiments, many of whom were in a poor state physically, a factor combined with the practicality of caring for such a large number that resulted in their eventual surrender to the authorities. In the event only Bushell and Preston managed to escape to Holland after crawling under the wire. Both men arrived in England on 4 January 1915 but received no decoration for their 4 month ordeal. Preston was mentioned in despatches for his bravery at Audregnies and ended the war with the rank of major. His award of the Military Cross was announced in the *London Gazette* in January 1918. Bushell ended his war with the same rank and retired in 1920 with the honorary rank of captain. He died in 1985, aged 94.

Several more successful escapes were recorded before the trench lines of the Western Front were fully established. Three men of 4/Hussars who became separated from the regiment after a skirmish on 25 August reached the channel ports. Major Hugh Mockett managed to reach Dunkirk after more than a month of hiding and moving by night, as did Privates James Marney and Reginald Hensler who likewise evaded capture and made it to Boulogne. All three survived the war, Mockett retiring with the rank of lieutenant colonel. Two medical officers who had remained behind with the wounded at Landrecies – Major Arthur Irvine and Captain Dywer – made their bid for freedom on 10 September 1914. Having being transferred to the Red Cross Hospital at Bavai they took full advantage of an unguarded exit and headed north to Valenciennes.

Reaching Lille, which they found in German hands, the pair finally made it to Dunkirk.

* * *

After the Battle of Le Cateau the countryside was strewn with isolated groups of British soldiers who had become detached from their regiments and cut off by enemy forces. The full story of the plight of these individuals will probably never be fully revealed. Some inevitably died of exposure whilst eking out an existence in the surrounding woodland and those who were given shelter by the local population either survived until 1918 or were later captured and, in most instances, subsequently shot as spies. Why so many chose to remain in hiding can probably be attributed to the expectation that the Allied forces would soon return; after all hadn't everyone expected the war to be over by Christmas? However, it must be said that the chances of making a successful escape from hiding after Christmas 1914 were slim. From the beginning of 1915 the only real option open to fugitive British soldiers was to remain in hiding or to surrender. I have often wondered if there were indeed any British soldiers who survived and, having been sheltered locally for several years, took the decision not to return after the Armistice in 1918, preferring instead to remain fully integrated and undiscovered in their new surroundings and content to build new lives amongst the people who had taken them in.

It is clear that where there was good leadership, men were happy enough to rely on their officers to get them back to Allied lines and numerous collections of stragglers found themselves successfully negotiating hazardous journeys through German held positions. One of these was the young Lieutenant Bernard Montomery who had been left behind with his company of 1/Royal Warwicks after 10 Brigade had retired from Haucourt on 26 August. Led by Major Arthur Poole the group moved south west to Gouy. Here Poole disposed of the company's machine guns before resuming their march to a wood near Ronssoy where they remained hidden until the next morning. On 28 August the party moved off at first light arriving at Bernes at 7.00 am where, apart from managing to commandeer enough food for all, they had sight of their first friendly faces in the form of French cavalry. That afternoon they rejoined the BEF at Matigny where they discovered Colonel Elkington had been cashiered over the St Quentin incident and at Brie Compte Robert on 5 September Poole found himself in command of the battalion – on the last day of the retreat.

Fighting alongside the Warwicks at Haucourt had been 2/Dublin Fusiliers. They too had received no order to retire and were still engaged with the enemy as darkness fell. General Haldane's diary recorded the retirement:

'I believe the order to retire went out about 3.30pm, when the 5ᵗʰ Division, which had born the brunt of the attack, was in imminent danger of being enveloped, a situation which would have imperilled the safety of the 3ʳᵈ and 4ᵗʰ Divisions on its left. The order reached me a few minutes before 5pm and directed me to cover the withdrawal of the division … from accounts which reached me later it seems that some remnants were still holding Haucourt under the command of Major Shewan, Royal Dublin Fusiliers.'[185]

Hugh Shewan's accidental rearguard fortuitously allowed the bulk of Haldane's brigade to get away and under the cover of darkness he led his 400 Dublin Fusiliers out of Haucourt as the Germans entered from the north. After a frustrating period of wandering about in the dark they reached the outskirts of Ligny in the dawn light of 27 August. Moving warily along the road to Clary they encountered what appeared to be friendly British troops on the outskirts of the village. Unconvinced by what he saw, Captain Alfred Trigona's suspicions were quickly confirmed when one of their number was shot down on the road. A wild fire fight ensued as German troops opened fire from their positions on the edge of the village. Captain Clarke recalled the chaos of the next few minutes:

'The rattle of musketry increased, and bullets came whizzing and flipping amongst us. The men spread out as they ran for greater safety … a retirement under fire is always nasty – this was positively horrid'.[186]

Corporal James O'Donnell also had vivid memories of the fight at Clary:

'We were surrounded and everybody realised that we had been trapped. It seemed to be the case of our surrendering, but this we did not do. There was then nothing left but to make a dash for it back in the teeth of their shells, and the officers determined to adopt this course than surrender. The only way it could be done was by dashing in small parties. I was with Lieut. Macky's party, [Second Lieutenant Francis Macky] and of our little contingent only our leader another lance corporal and myself escaped. We had to cover about 700 yards under a perfect rain of bullets, and those of us who escaped were saved by a beetroot field. About half way towards comparative safety we were forced to lie flat in the beetroot and were covered by the leaves'.[187]

Hugh Shewan – by now wounded along with 5 other officers – ordered a retirement and the Dublins fell back on Ligny leaving 1 officer and 44 other ranks dead or dying behind them. Shewan was taken prisoner along with Lieutenant Macky and the other wounded, spending the remaining period of the war in Germany.

The Dublins were now only some 40 strong and, led by the 2 surviving officers, Captains Alfred Trigona and Norman Clarke, struck north towards Caudry where they took advantage of the Warnelle valley and the railway line to remain undetected. Concealing themselves somewhere between Haucourt and Fontaine-au-Pire they watched local farm workers gathering up the bodies on the battlefield before slipping out to collect up anything edible they could salvage from the dead. 'Our object', wrote Clarke 'was to rejoin as soon as possible, and not to fight, for if we indulged in fighting there was small hope of ever rejoining'. Despite some very close calls with German troops they continued their journey crossing the Cambrai road on 29 August and heading north towards Naves on the Cambrai–Bavai road. During the night they increased their number by 8 men of 1/Gordon Highlanders who themselves had been in hiding for 3 days. Aided by the local population Clarke and Trigona led the group on what can only be described as an incredible journey which took them over the Sensée Canal and the busy Douai–Arras road towards Lens, arriving at Izel-lez-Equerchin at 2.30 am on 2 September. The next day they marched into Lens – the Germans were entering at the same time from the north – and boarded a train taking French reservists to their regimental depots. It would be another 24 hours before they were on a boat crossing the channel back to England.

Clarke and Trigona had begun their journey with 40 men and by the time they reached the safety of British lines they had collected another 36 stragglers from ten different regiments who had been scattered across the countryside. It had taken 8 days to march from Haucourt and judging from the evidence in Clarke's report there were plenty of stragglers still at large north of Le Cateau. Both Trigona and Clarke survived the war; Trigona – a member of an aristocratic Maltese family – died a baron in Malta in March 1975 whilst Lieutenant Colonel Clarke died in 1945 aged 66.

Another group of 2/Royal Irish led by Major Stratford St Leger managed a similar journey back to British lines after being cut off late on 26 August. The men of 8 Brigade were holding the ground to the east and north of Audencourt and with the pressure building up in the Caudry salient two companies of 2/Royal Irish – under the command of St Leger – were brought up at 8.30 am in support of 1/Gordons. Here they successfully held the advance of IR 93 from across the Cambrai road until 3.30 pm when 8 Brigade was given orders to begin retiring – orders which failed to reach the Royal Irish and the Gordons. It was a situation similar to that experienced by the Dublin Fusiliers and Warwicks, the men held on until nightfall after which every man for himself became the order of the day. Major St Leger – as we know from his command of the Royal Irish three days previously at Mons – was not a man to contemplate surrender and despite being surrounded he and a group of eight other ranks evaded capture by striking north towards Antwerp. With no maps the party marched only at night, lying up by day in barns provided by friendly Belgian farmers before finally reaching the safety of Belgian lines at Oudenarde.

* * *

But what of those individuals who remained behind in the care of the local population? The accounts which have come to light provide us with evidence of heroism and self-sacrifice on the part of local people whom, at huge risk to themselves, hid British soldiers from the Germans, often in their own homes. A typical act of selfless courage was that experienced by 19-year-old Private David Cruickshank of the 1/Cameronians. Cruickshank had enlisted only 6 months before the outbreak of war and after finding himself separated from his unit he had made his way into Le Cateau and threw himself on the mercy of Julie-Celestine Baudhuin, a local woman whose son and husband were fighting with the French Army. David remained in hiding in the home of the Baudhuin family until September 1916 when his presence was betrayed by a local woman. The Germans arrested not only David, but also Julie-Celestine and her son Leon. The courageous Julie-Celestine only avoided the death penalty by successfully pleading for her life along with that of David Cruickshank but both spent the remainder of the war in prison whilst Leon was sent to a work camp. Released after the war Julie-Celestine was reunited with her husband but tragically their eldest son Jules had been killed in September 1914.

Betrayal was the theme running through another story which involved 26-year-old Private Robert Digby of the Royal Hampshire Regiment who was one of four men stranded in the village of Villeret, northwest of St Quentin. On 16 May 1916, Privates Thomas Donohoe, David Martin, William Thorpe and Robert Digby were betrayed by one of the villagers and, all but Digby – who escaped through a window – were arrested, their trial at Le Câtelet was swift and all three were convicted of being spies, the sentence of death being carried out 11 days later. Digby was persuaded to surrender after hearing the villagers had been threatened with death unless he gave himself up, his trial lasted less than an hour and he followed his three comrades to the grave on 30 May 1916. But this was also a love story with a tragic ending for Robert Digby had fallen in love with a local girl with whom he had fathered a daughter. Claire Dessenne gave birth to their child, Hélène, on 14 November 1915 and thus the little girl was just 6 months old when her father was executed. Today the four men are remembered in Le Câtelet with a plaque erected in their memory on the only remaining piece of the château where they were executed. In the nearby communal cemetery the CWGC have erected headstones over their graves. As for Hélène, she grew up and remained in Villeret where she died, aged 90, in 2005. Her grave is in the village communal cemetery.

Betrayal was again to the fore in another story involving Trooper Patrick Fowler of 11/Hussars who became separated from his regiment after Le Cateau.

Until January 1915 he lived in the woods surrounding the battlefield – quite how he survived this ordeal is beyond belief – but survive he did until he was discovered by a local man named Louis Basquin who lived in the nearby village of Bertry. Basquin arranged for the soldier to be given shelter by his mother-in-law and for the next 4 years until the end of the war, Fowler spent much of his time hiding in a wardrobe.

But Fowler wasn't the only British fugitive being hidden in the village, Corporal Herbert Hull from the same regiment was living in the Cardon household and had he not been betrayed in September 1915 by local woman Irma Ferlicot, he too might have survived until liberated by British troops. When German troops arrived at the Cardon household and made straight for Hull's hiding place Monsieur Cardon managed to escape but Hull and Madame Cardon were arrested and sentenced to death – Madame Cardon's sentence was later commuted to 20 years hard labour but Herbert Hull was executed on 21 September 1915 and is buried at Caudry Old Communal Cemetery.[188] Fowler survived to be liberated at the end of the war.

Perhaps the most tragic case which came to light was the capture and execution of eleven British soldiers who had been taken in by the Chalandre and Logez families at Iron, a small village some 15 miles south east of Bertry. The men were fugitives from the rearguard actions at Le Grand Fayt and Etreux and were discovered by Vincent Chalandre in early October 1914. Initially there were nine soldiers but the number increased to eleven in December after the discovery of two more Irish soldiers hiding nearby. The driving force behind sheltering the eleven men seems to have been the courageous Madame Léonie Logez and until February 1915 the arrangements made for the eleven men worked well. Sensitive information in the hands of the wrong people, however, can lead to disastrous results. Whether it was prompted by sexual jealousy or revenge – or both – the betrayal of the soldiers and their benefactors centred on two of the lovers of a local woman named Blanche Maréchal.

Amongst her many suitors was Clovis Chalandre, the 16-year-old son of Vincent Chalandre, who let slip during one of their assignations that British soldiers were being sheltered by his family. Blanche passed on the information not only to her husband but to her other lovers, including the 66-year-old Bachelet. Young Clovis was jealous of Bachelet and on the night of 21 February, in a not untypical juvenile response, Clovis threw stones at Bachelet's window. This relatively harmless – if not rather pathetic fit of teenage jealousy – prompted an altogether more devastating reaction from Bachelet. In a desire for revenge, the old man drove to Guise the next morning and informed the German authorities of the presence of eleven British soldiers in the village. Vincent Chalandre was arrested with the eleven on 22 February, the following day his wife and two of their children – one being Clovis – were also arrested along with Léonie Logez and two of her children. Both the properties belonging to the two families were burnt to the ground in reprisal. On 25 February 1915 the so called

'Guise Eleven' were executed in the grounds of Guise Château along with Vincent Chalandre. The remaining members of the two families were sentenced to terms of imprisonment.

It appears that the 120 francs Bachelet received for his betrayal of what he called 'deserters' was not enough. He also informed the authorities about several other British soldiers in hiding locally and French sources indicate that an unknown number were afterwards captured and shot. At the end of the war Bachelet was arrested and taken into custody in September 1918 but died in custody whilst at the military prison in Châlons-sur-Marne before he could be brought to trial. The twelve executed men – five Munster Fusiliers, one cavalryman from 15/Hussars, five Connaught Rangers and Vincent Chalandre – are buried at Guise Communal Cemetery. Chalandre's grave has only recently been located in the Guise Communal Cemetery and there are plans to acknowledge his part in the episode with a plaque, linking him to the British soldiers buried close by.[189]

There is an intriguing footnote to this story, Michael Cary, the Munster Fusilier who crawled under the wire with Harry Beaumont, claimed to have been a member of the group at Iron but was apparently absent from the village on the day of the arrests. There is plenty of evidence – particularly when his account is compared to others –which suggests he may not be the twelfth man who escaped execution at Guise but he clearly knew of the incident in 1915 as he recounted it – albeit with inaccuracies – to Harry Beaumont whilst they were at the Berkendael Institute.

* * *

There were some truly remarkable escapes from prisoner of war camps in Germany made by British officers and men who had been captured in the first weeks of the war. One of the most prolific escapers was 20-year-old Second Lieutenant Jocelyn Hardy of the Connaught Rangers who had been taken prisoner at Maroilles after the ambush at Le Grand Fayt on 26 August. His first attempt at escape was made at Halle in 1915 when he broke through the wall of an adjacent factory. Although this failed he almost succeeded a few months later when he and another officer actually got aboard a Swedish steamer but he was arrested just before the ship was preparing to sail. Returned to Halle he made two further attempts – one with a party of Russian prisoners and another on his own when he caught a train to Bremen with the intention of reaching the Dutch border. Both these attempts failed as did his next which he made from Magdeburg. Here he teamed up with a Belgian officer and using Hardy's fluency in German, they caught a train to Berlin and then on to Stralsund on the Baltic coast where they were once again caught trying to find a fishing boat to take them to Sweden. Hardy's notorious record as an escaper resulted in him being sent to Fort Zorndorf from which escape was thought to be impossible.

Nevertheless, he made several more attempts, one nearly succeeding when he and two other prisoners disguised themselves as German soldiers. On another occasion he managed to break away from his guards whilst being marched to the *kommandatura* which was outside the camp, and got as far as the train before being recaptured.

Hardy's final attempt was made from Schweidnitz in Silesia in the company of Captain William Loder-Symonds of the Wiltshire Regiment. Carrying forged passes the two men caught a train to Aachen where they continued by tram to Richtericht and two days later crossed the nearby border into Holland. By the middle of March 1918 they were back in England and both officers were received by the King at Buckingham Palace on 18 March. Hardy – by now a captain – returned to the front a month later, this time to *the* 2/Inniskilling Fusiliers and in time to take part in yet another retreat in the teeth of the German 1918 offensives. In August 1918 he was awarded the Military Cross for bravery on the Ypres front but two months later, during a counter attack near Dadizeele, the wounds he received resulted in the loss of a leg. In 1920 the *London Gazette* announced his award of the DSO for his leadership at Dadizeele and a bar to his MC in recognition of his escape attempts and successful home run the previous year. William Loder-Symonds was less fortunate. He was the fourth of the five Loder-Symonds brothers to be killed in the Great War. Transferring to the newly formed Royal Air Force, he was killed in a flying accident in June 1918. His elder brother John had been killed in October 1914 serving in the South Staffordshire Regiment, Robert, who died in March 1915, was serving with the Cheshires and the youngest, Thomas, was killed on 9 May 1915 with the Cameronians. William is commemorated on the Beenham War Memorial in West Berkshire and in January 1918 he was mentioned in despatches in the *London Gazette* for gallant conduct and determination in escaping.

Several other soldiers who had been taken prisoner during the retreat also made successful home runs from German prisoner of war camps. Private Samuel Waugh of the Lancashire Fusiliers was captured on 26 August at Le Cateau and kept at Cambrai for two days before being sent to Sennelager. He appears to have been transferred to a number of camps before escaping from Dortmund in February 1916. This bid for freedom lasted for only 4 days but he was successful 6 months later when he got away from his working party on 2 August, crossing the Dutch border after 8 days on the run

Just 5 days after Samuel Waugh reached Holland Private Charles Brash of the Argyll and Sutherland Highlanders also successfully crossed the Dutch border after escaping from his prisoner of war camp near Hanover. Wounded and captured on Suffolk Hill, Waugh spent time in a variety of camps in Germany and made two attempts to escape before finally succeeding on 13 August in the company of Private Thomas McDonald of the Gordon Highlanders. Waugh, McDonald and Brash received the Military Medal in 1920.

Chapter 15

Aftermath

The Battle of the Marne is numbered amongst the great battles of history and was the turning point of the retreat in 1914. It is not within the scope of this book, however, to examine the battle which many feel changed the course of history. Suffice to say the Allied victory on the Marne shattered the Schlieffen Plan once and for all and concluded with the German armies retiring to the heights above the Aisne where the two sides dug in – trench warfare along with everything which that term came to stand for over the next four years and two months – had arrived. British casualties on the Marne numbered over 12,000 one of which was 20-year-old Drummer George Whittington from Wimbledon who was killed on 10 September during his battalion's attack on the village of Priez. He is buried at the Montreuil-aux-Lions British Cemetery a few miles to the south. In one of his last entries in his diary he writes of his friend George Scutt being taken off to hospital with fever. It was probably this sickness which accounted for his death in England in March 1915. He lies in the Bear Road Cemetery at Brighton.

The soldiers of 2/KOSB were only too aware that the Germans were retreating in front of them as they moved up towards Hartennes. The boot was now very much on the other foot and the newly promoted Captain Pennyman's delight at being in pursuit is evident from his diary entry on 10 September:

'Marched all day through unsavoury German remains. There was debris of all kinds along the road, consisting of wagons and things they had got rid of to hasten their progress, a dead horse every ten yards and a fair number of soldiers ... amongst other things was a deserted machine gun limber. It was a most beautiful little conveyance and all the fittings were A1. I remember finding, in a deserted German great coat, a French map of French roads and railways'.[190]

By 13 September the battalion was at Sermoise overlooking the Aisne and involved in the heavy fighting that was taking place as II Corps began crossing the river. The Germans had blown the main road bridge to Missy-sur-Aisne but the Sappers from 59/Field Company had begun to put men on the other side with makeshift rafts and in this rather precarious manner three battalions of 13 Brigade were put across the river by daybreak on 14 September. It was during these crossings under heavy fire that Lieutenant Robert Flint – whom readers last met blowing bridges on the Oise – won his DSO as James Pennycuick and Major Walker watched him and Captain William Johnston worked a raft across the river, taking ammunition one way and bringing wounded men back the other. Johnston was awarded the Victoria Cross but was killed near St Eloi less than 9 months later. Robert Flint was killed near Ypres in January 1915.[191]

Once the KOSB were established in the wooded area on the north bank at Missy, Captain Robert Dolbey – the medical officer attached to the battalion – established his forward dressing station in a nearby barn. Dolbey wrote a book of his experiences with the battalion and recalled the moment Gilbert Amos was killed:

> *'There lay young Amos, one of our junior subalterns. Only the day before I had spoken to him as we lay lazily listening to the overhead shelling in the woods behind La Sermoise ... I remember I told him he must have had a very watchful Guardian Angel. Now again his Guardian Angel had come to him, this time with a wreath'.*[192]

From his account of the battle on the Aisne it was clear that Dolbey was appalled by the extent of the casualties the battalion was taking, 'life was very short for the officers of the battalion', he wrote, 'and if death had not come now, it would surely have overtaken [them] in the next three months'. His prophecy was all too correct and proved to be the epitaph for the 1914 army. By the end of the year – after the First Battle of Ypres had taken its shocking toll of officers and men – the BEF had been reduced to a shadow of its former self. One of his next casualties was Jim Pennyman:

> *'Then Pennyman was brought in, all limp and grey and cold; there was blood on his shirt in front and my orderly, seeing the position of the wound, said, too loudly, that he was gone. This roused him, and I knew the age of miracles was not past and the bullet had just missed the big vessels at the base of the heart'.*[193]

Pennyman had been shot through the left side by a sniper, the bullet passing through his left hand before lodging in the lung where it remained. By 19 September after a rail journey of 48 hours, he was a patient at Number 8 Field Hospital, Rouen, and 10 days later arrived at the Edward VII Hospital for Officers in London. In August 1916 Pennyman was back on active service in the Ypres sector as second-in-command of 1/KOSB with the rank of acting major and still not fully recovered from his wounds. All too soon the battalion was moved to the Somme area to reinforce the bloody closing stages of that costly campaign before taking part in the Arras offensive in 1917. In June 1917 the *London Gazette* announced his secondment to the School of Musketry at Hythe – joining him at Hythe and announced in the same issue of the *Gazette* – was Norman Clarke of the Dublin Fusiliers, now a major. Pennyman's war was effectively over and apart from a brief return to the 1st Battalion in November 1918 when the battalion was in Germany, he soldiered on until 1921 when he retired through ill-health.

There were 40 more productive years before Lieutenant Colonel James Beaumont Worsley Pennyman died at home in September 1961. He is buried in St Cuthbert's Churchyard, Ormesby, in the family plot along with his second wife Ruth. After the war he kept in touch with many of the surviving Borderers and it would have been with some sadness that he learnt of the death of Private Charles Harding who had been in his machine gun section all during the retreat. Harding only got as far as Ypres before he was hospitalized after being buried by a shell in November 1914, an experience he never fully recovered from. Discharged in 1915 as unfit for further service, he was employed as a Draper's Porter before he died at home in March 1920 aged 28. Charles Harding left a widow, Margaret, and an 1- month-old daughter. In one of his last letters to Pennyman he recalled with some pride the battalion's actions at Mons and 'the little stunt I performed with you at Le Cateau'. Harding's story and those of the thousands of others who later died as a result of their injuries was part of the forgotten legacy of suffering of the Great War.

Kenneth Godsell – a member of the old established Gloucestershire brewing family – was also on the Aisne at Missy transporting men across the river and later served with his field company at Ypres where he won an MC in 1915. The award of the DSO followed in 1917 which he received at Buckingham Palace in September 1918. He retired from the army in 1919 with the rank of Brevet Lieutenant Colonel and died at Stroud in August 1959, aged 67. He had been fortunate in surviving the war intact, many of his contemporaries who left England in 1914 with him did not fare so well. Of the 69 RE officers in the eleven field companies serving with the BEF during the retreat over one third were killed in action and the majority of those were killed in 1914 or early 1915. Robert Egerton, the 26-year-old former Clifton College schoolboy who fought with 1/Field Squadron was an early casualty being killed in November 1914.[194] In one of his last letters home he complained at not getting enough action, 'I wish I had been in a field company when this war broke out', he wrote, 'the companies have had a much better show'.

November 1914 was a cruel month on the Ypres front. It was a month which saw the deaths of Lieutenant Arthur Carr and Lieutenant Neville Woodroffe – the Irish Guards officer who fell asleep at Landrecies – who was killed at

Zillebeke, four days before Major Bernard Gordon Lennox met his death at Bodmin Copse on 10 November.[195]

Many would say that 1915 was harder still. In the first 5 months of the year British and Dominion forces fought four major battles on the Western Front – battles which witnessed the death of Kenneth Godsell's comrade in arms, the ever resourceful Valdo Pottinger, who had fired his revolver at the detonator at Lock Number 4 on the canal at Mons. He died of his wounds in May at one of the field hospitals at Rouen.[196] 22-year-old Rowland Owen was killed on Hill 60, Ypres, in early May whilst fighting with 2/Duke of Wellington's. John Hamilton-Dalrymple was also a casualty of 1915, killed in April at Mauser Ridge, near Ypres, the 26-year-old lieutenant was one of the last officers left in 2/KOSB who had fought at Mons with Jim Pennyman.[197]

Where the death in action of a serving soldier left dependants, the bereaved were entitled to a war pension, unless the death was not deemed to be a result of wounds received in action. In November 1914 Charles Fishbourne – who had been involved in the action at Bailly – was wounded in the head at Ypres resulting in his eventual evacuation home. Sadly these wounds appear to have contributed to his death from Cerebro Spinal Meningitis in May 1915, and his widow applied for a war pension. However, the War Office did not agree and decided in its wisdom that all Mary Fishbourne and their 2-year-old son Charles were only entitled to was a compassionate allowance of £20 per year. Mary Fishbourne was devastated and immediately wrote to Winston Churchill – reminding him of the occasion when her husband had accompanied him on safari in Uganda in 1907 – and asking for his help. Churchill intervened and, needless to say, the allowance was increased to £75 in addition to the £20 already agreed.[198]

1915 was not a good year for Sir John French and Horace Smith-Dorrien. The animosity between the two men came to a head after Smith-Dorrien advocated a tactical withdrawal in April 1915 to consolidate the front line at Ypres. Haig wrote in his diary on 30 April:

> *Sir John also told me Smith-Dorrien had caused him much trouble. He was quite unfit (he said) to hold the Command of an Army, and so Sir J. had withdrawn all troops from his control except the II Corps. Yet Smith D stayed on! (He would not resign!) French is to ask Lord Kitchener to find him something to do at home … He also alluded to Smith-Dorrien's conduct on the retreat, and said he ought to have tried him by Court Martial, because (on the day of Le Cateau) he had ordered him to retire at 8 am and he did not attempt to do so'.*

Sir John was still bearing a grudge over Le Cateau and used Smith-Dorrien's suggestion of a withdrawal to remove him, accusing him of having a pessimistic outlook. Sir John had clearly chosen to forget his own behaviour during the retreat! To add insult to injury, several days later Sir John accepted the advice of General Herbert Plumer – Smith Dorrien's replacement – to perform a withdrawal almost identical to the one Smith-Dorrien had recommended. But Sir John's days as commander-in-chief were numbered as criticism mounted from all quarters, including Haig, who told the King in October 1915 that Sir John should have been removed after the retreat. French clung to command until the failures at Aubers Ridge and Loos forced Kitchener to replace him with Douglas Haig in December 1915. Smith-Dorrien died in August 1939 following a car accident.

For many others the war provided rapid promotion. Bernard Montgomery eventually rose to the exalted rank of field marshal but finished the war as a lieutenant colonel on the staff; Gerald Smyth began his war as a lieutenant and ended it as a 33-year-old Brigadier General commanding 93 Infantry Brigade four years later. He commanded 6/KOSB from November 1916 until October 1918, the regiment's history describing him as 'one of the best COs who commanded any unit of the regiment in the war'. Not a bad war record for a sapper! He finished his war with the DSO and bar, both the French and Belgian Croix de Guerre and five mentions in despatches – but without his left arm which he lost at Givenchy in October 1914. A passionate Ulster Unionist, Gerald became embroiled in the brutal turmoil of the Anglo-Irish War when he accepted the job of Divisional Commissioner of Police in Munster. It was to be a job that cost him his life in July 1920 when he was murdered by an IRA gang. He is buried at Banbridge in County Down.

James Pennycuick was mentioned in despatches three times in addition to his DSO, to which he added a bar in 1917. Like Gerald Smyth he also passed through Staff College after which he was appointed Brigade Major of 10 Infantry Brigade in 1925. Pennycuick retired from the army in 1945 as a Brigadier General and died in February 1966, aged 75. Percy Boulnois went to Italy in 1917 in command of 54/Field Company became a colonel and won the MC; Bernard Young who blew the bridge at Compiègne won a MC and became a major general serving in both wars and finally retiring in 1945. He died in 1969 aged 77. Henry Kane O'Kelly, the Dukes officer at Crépy-en-Valois who captured the two staff cars, retired as a lieutenant colonel as did CQMS Fitzpatrick of the Royal Irish who held the crossroads in the Nimy salient. Tom Bridges commanded a division in 1917 and lost his left leg in the process, whilst that able Grenadiers officer, Major 'Ma' Jeffreys, eventually commanded his battalion and was a major general in 1918. Captain Josslyn Vere Ramsden, the adjutant of XXVII Brigade RFA, retired as a lieutenant colonel with a DSO and Lieutenant William Tenison, who commanded a battery of guns so well at Crépy-en-Valois, also won a DSO, retiring with the rank of major.

Brigadier General Gleichen continued to command his brigade until March 1915. Subsequently, as a major-general, he commanded the 37th Division until October 1916. He was then appointed Director of the Political Intelligence Bureau of the recently established Department of Information, of which his close friend, the author John Buchan, was a deputy director; this post he held for the rest of the war. He retired from the Army in 1919 and died in December 1937. He changed his title in 1917 to Lord Edward Gleichen. Brigadier General Aylmer Haldane became a lieutenant general and commanded VI Army Corps before becoming GOC Mesopotamia from 1920-22. Sir James Aylmer Haldane died in 1950 and was buried at Brookwood Cemetery, he was 87.

But there were others, like the unfortunate Claude Bushell, whose promotion did not profit from war. Lance Corporal Alfred Jarvis, the reservist who won the VC at Mons, was still a private when he was discharged in 1917 and relatively young when he died aged 67 in 1948, but he was one of the more fortunate holders of the award, of the fifteen other VCs won during the retreat two were awarded posthumously and only seven of the other recipients survived. George Tailby, the subaltern who discovered von Garnier's cavalry division at Néry, retired as a lieutenant in 1919 but called himself Captain Tailby ever afterwards. He did serve as General Allenby's ADC but rank and promotion were in all probability of little importance to him as after the war he inherited his uncle's estate in Leicestershire and lived a very privileged life until his death in 1964.

Jack Giffard's adventures on 1 September at Néry did not conclude with his evacuation to Baron. The next morning the hospital was overrun by the Germans and for the next four or five days they were technically prisoners of war during which time Giffard's diary noted the death of his friend Lionel Mundy.[199] On the morning of Saturday 5 September Sergeant Nelson managed to escape from the hospital grounds and, still wearing his hospital slippers, climbed the perimeter wall and ran into a French cavalry patrol. Help was not far away and before long the advancing French 14th Division was back in charge. Giffard reached Le Havre on 10 September and was taken to the Frascati Hotel which had been turned into a military hospital.[200] A week later he was home but would never be passed fit for active duty again. His wounds – which he makes light of in his diary – were evidently serious enough to ensure he spent the remainder of his war service with the British War Mission to the United States, his work there recognised by the OBE. Invalided out of the army, he retired to grow tobacco in Southern Rhodesia. He died, aged 72, in 1956.

Cyril Helm ended his war in command of 42/Field Ambulance and with the ribbons of the MC and DSO on his chest. He retired from the RAMC in 1923 and went into private practice near Colchester only to be recalled in 1939 to take a mobile general hospital to Nigeria. Returning from the Gold Coast he landed in Normandy on D Day+7 in command of the first 600-bed hospital to be established in occupied Europe. In 1947 he retired again, this time to take up general practice in Plymouth. This grand old warrior died, aged 83, in 1972. Arthur Habgood, who served with 9/Field Ambulance during the retreat, also finished his war with the DSO and in command of 142/Field Ambulance and lived until he was 96. Gerard Kempthorne, the 1/Lincolns medical officer, was awarded the DSO and died in 1939. His army career, which began in 1903, ended after 28 years service in 1931with the rank of lieutenant colonel. Captain Eburne Hamilton the 7/Field Ambulance doctor who was captured on 23 August near Mons, was eventually repatriated and returned to England in 1915 along with Captain Robert Dolbey, whom, after moving to the La Bassée front with 2/KOSB in October 1914, was captured shortly afterwards.

Promotion for Thomas Wollocombe – the adjutant of the 4/Middlesex at Mons – followed quickly. He was promoted to captain in 1915 – the year in which he won his MC – and less than a year later he was promoted to major. Command of a battalion came in February 1917 when he took over the 11th (Service) Battalion of the Middlesex from Lieutenant Colonel Pargiter, remaining as colonel of the battalion until it was disbanded a year later. After his death in 1957, his son Richard published his father's diary, an account which remains to this day as one of the classic narratives by an infantry officer in the Great War. In its pages Wollocombe recounts his admiration of 2/Royal Irish as an effective fighting unit which he formed at Mons when the two battalions fought side by side, an impression that was added to when the Irish battalion took Le Pilly, a village to the north of La Bassée, 2 months later.

Command of the Royal Irish at Le Pilly was in the hands Lieutenant Colonel Edward Daniell who was killed 2 days later, had Major Stratford St Leger not become separated from the regiment at Audencourt, in all probability, as senior major, he would have been in command himself at the time. However, St Leger was back with the battalion by 25 October – to the delight of all ranks – assuming command until December when he joined the General Staff. He was awarded the DSO in 1916, made a CMG in 1918 and a CVO in 1921.[201] One of St Leger's lasting legacies is *War Sketches in Colour*, which contains sixty-six of his sketches and water colours made in South Africa during his time with the mounted Infantry fighting the Boers, recently a copy was sold for over £500. Stratford 'Zulu' St Leger died at Hove in 1935.

Aubrey Herbert's account of his experiences during the retreat was published in 1919 under the title *Mons, Anzac and Kut*. Born into a world of wealth and privilege at Highclere – the magnificent ancestral home of the Earls of Carnarvon – he was the half brother of George, the 5th Earl, who discovered Tutankhamun's tomb. Educated at Eton and Balliol, he became honorary attaché first in Tokyo, then in Constantinople. In 1911 he entered Parliament as Conservative member for the Yeovil Division of Somerset, a constituency which continued to elect him until his death. On the outbreak of war – despite his poor eyesight – he went to war with 1/Irish Guards. As readers will recall he was captured at Villers-Cotterêts on 1 September 1914 after being badly wounded during the retirement in the forest. Herbert was taken with the other Guards Brigade wounded to Viviers where they remained until the advancing French arrived on 11 September. In the last months of the war he was the head of the English Mission attached to the Italian Army in Albania. He died prematurely – aged 43 – in September 1923 from blood poisoning.

After the Royal Berkshires' attack on the bridge at Maroilles on the night of 25 August the recovered dead were buried in a mass grave at Maroilles communal cemetery. The only officer amongst those killed in action was Captain Henry Shott and once his death had been confirmed, his widow Hazel returned to the United States. However, in 1920 she received a letter from the War Office to the effect that her late husband's ring had been found having been in the possession of a Monsieur Wattrelos. Presuming it had been found near Maroilles, Hazel Shott was a little surprised to hear it had been picked up near the canal at Tertre in Belgium on 24 August 1914.

The Berkshires had been at Bavai on 24 August – nowhere near Tertre – and initially it was thought the ring had been the property of an officer of 2/KOSB but the initials 'HS' engraved on the ring's crest eventually led to the Shott family. So what was Henry Shott doing at Tertre? We know he was at Maroilles on 25 August so presumably he was north of the canal sometime before the 23rd. The battalion war diary gives nothing in the way of supplementary information and makes no mention of officers being detached on other duties leaving a question mark remaining over the intriguing tale of Henry Shott's ring.

Returning prisoners of war were required to make statements on their return giving an account of the circumstances of their capture and their experiences in prisoner of war camps. Arthur Peebles' statement, which he made in Switzerland in 1917 after repatriation, runs to nine pages in which he details the appalling treatment suffered by British officers and men at the hands of their captors. Following the train journey from Cambrai he was taken to Torgau, an old fort on the banks of the River Elbe, where each officer:

'*was supplied with a plank bed, straw mattress and blankets, a stool, earthenware basin and jug … the sanitary arrangements were very bad, the latrine consisted of an enormous hole in the ground which was emptied at intervals*'.[202]

At Torgau he shared a room with Major Charles Yate, the VC winner at Le Cateau, and described the refusal of the German authorities to allow any British officers to see Yate's body after his attempted escape or to allow any of them to attend his funeral. The 2/KOYLI commanding officer, Colonel Reginald Bond, did all he could to establish the true facts of the case but to no avail and could only conclude Yate's death was the result of foul play.

Lieutenant Colonel Alexander Abercrombie's capture at Maroilles eventually took him first to Torgau with Arthur Peebles and then to the notorious camp at Magdeburg where he died in captivity in early November 1915. It was a particularly sad end to an army career that began in 1885 and a tragedy for the family which was unfortunately compounded by the death of his eldest son, Captain Alexander Ralph Abercrombie DSO, MC, who died of wounds on 31 December 1918. Elspeth Abercrombie – who was 12-years-old in 1918 – joined the Queen Alexander's Imperial Military Nursing Service and was present at Dunkirk in 1940 on a hospital ship which survived two very near misses from marauding German dive bombers.

Lieutenant Arthur Chitty, who was captured at Mons, was another officer who fought at Dunkirk in 1940. Having survived his term as a prisoner in Germany, Chitty commanded 4/Royal West Kents and won a DSO during the battalion's retreat to that channel port. His company commander at Mons, Captain George Lister, although in command of the 1st Battalion in 1920, fared less well. Lister was not a well man when he rejoined the regiment after the Armistice and died in November 1921.

Captain Stewart Newcombe, the officer whom Bernard Young was so glad to see at the Compiègne bridge, was taken prisoner in 1917 by the Turks. He was captured during the Third Battle of Gaza in Palestine after he led a party of men behind the lines. Forced to surrender after being surrounded, he was imprisoned in Constantinople and later at Brusa, from where he successfully escaped. Newcombe was a close associate of T E Lawrence – who was godfather to Newcombe's son Lawrence – and was one of the six pallbearers at Lawrence's funeral in 1935.

Being a prisoner of war was hard enough but readers might spare a thought for Major Abingdon Bayly who commanded 118 Battery's guns at Etreux. In June 1915, whilst he was a prisoner in Germany, he received the classic *Dear John* letter from his wife asking for a divorce:

'My dear Bill,

This letter that I am writing to you now is the hardest that I have ever written in my life, because I would do anything sooner than give you pain, but I am afraid that is impossible. For the last six months I have been most unhappy because an influence has come into my life which would make it absolutely impossible for me to ever live again with you as your wife, and after much deliberate thought I have come to the conclusion that it is much better for you to hear all this whilst you are away.

You will find the necessary evidence for obtaining a divorce from me at the Great Central Hotel, London, W., where I stayed with someone on June 18 as Mr. and Mrs. A. B——. You will not find out who it is or will ever do so, but I beg of you to instruct Messrs. Hennen and Co., of Quality-court, Chancery-lane, to send you the necessary papers so that proceedings can at once be taken against me.

I have made inquiries and find that your being a prisoner of war in Germany does not impede matters, and there are reasons why I beg of you to do this for me at once and to try and think as leniently of me as you can.

If this matter is carried through now during the war I feel sure that your name will be saved from any scandal, as people are far too busy to worry themselves over divorce cases these days. Please do not think that I did not try to fight against things, because I did; but I am not very old, and why should we both be miserable for the rest of our lives, because I never could return to you now and I feel sure that you, with your great sense of justice, would be the last person in the world to wish to see me unhappy for the rest of my life. I should suggest that Yvonne and Gerald stay with nurse until the war is over.

Yours regretfully,
Viola.'[203]

Bayly remarried after his return to England but his son Gerald, a lieutenant in the Fleet Air Arm, was killed at Taranto in 1940 flying from HMS *Eagle*.

Major Herbert Stewart's son Paul was also a lieutenant in the Royal Navy and he too was killed in 1940 serving on HMS *Bideford*. Stewart became a lieutenant colonel in charge of the Base Supply Depot at Le Havre. He was awarded the DSO in 1915 for 'services in connection with operations in the field' and in 1916 became Assistant Director of Supplies on the Lines of Communication in France, an appointment he held until the end of the war. He was made an OBE in 1919. Like Jack Giffard, Stewart retired to Southern Rhodesia.

Edward Spears died in 1974 after a career which spanned the two world wars and brought him into contact – and conflict – with the political backroom of both wars. A confidant of Winston Churchill, he began his military career as a subaltern in 11/Hussars but his love of all things French and his fluency in the language meant that his skills were put to better use as a liaison officer, first with the Fifth and later with the Tenth French Army. In 1915 he won the MC and was appointed head of the British Military Mission in Paris, retiring from the army as a brigadier general in 1920. He later described his part in the BEF's advance and retreat from Mons in *Liaison 1914* which was published in 1930, the first of several books which chronicled events in France. He was made a KBE in 1942 and a baronet in 1953.

In March 1921 the family of Lieutenant Frederick Styles bought the orchard at Etreux where the Munsters made their last stand on 27 August. The owner, a Monsieur Charles Dauzet, agreed the sum of 500 Francs for the land with Frederick's elder brother William, a major serving with 12/Lancers. Eight month later, after Dauzet realised the significance of the sale, he attempted unsuccessfully to double the sale price of the plot. This obvious attempt to cash in on the grief of the bereaved was ignored and work began to turn the small orchard on the Landrecies road into a permanent memorial to the officers and men of 2/Munsters. The cemetery was consecrated by the Dean of Wassigny on 5 October 1921 and amongst those who attended the ceremony were the parents of Lieutenant Vere Awdry, Captain Richard Chute – the brother of the battalion's machine-gun officer – and Frederick Style's two brothers and sister. On the rear wall of the cemetery a plaque was fixed which included the words:

> *'The action is likely to become the classical example of the performance of its functions by a rearguard; the battalion not only held up the attack by a strong hostile force in its original position, thereby securing the unmolested withdrawal of its division, but in retiring drew onto itself the attack of very superior numbers of the enemy'.*

Today a magnificent Celtic Cross stands defiantly at the entrance to the orchard at Etreux – just as the men of the Munsters stood and fought to the bitter end on 27 August 1914 – as an enduring reminder of this classic example of a dogged and disciplined rearguard action fought during a retreat that has long since passed beyond the realm of living memory. At the time of writing and with the centenary of the start of the Great War fast approaching it is fitting that we should remember this and numerous other gallant actions of the BEF as it fought to remain intact and stay in the fight in the face of a relentless pursuit by an aggressive and determined German Army almost a century ago.

Notes

Introduction
1. The Diary of J B W Pennyman. Teesside Archives U. PEN/7/150.

Chapter 1
2. Major Hubert Dunsterville Harvey-Kelly was shot down and killed on 21 December 1916 while flying as CO of 56 Squadron. He is buried at Brown's Copse Cemetery, Roeux – Special Memorial 7. He was 26-years-old and had been awarded the DSO and mentioned in despatches.
3. Haldane, a prominent Liberal and close associate of Asquith, was a strong advocate of British commitments on the continent. He implemented the Haldane Reforms, a wide-ranging set of reforms aimed at preparing the army for participation in a possible European war. The main element of this was the establishment of the British Expeditionary Force, along with the creation of the Imperial General Staff, the Territorial Force, the Officer Training Corps and the Special Reserve.
4. de Symons Barrow later became a Major General whilst Home was eventually promoted to Brigadier General.
5. Haig married the Hon. Dorothy Vivian who was a lady-in-waiting at the court of King Edward VII. She was a daughter of Hussey Vivian, 3rd Baron Vivian.
6. Letter written by L E O Charlton and held in the Fusilier Museum Archive.

Chapter 2
7. 4th Middlesex Regiment War Diary, TNA WO 95/1422.
8. A German infantry regiment in 1914 was of comparable size to that of a British brigade, consisting of three battalions and a machine-gun company. Each battalion was of a similar size to its British equivalent; 4/Middlesex for example, mustered 31 officers and 1,076 men on 5 August compared to 26 officers and 1,054 men of I/IR 86.
9. Lieutenant Herbert Wilfred Holt is buried at St Symphorien Military Cemetery. Grave Reference: V.A.4.
10. 4th Middlesex Regiment War Diary. TNA WO 95/1422.
11. Ibid.
12. POW Report. TNA WO 161.
13. 4th Middlesex Regiment War Diary. TNA WO 95/1422.
14. 2nd Royal Irish Regiment War Diary. TNA WO 95/1421.
15. Private Papers of E S B Hamilton. IWM Dept. of Documents 87/33/1.

16. Ibid.
17. John Denys Shine died of wounds on 25.8.14 and is buried at Mons (Bergen) Communal Cemetery. Grave Reference: IV.B.18
18. Private Papers of G A Kempthorne. IWM Dept. of Documents 79/17/1.
19. Soldiers Died in the Great War database.
20. Royal Anglian and Royal Lincolnshire Regimental Archive.

Chapter 3
21. The Diary of J B W Pennyman. Teesside Archives U. PEN/7/150.
22. Ibid.
23. Moloney C V, *Invicta – With the Queen's Own Royal West Kent Regiment in the Great War*. Nisbet & Co. 1923, p.9.
24. Bloem W, *The Advance From Mons*, Tandem 1967, p68.
25. The Diary of J B W Pennyman. Teesside Archives U. PEN/7/150.
26. Bloem, *The Advance From Mons*, p.80.
27. Moloney C V, *Invicta*, p.12.
28. The Diary of J B W Pennyman. Teeside Archives U. PEN/7/150.
29. The Personal Diary of Kenneth Godsell RE Journal Archive.
30. Private Papers of B T St John. IWM Dept. of Documents 83/17/1.
31. TNA WO 339/7224.
32. Private Papers of B T St John. IWM Dept. of Documents 83/17/1.
33. 2nd Royal Irish Regiment War Diary. TNA WO 95/1421.
34. Zuber T, *The Mons Myth*, The History Press 2010, p.167.
35. POW Report in TNA WO 161/95.

Chapter 4
36. Private Papers of G A Kempthorne. IWM Dept. of Documents 79/17/1.
37. Stewart H A, *From Mons to Loos – Being the Diary of a Supply Officer*. Blackwood 1916, p.25.
38. Private Papers of G A Kempthorne. IWM Dept. of Documents 79/17/1. Cecil Holmes is buried at Frameries Communal cemetery. Grave Reference: III.A.B
39. Stewart H A, *From Mons to Loos* op.cit.
40. Nurse F Aggasiz from an account in TNA WO 339/9412. Malcolm Leckie is buried at Frameries Communal Cemetery. Grave Reference: I.B.1
41. Private H J Halsey died of wounds on 13 September 1914, Lance Corporal H A Herriot died of wounds on 28 August 1914. These two men along with the five others who were killed in the action at Blaugies are buried at Hautrage Military Cemetery, Belgium.
42. Personal Papers of R H Owen. IWM Dept. of Documents 90/37/1.
43. Beaumont H, *Old Contemptible*. Hutchinson 1967, p.38.
44. Maximilian Francis Broadwood, aged 21 is buried at Hautrage Military Cemetery. Grave Reference: I.E.18. Charles George Pack-Beresford's name is commemorated on the La Ferté-sous-Jouarre Memorial.
45. Personal Papers of R H Owen. IWM Dept. of Documents 90/37/1.
46. The Diary of J B W Pennyman. Teesside Archives U.PEN/7/150.

Chapter 5
47. John Stirling Ainsworth, aged 23, was killed in action on 14 October 1914 near Ypres. He is buried at Meteren Military Cemetery. Grave Reference: IV.E.677.

48. Kenneth Croft North, aged 27, was killed in action on 31 October 1914 at Ypres. He is buried at Oak Dump Cemetery. Grave Reference: F.5.
49. Private Papers of J Giffard. IWM Dept. of Documents 05/9/1.
50. Anglesey, *A History of British Cavalry Vol 7*. Leo Cooper 1996, p.140.
51. Ibid, p.122.
52. an Emden R, *Tickled to Death to Go*. Spellmount 1996, p.53.
53. POW Report in TNA WO 161.
54. The controversy over whether there was actually a wire fence or not was fuelled by evidence from Major A H Burne in September1921when he revisited the battlefield and was informed by local people who knew the area intimately that no wire fences had ever been used in the neighbourhood. This is in direct variance to accounts given by officers and men who took part in the charge who remember being brought up by a wire fence before swinging off to the right and with Lieutenant Matterson's account of Dyer's charge which also mentions a wire fence which he had to climb through.
55. Major John Boyd Orr is buried at Cement House Cemetery, near Langemark. Grave Reference: XVIII.B.6. Captain Francis J Cresswell is buried at Auberchicourt British Cemetery, Grave Reference: IV.B.17 and Captain Ernest Felix Victor Briard is remembered on Special Memorial C.1 in Elouges Communal Cemetery. Lieutenant Harold Openshaw died of wounds 4 days later and was originally buried at Thulin New Communal Cemetery but his grave was subsequently lost. He is now commemorated on the Kipling Memorial at Cement House Cemetery.
56. Francis Octavius Grenfell, aged 35, was killed in action on 24 May 1915. He is buried at Vlamertinghe Military Cemetery, Grave Reference: II.B.14. His twin brother, Riversdale, also in the 9th Lancers, was killed in action on 14 September 1914. The Grenfell twins were from a notable military family. Their maternal grandfather was Admiral John Pascoe Grenfell and other relatives included their uncle, Field Marshal Francis Grenfell, 1st Baron Grenfell. An older brother, Lieutenant Robert Septimus Grenfell, 21st Lancers, was killed in a cavalry charge during the Battle of Omdurman in 1898. Three other brothers, Cecil Alfred, Howard Maxwell and Arthur Morton Grenfell, all reached the rank of Lieutenant Colonel. A cousin, Lieutenant Claude George Grenfell was killed at Spion Kop during the Boer War and two other cousins Julian Grenfell, the poet, and his brother, Gerald William Grenfell, were killed in the Great War.
57. POW Report in TNA WO 161.
58. 1st Cheshire Regiment War Diary. TNA WO 95/1571.
59. William Suttor Rich, aged 35, was twice mentioned in despatches before he was killed in action at Violaines on 9 November 1914. He is buried at Douai Communal Cemetery. Grave reference: D.1.
60. Gleichen Count E, *Infantry Brigade 1914* Blackwood 1917, p.31.
61. Zuber, *The Mons Myth*, p.193.

Chapter 6

62. Interestingly Lieutenant Cyril Helm's diary confirms the forest had provided suitable paths for 2/KOYLI 'for the greater part of the day' as they had marched up through the Forest on 20 August en route to Mons. L Battery had also used the forest tracks, its guns and limbers using white triangle markers to assist with recognition in the gloom.

63. Lord Bernard Charles Gordon Lennox, aged 35, was killed in action near Bodmin Copse, Ypres, on 10 November 1914. He is buried in the Zillebeke Churchyard Cemetery, Grave Reference: E.3.
64. Private Diary of Bernard Gordon Lennox. Grenadier Guards Archive.
65. Private Papers of R Whitbread. IWM Dept of Documents 8/30/1. The Hon Charles Henry Stanley Monck, aged 37, was killed on 21 October 1914 at St Julien. His name is commemorated at the Perth Cemetery (China Wall) near Ypres. David Cecil Bingham, aged 27, was killed in action on 14 September 1914 during the Battle of the Aisne. His name is commemorated on the La Ferté-sous-Jouarre Memorial.
66. Private Diary of Bernard Gordon Lennox.
67. Private Papers of R Whitbread. IWM Dept of Documents 8/30/1.
68. Ibid. Private Thomas Robson is buried at Landrecies Communal Cemetery, Grave Reference: B.6.
69. Ibid.
70. George Harry Wyatt survived the war. He was wounded twice and was mentioned in despatches. In 1919 he resumed his career with the Police. After retiring from the Police Force in February 1934, he died at Doncaster on 22 January 1964. He is buried at Cadeby Cemetery, Doncaster.
71. Private Diary of Bernard Gordon Lennox. Grenadier Guards Archive.
72. Herbert A, *Mons, Anzac and Kut* . Hutchinson 1925. www.gwpda.org – accessed 16 July 2010. Lord Desmond FitzGerald died of wounds on 3 March 1916. He was 28-years-old and had recently been promoted to Major. Wounded on two occasions, he was awarded the MC in 1915 and had been mentioned in despatches. He is buried in Calais Southern Cemetery. Grave Reference: Plot A. Row Officers. Grave 5.
73. Personal Papers of N L Woodroffe. IWM Dept. of Documents 95/31/1.
74. Private Papers of R Whitbread IWM Dept of Documents 8/30/1. Sir Robert Cornwallis Maude, 6th Viscount Hawarden, died of his wounds on 26 August 1914. He was 23-years-old. He is buried at Landrecies Communal Cemetery, Grave Reference: B.3.
75. Robert Humphrey Medlicott Vereker, aged 27, is buried at Landrecies Communal Cemetery, Grave Reference B.2.
76. War Diaries and Letters 1914-1918.
77. Cull I, *The China Dragon's Tales* The Wardrobe Museum.
78. The Hon William Andrew Nugent died of wounds received during the Second Battle of Ypres on 29 May 1915. He was 39-years-old. He is buried at Kensal Green Cemetery, London.
79. TNA WO 374/62200.
80. Walter Brindle is buried in the mass grave at Maroilles Communal Cemetery.
81. TNA WO 374/62200.
82. POW Report in TNA WO 161.
83. Possibly Private William W Totman, who is buried in the south part of Bavai Communal Cemetery.
84. John Ardkeen Savage was 31-years-old when he was killed in action near Troyon on 14 September 1914. His name is commemorated on the La Ferté-sous-Jouarre Memorial. He served for a short period with Captain Henry Shott in the West African Frontier Force.
85. 1/Northants War Diary TNA WO 95/1271.

86. In actual fact the diary he was writing in did not belong to him, he had come across it by chance on 23 August and he and his friend Private George Scutt resolved to keep it and continue the daily recording between them.

Chapter 7
87. Private Papers of A H Habgood. IWM Dept. of Documents PP/MCR/C57.
88. There are five soldiers of the 2/South Lancs recorded as killed in action on 25 August and all five are commemorated on the Memorial at La Ferté-sous-Jouarre.
89. Robert Charles Partridge was killed in action at Sablonnières on 8 September 1914. He was 32-years-old. He is buried at Sablonnières New Communal Cemetery. Grave Reference: 3.
90. The Private Diary of Cyril Helm. Western Front Association 2008.
91. Ballard J, *Smith-Dorrien*. Constable 1931, p.173.
92. Brigadier General Edward Stanislaus Bulfin (1862-1939) was GOC 2 Brigade in 1914. He was wounded at Ypres later in the year and went on to become GOC XXI Corps in 1917. The quote from his diary is cited in Gardner, *Trial by Fire* p.56.
93. Brigadier General Cecil de Sausmarez DSO died in August 1966 aged 95. He was commissioned in 1889 in the Royal Artillery and saw action in South Africa. At the Battle of the Aisne he was severely wounded. He was mentioned in dispatches three times.
94. The Diary of J B W Pennyman. Teesside Archives U.PEN/7/150.
95. John Edmund William Dennis is commemorated on the La Ferté-sous-Jouarre Memorial.
96. Edward Geoffrey Myddelton is commemorated on the La Ferté-sous-Jouarre Memorial and on the Suffolk Memorial on Suffolk Hill.
97. Walker G, From the Curragh to the Aisne 1914. *RE Journal*, April 1919, p.171-175.
98. The Diary of J B W Pennyman. Teesside Archives U.PEN/7/150.
99. The Private Diary of Cyril Helm.
100. William Henry Joseph Barber-Starkey died of wounds on 11 September 1914. He was 34-years-old and is buried at Le Cateau Communal Cemetery, Grave Reference: III.B.8. 31-year-old Sergeant Jesse Woolger is commemorated on the La Ferté-sous-Jouarre Memorial. Both men are also commemorated on the Suffolk Memorial on Suffolk Hill.
101. Benjamin George Cobey is commemorated on the La Ferté-sous-Jouarre Memorial and on the Suffolk memorial on Suffolk Hill. Job Henry Charles Drain survived the war and died in 1975. He is buried at Rippledale Cemetery, Barking. Frederick Luke also survived the war and died in 1983 in Glasgow.
102. Holmes R, *Riding the Retreat*, Jonathan Cape 1995, p.189.
103. Holmes was promoted to sergeant when he returned to the Western Front in October 1915. In December he was transferred to India and in March 1917 was commissioned and sent to Mesopotamia, where he fractured his skull. No longer fit enough for active service, Holmes worked in the Military Record Office in London. He died at Port Augusta, Australia on 22 October 1969.
104. POW Report in TNA, WO 161.
105. The Diary of J B W Pennyman. Teesside Archives U.PEN/7/150
106. The Personal Diary of Kenneth Godsell RE Journal Archive
107. Charles Allix Lavington Yate is buried at the Berlin South-Western Cemetery, Grave Reference: II.G.8.

Chapter 8

108. Nigel Cave and Jack Sheldon, *Le Cateau,* Pen and Sword 2008, p.9.
109. The Seydoux family began manufacturing textiles at Le Cateau at the beginning of the 19th Century. Much of the textile factory was dismantled by the Germans during the war and finally destroyed in the 1918 Battle of Le Cateau. Rebuilt in 1921 the family continued manufacturing until 1981. Andre Seydoux was very much involved with the International Red Cross, hence his involvement with the British wounded in August 1914.
110. James Richard Lander is buried at Landrecies Communal Cemetery, Grave Reference: B.13.
111. Guy Maxwell Shipway, aged 37, is buried at Etreux Communal Cemetery, Grave Reference: 50/51.
112. Private Papers of J Mcllwain. IWM Dept. of Documents 96/29/1.
113. 23- year-old Robert Burton Benison was killed in action on 20 September 1914. He is buried at Vendresse British Cemetery, Grave Reference: III.C.7.
114. Private Papers of J Mcllwain. IWM Dept of Documents 96/29/1. 21-year-old Victor Aloysius Lentaigne was killed in action on 14 September 1914 and is commemorated on the La Ferté-sous-Jouarre Memorial. Private Patrick Sweeney died in captivity in 1919.
115. Ibid.
116. POW Report in TNA, WO 161
117. William Gordon Steiglitz Barker, aged 32, is buried at Shere (St James) Churchyard, Surrey.
118. Robert Andrew de Stacpoole, aged 22, was killed in action on 20 September 1914. His name is commemorated on the La Ferté-sous-Jouarre Memorial.

Chapter 9

119. The Personal Diary of Kenneth Godsell RE Journal Archive.
120. The Diary of J B W Pennyman. Teesside Archives U.PEN/7/150.
121. Bridges T, *Alarms and Excursions,* Longman 1938, pp.87-8.
122. Report by Brigadier General Maxse on Etreux, TNA WO 95/588. Adrian Grant-Duff was killed on 14 September 1914 during the Battle of the Aisne. He was 44-years-old and is buried at Moulins New Communal Cemetery, Grave Reference: 1.
123. William Wilkes is buried at Etreux British Cemetery, Grave Reference: III.B.2.
124. Edward Charles Hardinge was 22-years-old when he died of his wounds. He had been awarded the DSO and mentioned in despatches. He is buried in the churchyard at Fordcombe (St Peters), Penshurst. He was the godson of Queen Alexandra.
125. 2nd Royal Munster Fusiliers War Diary TNA WO 95/1279.
126. Ibid.
127. Ibid.
128. *Faithful unto Death* is a painting by Edward Poynter. The work illustrated the epitome of devotion to duty for Victorian morals. It depicts a Roman sentry standing at his post whilst Pompeii and its citizens are destroyed by the eruption of Vesuvius in 79 AD. Despite this and his obvious trepidation, the soldier stands firm.
129. POW Report in TNA WO 161
130. Ibid.
131. The Personal Diary of Kenneth Godsell RE Journal Archive.

132. Buckland, Major General Sir U H, Demolitions Carried Out at Mons and during The Retreat. *RE Journal*, March 1932. pp.18-40.

Chapter 10

133. Spears, Sir E, *Liaison 1914*, Eyre & Spottiswoode 1930, p.268.
134. The Personal Diary of Kenneth Godsell RE Journal Archive.
135. John Kirwan Gatacre was killed on 12 October 1914 and is buried at Meteren Military Cemetery, Grave Reference: II.N.352.
136. Anglesey, *A History of the British Cavalry Volume 7*, p.142.
137. Captain John Clive Darling was the 20/Hussars signalling officer in 1914. He was awarded the DSO and mentioned in despatches. He finished the war a major and wrote the history of the regiment. He died in 1933, aged 45.
138. Later, as Brigadier General Frank Wormald, he was killed in action near Loos on 3 October 1915. He is buried in the village churchyard at Nedonchel. There is one other CWGC burial in the cemetery, that of Private Hardy who was killed on 30 March 1917.
139. Anglesey, *A History of the British Cavalry Volume 7*, p.138.
140. Ibid, p.139.
141. Ibid.
142. The Diary of J B W Pennyman. Teesside Archives U.PEN/7/150.

Chapter 11

143. Private Papers of J Giffard. IWM Dept. of Documents 05/9/1.
144. Stewart, *From Mons To Loos*, p.161.
145. Lieutenant Arthur Clunes Hooper Carr was killed in action on 14 February 1915 at Ypres. His name is commemorated on the Menin Gate, Panel 9.
146. Private Diary of J A C Pennycuick. Privately held manuscript.
147. Ibid.
148. Haldane, Lieutenant General Sir A, *A Brigade of the Old Army*, Arnold 1920, p.50
149. 41-year-old John Baillie Barstow is buried at Noyon New British Cemetery, Grave Reference: IV.B.5.
150. Young B, The Diary of an RE Subaltern with the BEF in 1914. *RE Journal*, December 1933, pp.550-561.
151. Frustratingly at the time of writing the author has been unable to find the name of this officer, although under the circumstances one would imagine he would probably have wished it to remain so!
152. Stewart, *From Mons To Loos*, pp.62-3.
153. Poseck von M, *The German Cavalry 1914 in Belgium and France*. Naval and Military Press, 2007, p.87. George Critchett Juler and Charles Dale are commemorated on the La Ferté-sous-Jouarre Memorial.
154. The Diary of J B W Pennyman. Teesside Archives U.PEN/7/150.

Chapter 12

155. Takle P, *The Affair at Néry* Pen and Sword 2006, p.50.
156. Ibid.
157. The exact time is courtesy of Lieutenant Guy Norrie who looked at his watch when the first shell exploded.

158. Private Papers of J Giffard. IWM Dept. of Documents 05/9/1. Charles Bull Weedon, aged 36, died of wounds on 8 September 1914 and is buried at Baron Communal Cemetery, Grave Reference: 1.

159. Private Papers of W Bull. IWM Dept. of Documents 02/40/1.

160. Private Papers of J Giffard. IWM Dept. of Documents 05/9/1.

161. The Private Papers of D Nelson, IWM Dept. of Documents Misc 54 (525).

162. Hugh Ponsonby Burnyeat (then lieutenant colonel) was killed on 31 October 1918. He is buried at Bousies Communal Cemetery, near Le Cateau, Grave Reference: 9. He was 37-years-old.

163. The Middlesex history says it was 6.00 am when they were met by a messenger from Néry, Becke says it was at 7.00 am, giving the time Major Rowley arrived at the village – ahead of the battalion – as 8.00 am. The brigade war diary records that the action was over by 8.45 am and all firing had ceased – which according to Becke's timings would have given 1/Middlesex less than 45 minutes to capture the guns on the plateau. I suspect 6.00 am is the more accurate of the two.

164. From an address by Lord Norrie to the Royal Artillery Historical Society 1967.

165. Wyrall E, *The Die-Hards in the Great War* Harrison & Son 1926, p.39.

166. This number of wounded is at odds with the official figure of 91 British wounded. The figure is quoted by Lieutenant Colonel Frederick Brereton in his account of the RAMC published in 1919 and presumably includes German wounded.

167. Herwig, H, *The Marne 1914*, Random House 2011, p277

Chapter 13

168. Private Diary of Bernard Gordon Lennox. Grenadier Guards Archive.

169. Herbert, *Mons, Anzac and Kut,* op.cit.

170. Craster J M, *Fifteen Rounds a Minute,* Macmillan 1976, p.53.

171. Herbert, *Mons, Anzac and Kut.* op.cit.

172. Craster, *Fifteen Rounds a Minute,* p.54.

173. Private Diary of Bernard Gordon Lennox. Grenadier Guards Archive.

174. Craster, *Fifteen Rounds a Minute,* p.56.

175. Herbert, *Mons, Anzac and Kut..* op.cit.

176. Captain Lightly Harold Birt was killed in action on 5 January 1915. He is buried at Le Touret Military Cemetery, Richebourg L'Avoué, Grave Reference: I.C.19.

177. Private Papers of Rev. F F S Smithwick. IWM Dept. of Documents 01/59/1.

178. The Diary of J B W Pennyman. Teesside Archives U.PEN/7/150.

179. Private Papers of J V Ramsden. IWM Dept. of Documents 88/52/1.

180. Fisher, J, *History of the Duke of Wellington's West Riding Regiment. from August 1914 to December 1917* Halifax Exors of Geo 1917.

181. The Personal Diary of Kenneth Godsell, RE Journal Archive.

182. Spears, E, *Liaison 1914.* p.415.

183. Ernie Rumbolt Taylor was killed in action on 18 May 1915. He is buried at Oosttaverne Wood Cemetery, Grave Reference: VIII.J.9. Albert Clarke died of wounds on 18 May 1915. He is buried at the First DCLI Cemetery, The Bluff, Grave Reference: D.4. Thomas Martin Ellis was killed in action on 13 May 1915. He is buried at Perth Cemetery (China Wall), Grave Reference: IV.L.8.

184. Beaumont, *Old Contemptible*, p.148.

185. Haldane, *A Brigade of the Old Army 1914.*p.24.

186. Scott P, *Dishonoured,* Tom Donovan 1994, p.61.
187. *Kildare Observer* October 1914. www.athyheritagecentre-museum.ie – accessed 4 September 2010.
188. Grave Reference: B.7.
189. Malloch, H, Behind the Lines: The Story of the Iron 12 – Part 1, *Stand To! The Journal of the Western Front Association* No. 87 December/January 2010 pp. 6-11 and Part 2, *Stand To!* No. 88 April/May 2010 pp. 11-15.

Chapter 15

190. The Diary of J B W Pennyman. Teesside Archives U.PEN/7/150.
191. Robert Bradford Flint is buried at Dranouter Churchyard, near Ypres, Grave Reference: II.A.2. William Henry Johnston is buried at Perth Cemetery (China Wall), Grave Reference: III.C.12.
192. Dolbey R V, *A Regimental Surgeon in War and Prison,* John Murray 1917, p.55. Gilbert Stratton Amos is buried at Vauxbuin French National Cemetery, Grave Reference: II.C.16.
193. Ibid.
194. Robert Randle Egerton is buried at New Irish Farm Cemetery, Ypres, Grave Reference: XXXIII.C.2.
195. The name of 21-year-old Neville Leslie Woodroffe is commemorated on the Menin Gate Panel 11.
196. Charles Evan Roderick Pottinger is buried at St Sever Cemetery, Rouen, Grave Reference: A.1.11.
197. John Raphael Hamilton-Dalrymple was killed in action on 23 April 1915. His name is commemorated on the Menin Gate Panel 22.
198. Charles Eustace Fishbourne is buried at Gresford (All Saints) Churchyard in Denbighshire.
199. Lionel Frank Hastings Mundy died of his wounds on 3 September 1914. He is buried at Baron Communal Cemetery. He was 28-years-old.
200. This majestic building was destined not to survive beyond 1944 when in the September of that year it was almost totally destroyed by Allied bombing.
201. CMG – Companion of the Order of St Michael and St George. CVO – Commander of the Royal Victorian Order.
202. POW Report in TNA WO 161/95.
203. See 'Suit by a Prisoner Of War, BAYLY v. BAYLY AND CAIRD AND KEEN'. *The Times.* 11 November 1916 on the Great War Forum discussion group – http://1914-1918.invisionzone.com/forums/index.php?showtopic=127747&st=0&p=1218391&hl=bayly&fromsearch=1&#entry1218391- accessed 12October 2010.

BEF Order of Battle August 1914

(Excluding some support units)

I Corps – Lieutenant General Sir Douglas Haig

1st Division – General Officer Commanding – Major General S H Lomax

Brigades	Battalions	Artillery	Engineers	Field Ambulance
1 (Guards) Brigade (*Brig Gen F I Maxse*)	1/Coldstream (*Lt Col J Ponsonby*) 1/Scots Guards (*Lt Col H C Lowther*) 1/Black Watch (*Lt Col A Grant–Duff*) 2/Munster Fusiliers (*Major P Charrier*) ◗	XXV Brigade (113, 114, 115 Btys) XXVI Brigade (116, 117, 118 Btys) XXXIX Brigade (46, 51, 54 Btys) XLIII Howitzer Brigade (30, 40, 57 Btys)	23 Field Company (*Maj C Russell–Brown*) 26 Field Company (*Maj H L Pritchard*) 1st Signal Company	1 Field Ambulance 2 Field Ambulance 3 Field Ambulance (*Lt Col G Cree*)
2 Infantry Brigade (*Brig Gen E S Bulfin*)	2/Royal Sussex Regiment (*Lt Col E H Montresor*) 1/Loyal North Lancs (*Lt Col G C Knight*) 1/Northamptonshire Regiment (*Lt Col E Osborne Smith*) 2/Kings Royal Rifle Corps (*Lt Col E Pearce–Serocold*)	26 Heavy Bty RGA In addition to the individual brigade ammunition columns and 26 Heavy Battery Ammunition Column, the divisional artillery was supported by the 1st Divisional Ammunition Column.	*Divisional Mounted Troops* A Squadron 15/(The King's) Hussars (*Capt O B Walker*) 1/Cyclist Company	
3 Infantry Brigade (*Brig Gen H S Landon*)	1/Queen's Royal West Surrey (*Lt Col D Warren*) 1/South Wales Borderers (*Lt Col H E B Leach*) 1/Gloucestershire Regiment (*Lt Col A C Lovett*) 2/Welch Regiment (*Lt Col B Morland*)			

* 4th Division units not present at Le Cateau on 26 August 1914.

◗ Killed in action during the retreat.

▣ Taken prisoner during the retreat.

2nd Division – General Officer Commanding – Major General C C Monro

Brigades	Battalions	Artillery	Engineers	Field Ambulance
4 (Guards) Brigade (*Brig Gen R Scot-Kerr*)	2/Grenadier Guards (*Lt Col N A Corry*) 2/Coldstream Guards (*Lt Col C E Pereira*) 3/Coldstream Guards (*Lt Col G P Fielding*) 1/Irish Guards (*Lt Col Hon G Morris*) ♥	XXXIV Brigade (22, 50, 70 Btys) XXXVI Brigade (15, 48, 71 Btys) XLI Brigade (9, 16, 17 Btys) XLIV Howitzer Brigade (47, 56, 60 Btys)	5 Field Company (*Maj C N North*) 11 Field Company (*Maj P Denis de Vitre*)	4 Field Ambulance 5 Field Ambulance 6 Field Ambulance
5 Infantry Brigade (*Brig Gen R C Haking*)	2/Worcestershire Regiment (*Lt Col C B Westmacott*) 2/Ox and Bucks Light Infantry (*Lt Col H R Davies*) 2/Highland Light Infantry (*Lt Col A A Wolfe-Murray*) 2/Connaught Rangers (*Lt Col A W Abercrombie*) ◉	35 Heavy Bty RGA In addition to the individual brigade ammunition columns and 35 Heavy Battery Ammunition Column, the divisional artillery was supported by the 2nd Divisional Ammunition Column	*Divisional Mounted Troops* B Squadron 15/(The Kings) Hussars (*Capt Hon W A Nugent*) 2/Cyclist Company	
6 Infantry Brigade (*Brig Gen R H Davies*)	1/King's Liverpool Regiment (*Lt Col W S Bannatyne*) 2/South Staffordshire Regiment (*Lt Col C S Davidson*) 1/Royal Berkshire Regiment (*Lt Col M D Graham*) 1/Kings Royal Rifle Corps (*Lt Col E Northy*)			

II Corps – General Sir Horace Smith-Dorrien (after 17 August 1914)

3rd Division – General Officer Commanding – Major General H I W Hamilton

Brigades	Battalions	Artillery	Engineers	Field Ambulance
7 Infantry Brigade (*Brig Gen F McCracken*)	3/Worcestershire Regiment (*Lt Col B F Stuart*) 2/South Lancashire Regiment (*Lt Col C Wanliss*) 1/Wiltshire Regiment (*Lt Col A W Hastead*) 2/Royal Irish Rifles (*Lt Col W D Bird*)	XXIII Brigade (107, 108, 109 Btys) XL Brigade (6, 23, 49 Btys) XLII Brigade (29, 41, 45 Btys) XXX Howitzer Brigade (128, 129, 130 Btys)	56 Field Company (*Maj N J Hopkins*) 57/Field Company (*Maj F G Howard*) 3rd Signal Company	7 Field Ambulance (*Lt Col A Kennedy*) 8 Field Ambulance (*Lt Col C A Stone*) 9 Field Ambulance
8 Infantry Brigade (*Brig Gen B Doran*)	2/Royal Scots (*Lt Col H McMicking*) 2/Royal Irish Regiment (*Lt Col St J A Cox*) 4/Middlesex Regiment (*Lt Col C P Hull*) 1/Gordon Highlanders (*Lt Col E H Neish*) ◉	48 Heavy Bty RGA In addition to the individual brigade ammunition columns and 48 Heavy Battery Ammunition Column, the divisional artillery was supported by the 3rd Divisional Ammunition Column.	*Divisional Mounted Troops* C Squadron 15/(The King's) Hussars (*Major F C Pilkington*) 3/Cyclist Company	
9 Infantry Brigade (*Brig Gen F Shaw*)	1/Northumberland Fusiliers (*Lt Col H S Ainslie*) 4/Royal Fusiliers (*Lt Col N R McMahon*) 1/Lincolnshire Regiment (*Lt Col W Smith*) 1/Royal Scots Fusiliers (*Lt Col D Smith*)			

* 4th Division units not present at Le Cateau on 26 August 1914.
▶ Killed in action during the retreat.
◉ Taken prisoner during the retreat.

5th Division – General Officer Commanding – Major General Sir C Fergusson

Brigades	Battalions	Artillery	Engineers	Field Ambulance
13 Infantry Brigade (*Brig Gen G Cuthbert*)	2/King's Own Scottish Borderers (*Lt Col C N Stephenson*) ◉ 2/Duke of Wellington's Regiment (*Lt Col J A C Gibbs*) ◉ 1/Queen's Royal West Kent (*Lt Col A Martyn*) 2/King's Own Yorkshire Light Infantry (*Lt Col R Bond*) ◉	XV Brigade (11, 52, 80 Btys) XXVII Brigade (119, 120, 121 Btys) XXVIII Brigade (122, 123, 124 Btys) VIII Howitzer Brigade (37, 61, 65 Btys)	59/Field Company (*Maj G Walker*) 17/Field Company (*Maj C W Singer*) 5th Signal Company	13 Field Ambulance 14 Field Ambulance 15 Field Ambulance
14 Infantry Brigade (*Brig Gen S P Rolt*)	2/Suffolk Regiment (*Lt Col C A Brett*) ♥ 1/East Surrey Regiment (*Lt Col J R Longley*) 1/Duke of Cornwall's Light Infantry (*Lt Col M N Turner*) 2/Manchester Regiment (*Lt Col H L James*)	108 Heavy Bty RGA In addition to the individual brigade ammunition columns and 108 Heavy Battery Ammunition Column, the divisional artillery was supported by the 5th Divisional Ammunition Column.	*Divisional Mounted Troops* A Squadron 19/(Queen Alexandra's Own) Royal Hussars 5/Cyclist Company	
15 Infantry Brigade (*Brig Gen Count Gleichen*)	1/Norfolk Regiment (*Lt Col C R Ballard*) 1/Bedfordshire Regiment (*Lt Col C R Griffith*) 1/Cheshire Regiment (*Lt Col D C Boger*) ◉ 1/Dorsetshire Regiment (*Lt Col L J Bols*)			

III Corps – **Major General W P Pulteney** (formed in France on 31 August 1914) 4th Division – General Officer Commanding – **Major General T D'O Snow** (Landed in France on 22/23 August 1914)

Brigades	Battalions	Artillery	Engineers	Field Ambulance
10 Infantry Brigade (*Brig Gen J A Haldane*)	1/Royal Warwickshire Regiment (*Lt Col J F Elkington*) 2/Seaforth Highlanders (*Lt Col Sir E Bradford*) 1/Royal Irish Fusiliers (*Lt Col D W Churcher*) 2/Royal Dublin Fusiliers (*Lt Col A E Mainwaring*)	XIV Brigade (39, 68, 88 Btys) XXIX Brigade (125, 126, 127 Btys) XXXII Brigade (27, 134, 135 Btys) XXXVII Howitzer Brigade (31, 35, 55 Btys)	* 7 Field Company (*Maj S G Faber*) * 9 Field Company (*Maj J B Barstow*) ◗ * 4th Signal Company	* 10 Field Ambulance * 11 Field Ambulance * 12 Field Ambulance
11 Infantry Brigade (*Brig Gen A Hunter-Weston*)	1/Somerset Light Infantry (*Lt Col E H Swayne*) 1/East Lancashire Regiment (*Lt Col L St G Marchant*) 1/HampshireRegiment (*Lt Col S C Jackson*) 1/Rifle Brigade (*Lt Col H M Biddulph*)	* 31 Heavy Bty RGA In addition to the individual brigade ammunition columns and * 31 Heavy Battery Ammunition Column, the divisional artillery was supported by the * 4th Divisional Ammunition Column.	*Divisional Mounted Troops* * B Squadron 19/(Queen Alexandra's Own) Royal Hussars * 4/Cyclist Company	
12 Infantry Brigade (*Brig Gen H F Wilson*)	1/King's Own (*Lt Col A McNair Dykes*) ◗ 2/Lancashire Fusiliers (*Maj C J Griffin*) 2/Inniskilling Fusiliers (*Lt Col H P Hancox*) 2/Essex Regiment (*Lt Col G Anly*)			

* 4th Division units not present at Le Cateau on 26 August 1914.
◗ Killed in action during the retreat.
▣ Taken prisoner during the retreat.

19 Infantry Brigade (formed from lines of communication troops at Valenciennes on 22 August)

General officers commanding	Battalions	Background
Initially the brigade was under the independent command of Major General L G Drummond. Lieutenant Colonel B E Ward assumed command of the brigade after Drummond was wounded on 27 August, relinquishing command on 3 September 1914, when Brig Gen F Gordon was appointed.	1/Devonshire Regiment *(Lt Col G M Gloster)* 2/Royal Welch Fusiliers *(Lt Col D Radcliffe)* 1/Cameronians *(Lt Col P R Robertson)* 1/Middlesex Regiment *(Lt Col B E Ward)* 2/Argyll and Sutherland Highlanders *(Lt Col H P Moulton-Barrett)*	Infantry brigades were generally deployed as part of an infantry division. However the role of 19 Brigade in August 1914 was to hold key towns and bridges along the route which connected the BEF to its supply bases on the coast. Hence the term 'lines of communication'. At Mons for example, 1/Middlesex was ordered to hold bridges and locks over the canal in anticipation of the general advance. In this manner it became embroiled in the retreat. On 25 August the brigade was called upon to support the cavalry near Haussy before moving on to Solesmes and Le Cateau. At Le Cateau, the brigade was used on the right flank and was in action with 2/Suffolks on the Montay Spur.
		However, although it remained independent as such, it served as reinforcement troops for the remainder of the retreat and was later attached to 6th Division
		The brigade continued in this role until May 1915 when it finally found a permanent home with the 27th Infantry Division.

Cavalry Corps – Major General E H Allenby

Brigades	Regiments	Horse Artillery	Engineers	Field Ambulance
1 Cavalry Brigade (*Brig Gen C J Briggs*)	2/Dragoon Guards (Queens Bays) (*Lt Col H W Wilberforce*)	III Brigade RHA D and E Batteries III Brigade Ammunition Column	1 Field Squadron RE 1 Signal Troop	1 Cavalry FA
	5/(Princess Charlotte's) Dragoon Guards (*Lt Col G K Ansell*) ♥			2 Cavalry FA
	11/(Prince Albert's Own) Hussars (*Lt Col T T Pitman*)	VII Brigade RHA I and L Batteries VII Brigade Ammunition Column		3 Cavalry FA
2 Cavalry Brigade (*Brig Gen H de B de Lisle*)	4/(Royal Irish) Dragoon Guards (*Lt Col R L Mullens*)			4 Cavalry FA
	9/(Queen's Royal) Lancers (*Lt Col D Campbell*)			
	18/(Queen Mary's Own) Hussars (*Lt Col C K Burnett*)			
3 Cavalry Brigade (*Brig Gen H de la P Gough*)	4/(Queen's Own) Hussars (*Lt Col I G Hogg*) ♥			
	5/(Royal Irish) Lancers (*Lt Col A Parker*)			
	16/(The Queen's) Lancers (*Lt Col M L MacEwen*)			
4 Cavalry Brigade (*Brig Gen C E Bingham*)	Composite Household Cavalry Regiment (*Lt Col Cook*)			
	6/Dragoon Guards (Carabiniers) (*Lt Col J W A Annesley*)			
	3/(King's Own) Hussars (*Lt Col A A Kennedy*)			
5 Cavalry Brigade (*Brig Gen Sir P W Chetwode*)	2/Dragoons (Royal Scots Greys) (*Lt Col C B Bulkeley-Johnston*)	J Battery RHA and Ammunition Column	4 Field Troop 5 Signal Troop	5 Cavalry FA
	12/(Prince of Wales' Own) Lancers (*Lt Col F Wormald*)			
	20/Hussars (*Lt Col G T Edwards*)			

* 4th Division units not present at Le Cateau on 26 August 1914.

♥ Killed in action during the retreat.

◙ Taken prisoner during the retreat.

Appendix 2

The Cemetery Trail

The graves of the men of the BEF who fought at Mons and during the subsequent retreat are scattered along the 200 mile retirement that ended south of the Marne. The great tragedy in many of these cemeteries is the number of unidentified graves of men whose name will never stand above them. For more precise information on the location of each cemetery visit the Commonwealth War Graves Commission website at: www.cwgc.org. The cemeteries listed are in approximate geographical order, beginning at Tournai and finishing at Verberie.

Cemetery	Number of identified burials	Number of identified 1914 burials (Aug and Sept)	Cemetery Detail
Tournai Communal Cemetery Allied Extension	819	3	Not technically during the period of the retreat but very much part of the build up to Mons: Private James Hawes, 4/Dragoon Guards (24.8.14) Lt Vincent Waterfall and Lt Charles Bayly, RFC (22.8.14) are buried here.
Hautrage Military Cemetery	358	150	The military cemetery was begun by the Germans in August and September 1914, and in the summer of 1918 they brought into it a large number of British graves of 1914, mostly of the 2nd Cavalry and 5th Infantry Divisions. Buried here are Lt Max Broadwood (1/RWK), Cpl Edwin Marsden (17/Field Company), Maj Chandos Leigh (2/KOSB), Capt John Benson (1/East Surreys)
Mons Communal Cemetery	490	34	Including men of 8 and 9 Infantry Brigades who fought in the Nimy Salient on 23 August. Lt John Shine, the Royal Irish Machine-Gun Officer is buried here.
Cuesmes Communal Cemetery	9	6	Six men of 2/South Lancs are buried here including 16-year-old Private James Price.
St Symphorien Military Cemetery	408	134	The cemetery was made by the Germans in August 1914, after the Battle of Mons. It has the distinction of containing the graves of some of the first and last casualties of the Great War. Contains the largest concentration of men from 4/Middlesex and 2/Royal Irish. Also buried here are Lt Maurice Dease VC, Lt Wilfred Holt (RE) and Capt Kenneth North (4/Middlesex)

Cemetery	Number of identified burials	Number of identified 1914 burials (Aug and Sept)	Cemetery Detail
Frameries Communal Cemetery	28	19	Men from 1/Lincolnshire, 2/South Lancs, 1/Northumberland Fusiliers and 2/HLI including Capt Cecil Holmes (1/Lincolns) and Capt Malcolm Leckie.
Quievrain Communal Cemetery	45	1	All 1918 burials apart from Private J Clarke of 1/Cheshire Regiment.
Auberchicourt British Cemetery	271	4	Casualties from Audregnies including Capt Francis Cresswell (1/Norfolks) and Private Frederick Garrad (1/Cheshires)
Audregnies Communal Cemetery	9	8	Men from 1/Cheshires and 1/Norfolks
Elouges Communal Cemetery	55	39	The 1914 burials are mainly from the units deployed at Audregnies on 24 August 1914. They are in trench graves, and the actual position of each body in the row is not known.
Wihéries Communal Cemetery	10	5	Casualties from Audregnies on 24 August including Capt Ernest Jones, Lt Kingdon Frost and Drummer Ernest Hogan of 1/Cheshires. Lt Frost's grave was unknown for 80 years until Alan Gregson presented evidence to the CWGC which led to them recognising his last resting place with a named headstone on the 80th anniversary of his death in action in 1914.
Angre Communal Cemetery	11	2	Cpl Edward Warde, 5/Lancers (26.8.14) and Private R Walker, ASC (27.8.14)
Bavai Communal Cemetery	12	3	Buried here are: Sapper E Ezard (24.8.14), Private C Hunt, 12/Lancers (29.8.14) and Private W Totman, 12/Lancers (25.8,14)

Cemetery			
Houdain-les-Bavai Communal Cemetery	1	1	L/Cpl A Appleton, 1/Dorsetshire Regiment (28.8.14).
Avesnes-sur-Helpe Communal Cemetery	205	1	Private Michael Molloy, 2/Connaught Rangers (4.9.14)
Landrecies Communal Cemetery	54	35	Mainly men of the Coldstream and Grenadier Guards who fought the rearguard action at Landrecies on 25 August, including Lt Robert Vereker and Lt Viscount Hawarden and Private James Lander 1/Gloucesters.
Maroilles Communal Cemetery	20	18	Eighteen of the men who fought in the rearguard action at Maroilles on 25 August, including Capt Henry Shott.
Le Grand Fayt Communal Cemetery	5	3	The scene of the rearguard action on 26 August. Three Connaught Rangers are buried here: Capt Francis Leader, L/Cpl E McCann and L/Cpl J Wyley.
Prisches Communal Cemetery	3	1	Private Tom Hazelwood of 1/Gloucesters is buried here. (27.8.14)
Haucourt Communal Cemetery	2	2	The majority of burials here are unidentified apart from Capt Henry Clutterbuck and CSM William Sharp of the 1/King's Own, killed on 26.8.14.
Fontaine-au-Pire Communal Cemetery	70	47	The northwest end of the Communal Cemetery was used by the Germans after Le Cateau, and the British wounded who died in the Mairie were buried there.
Esnes Communal Cemetery	55	53	Casualties from Le Cateau including men from 2/Lancashire Fusiliers, 2/Essex, Royal Irish Fusiliers and Inniskilling Fusiliers.
Bethencourt Communal Cemetery	75	19	A German hospital was posted in the village of Bethencourt in August and September, 1914. Most of the 1914 casualties buried here were either killed on 26 August or later died of their wounds.
Montigny Communal Cemetery	38	6	Six casualties of Le Cateau: Two Royal Warwicks, two Dublin Fusiliers, one from the 1/King's Own and an RFA gunner.

Cemetery	Number of identified burials	Number of identified 1914 burials (Aug and Sept)	Cemetery Detail
Caudry Old Communal Cemetery	98	17	Battle casualties from Le Cateau and Cpl Herbert Hull executed by the Germans in September 1915.
Caudry British Cemetery	654	19	1914 burials mainly Royal Scots and Gordon Highlanders who fought at Audencourt on 26 August.
Le Cateau Military Cemetery	513	29	The majority of the graves in Plots I, III, IV and V are those of the British dead buried by the Germans, mainly from Le Cateau. Men of 2/Argyll and Sutherland Highlanders, 2/Suffolks, 2/Manchesters and 2/KOYLI.
Le Cateau Communal Cemetery	101	24	A third of the burials are unidentified. Men from 2/Suffolks, 2/Argyll and Sutherland Highlanders, 2/Manchesters.
Troisvilles Communal Cemetery	17	8	All casualties of Le Cateau apart from Private W Oakley, 1/Dorsetshire Regiment who died on 24.8.14.
Bertry Communal Cemetery	40	3	The identified 1914 burials are: Private William Addlestone, RE (26.8.14), Lt Alexander Lyon, 1/Gordons (27.8.14) and Private Harry Stanford, 1/Bedfordshire Regiment (27.8.14)
Reumont Churchyard	11	2	Two Argyll and Sutherland Highlanders are buried here: Capt John Fraser (28.8.14) and Private Scott McKay (26.8.14).
Maurois Communal Cemetery	78	1	The only identified burial from 1914 is L/Cpl W Shenton, 11/Hussars (27.8.14).
Le Catelet Churchyard	5	4	Contains the graves of the 'Le Catelet Four', Privates Digby, Donohoe, Martin and Thorpe. Shot by the Germans in 1916.

Cemetery			
St Souplet British Cemetery	590	12	Several Munster Fusiliers brought in after the war from Fesmy and Oisy but a mixture of other regiments, some of whom must have died of wounds after being taken prisoner.
St Quentin Northern Communal Cemetery	7	3	Probably casualties from Le Cateau who died of wounds in the area: Private G Irwin, 2/Manchesters (26.8.14) Private E Locke, 1/Lincolnshires (28.8.14) and Private John Pearson, 2/KOSB (26. 8.14)
Moÿ-de-l'Aisne Communal Cemetery	7	5	The casualties from the cavalry rearguard at Cerizy on 28 August including Capt John Michell and Maj Foster Swetenham.
Etreux British Cemetery	99	99	The scene of the rearguard in which 2/Munster Fusiliers were overwhelmed on 27 August. The British Cemetery is in an old orchard on the Landrecies road. It was created by the survivors on the 28 August. Private William Wilkes (15/Hussars) is also buried here
Etreux Communal Cemetery	9	6	There are ten burials on this site and of the indentified 1914 casualties there are four 2/Munster Fusiliers and two 1/Gloucesters, including Capt Guy Shipway.
Guise Communal Cemetery	12	12	The 'Guise Eleven' are buried here after they were shot by the enemy at the château in February, 1915. The recently discovered grave of Vincent Chalandre is nearby. Also here are Driver J Yarnell, RFA, (25. 8.14) and L/Cpl John Stent 15/Hussars.
Noyon New British Cemetery	165	1	Maj John Barstow is buried here (9/Field Company).
Noyon Communal Cemetery	1	1	Gunner Rowland Smith, RGA, was buried by the Germans in August 1914.
Guards Grave Cemetery, Villers-Cotterêts	78	78	The men of the 4 (Guards) Brigade who died in the rearguard action on 1 September. Amongst those buried here is Lt Col Hon George Morris.

Cemetery	Number of identified burials	Number of identified 1914 burials (Aug and Sept)	Cemetery Detail
Haramont Communal Cemetery	2	1	Lt Col Ian Hogg, 4/Hussars is buried here (2.9.14)
Crépy-en-Valois Communal Cemetery	7	4	Four of the men from 2/KOSB and 1/RWK who fought in the rearguard action on 1 September.
Néry Communal Cemetery	20	19	The men of 1 Cavalry Brigade and L Battery RHA who were killed on 1 September. Included here are: Capt Edward Bradbury VC, Lt John Campbell and Maj Hon John Cawley. John Cawley's brother, Oswald, who was killed on 22.8.18, is also buried here.
Baron Communal Cemetery	16	16	Further casualties from Néry who died later at the field hospital at Baron. Buried here are Lt Lionel Mundy and Sgt Charles Weedon.
Verberie French National Cemetery	52	30	More of the Néry casualties including Lt Col George Ansell, 5/Dragoon Guards.
Verberie Communal Cemetery	4	4	Twenty-six British soldiers, all unidentified, are buried in one big grave – but a special inscription records the names of twelve men of L Battery, RHA, and twelve of the 2/Dragoon Guards and 5/Dragoon Guards, who fell at Néry. There are four identified graves of men of 2/Inniskilling Fusiliers.

Select Bibliography

Unpublished sources

The National Archives
Unit War Diaries in WO 95.
Service Records in WO 339.
Personal Papers in WO 106 and CAB 45.
Prisoner of War Reports in WO 161.

Private Papers
The Private Papers of G W Beer, 11/Field Ambulance.
The Private Papers of W Bull, L Battery RHA.
The Private Papers of J Giffard, L Battery RHA.
The Diary of K B Godsell, 17/Field Company RE.
The Diary of C Helm, RAMC.
The Diary of A H Habgood, 9/Field Ambulance.
The Private Papers of ESB Hamilton, 7/Field Ambulance.
The Private Papers of GA Kempthorne, RAMC.
The Diary of Major Lord Bernard Gordon Lennox, 2/Grenadier Guards.
The Private Papers of J McIIwain, 2/Connaught Rangers.
The Private Papers of D Nelson, L Battery.
The Letters of R H Owen, 2/Duke of Wellington's Regiment.
The Personal Papers of J A C Pennycuick, 59/Field Company, RE.
The Diary and Private Papers of J B W Pennyman, 2/KOSB.
The Private Papers of J V Ramsden, XXVII Brigade RFA.
The Private Papers of Rev F F S Smithwick, 5/Field Ambulance.
The Private Papers of B T St John, 1/Northumberland Fusiliers.
The Private Papers of R Whitbread, 3/Coldstream Guards.
The Letters of N L Woodroffe, 1/Irish Guards.
The Diary of Drummer George Whittington, 2/Royal Sussex.

Published Sources

Books

The Marquess of Anglesey, *A History of the British Cavalry 1816–1919* (Vol. 7), Leo Cooper, 1973–1982.

David Ascoli, *The Mons Star*, Harrap, 1981.

R Barker, *A Brief History of the Royal Flying Corps in World War 1*, Robinson, 2002.

C Ballard, *Smith-Dorrien*, Constable, 1931.

Arthur Banks, *A Military Atlas of the First World War*, Leo Cooper, 2004.

Walter Bloem, *The Advance From Mons*, Tandem, 1967.

Sir Tom Bridges, *Alarms and Excursions*, Longmans, 1938.

Lord Carnock, *The History of the 15th The King's Hussars 1914–1922*, Crypt House Press, 1932.

Nigel Cave, and Jack Sheldon, *Le Cateau*, Pen and Sword Books, 2008.

A E Clarke-Kennedy, (Ed.) *Old Contemptible*, Hutchinson, 1967.

Frederick Coleman, *From Mons to Ypres with General French*, A L Burt Company, 1916.

Rose Coombes, *Before Endeavours Fade*, After the Battle, 2006.

Sir Arthur Conan Doyle, *The British Campaign in France And Flanders 1914*, Hodder & Stoughton, 1916.

A Crookenden, *The Cheshire Regiment in the Great War*, Privately published, 1956.

J M Craster, *Fifteen Rounds a Minute*, Macmillan, 1976.

Ian Cull, *The China Dragon's Tales*, The Wardrobe, 2004.

David Daniel, *Cap of Honour*, White Lion, 1951.

J C Darling, *20th Hussars in the Great War*, Privately published, 1923.

R V Dolbey, *A Regimental Surgeon in War and Prison*, John Murray, 1917.

J Dunn, *The War The Infantry Knew*, Abacus, 1994.

Sir J E Edmonds, *Military Operations France and Belgium 1914 Vol. 1*, Macmillan, 1926.

Max Egremont, *Under Two Flags*, Weidenfeld & Nicholson, 1997.

H Evans and N Laing, *The 4th (Queen's Own) Hussars in the Great War*, Gale and Polden, 1920.

Anthony Farrar-Hockley, *Death of an Army*, Arthur Barker, 1967.

Nikolas Gardner, *Trial by Fire*, Praeger, 2003.

H Gibb, *Record of the 4th Royal Irish Dragoon Guards in the Great War 1914–1918*, Canterbury, 1925.

Stair Gillion, *The KOSB in the Great War*, Thomas Nelson, 1930.

Gerald Gliddon, *VCs Handbook*, Sutton, 2005.

Count E Gleichen, *The Doings of the Fifteenth Infantry Brigade*, Blackwood, 1917.

Sir Aylmer Haldane, *A Brigade of the Old Army 1914*. Edward Arnold, 1920.

Lord E Hamilton, *The First Seven Divisions*, Hurst & Blackett, 1916.

Holger H Herwig, *The Marne 1914*, Random House, 2011.

Richard Holmes, *Riding the Retreat*, Jonathan Cape, 1995.

Brigadier General Sir Archibald Home, *The Diary of a World War I Cavalry Officer*, Costello, 1985.

Jack Horsfall and Nigel Cave, *Mons*, Pen and Sword Books, 2000.

Basil Liddell Hart, *History of the First World War*, Book Club, 1973.

J T Long, *Three's Company, A History of No.3 (Fighter) Squadron RAF*, Pen & Sword, 2005.

C V Maloney, *Invicta, With the 1st Battalion The Queen's Own Royal West Kent Regiment in The Great War*, Nisbet & Co., 1923.

C C R Murphy, *The History Of The Suffolk Regiment 1914–1927*, Hutchinson & Co., 1928.

Ponsonby, F, *The Grenadier Guards In The Great War of 1914–1918*, Macmillan 1920.

M von Posek, *The German Cavalry 1914 in Belgium and France*, Naval & Military Press, 2007.

Major General H L Pritchard, (Editor) *History of The Corps Of Royal Engineers (Volume 5)*, Institute of Royal Engineers, 1951.

Sir J Ross of Bladensburg, *The Coldstream Guards 1914–1918*, Oxford University Press, 1928.

Peter T Scott, *Dishonoured*, Donovan, 1994.

Gary Sheffield and John Bourne, *Douglas Haig War Diaries and Letters 1914–1918*, Orion, 2005.

Andy Simpson, *The Evolution of Victory*, Donovan, 1995.

Sir Edward Spears, *The Picnic Basket*, Secker & Warburg, 1967.

Sir Edward Spears, *Liaison 1914*, Eyre & Spottiswoode, 1930.

John Strawson, *Gentlemen in Khaki*, Secker & Warburg, 1989.

Major A S Stewart, *From Mons To Loos*, Blackwood, 1916.

Patrick Takle, *The Affair at Néry*, Pen and Sword Books, 2007.

John Terraine, *Mons, Retreat to Victory*, Wordsworth, 2002.

Barbara Tuchman, *The Guns of August – August 1914*, Four Square, 1962.

Richard Van Emden, *Tickled To Death To Go*, Spellmount, 1996.

M Whyman, *The Last Pennymans of Ormesby*, Bargate, 2008.

T S and R H Wollocombe, *Diary of the Great War*, Privately published, 1989.

Everard Wyrall, *The Gloucestershire Regiment in the War 1914–1918*, Methuen, 1931.

Everard Wyrall, *The History of the Duke of Cornwall's Light Infantry 1914–1919*, Methuen & Co 1932.

Everard Wyrall, *The Diehards in the Great War*, Harrisons and Sons, 1926.

Terence Zuber, *The Mons Myth*, The History Press, 2010.

Articles

Captain H A Baker, History of the 7th Field Company, RE, During the War 1914–1918, *RE Journal*, June 1932.

Major General Sir R Buckland, Demolitions Carried Out at Mons and During the Retreat, 1914, *RE Journal*, March and June 1932.

Colonel W H Evans, A Brief History of the RE with Cavalry in France During the War 1914–1918, *RE Journal*, March 1926.

Brigadier General G Walker, From the Curragh to the Aisne, 1914, *R E Journal*, April 1919.

Major B K Young, The Diary of an RE Subaltern with the BEF in 1914, *RE Journal*, December 1933.

Index

General Index

British Expeditionary Force
Corps:

Infantry Divisions:

Infantry Brigades:

Infantry Battalions: